THE RAILWAYS OF BECKENHAM

The classic picture of Beckenham Junction taken about 1864, with Michael Moore, Beckenham's first stationmaster standing next to the down main line next to the Southend Road bridge. Note the overall roof and the way in which the station name has been picked out in whitewashed pebbles and, in the background, the cottage known as Rutland Lodge which later became the stationmaster's official residence and which survived until 1983. (Bromley Libraries)

THE RAILWAYS OF BECKENHAM

NON NOBIS SOLUM

Andrew Hajducki

Published by The Ardgour Press in association with Noodle Books

© The Ardgour Press, Andrew Hajducki and Noodle Books 2011

ISBN 978-1-906419-59-2

First published in 2011 by The Ardgour Press, 16 Howard place, EDINBURGH. EH3 5JZ

NOODLE BOOKS.PO Box 279, Corhampton, SOUTHAMPTON. SO32 3ZX

www.noodlebooks.co.uk

Typeset and Design by Bruce Murray
Printed in England by Ian Allen Printing Limited.

Front cover - *"Golden Days at Beckenham Junction" depicting 34092 'City of Wells' on the down 'Golden Arrow' passing through Beckenham Junction on a winter's day in the 1950s (Eric Bottomley)*

Full Page 6 & 7 - A chilly scene as Wainwright "D" class 4-4-0 No. 731 passes Shortlands with a down express in about 1920. These locomotives were often regarded as the epitome of SECR elegance and No. 731 was in service for some fifty years from 1901; No, 373 of the same class has been restored to full SECR Brunswick green livery and is now part of the national collection at York Musuem . (John Minnis Collection)

Full Page 212 (Endpiece) - Junction starter signals and locomotive water supply column on the up side of Beckenham Junction Station in 1952 (Kevin Robertson Collection)

Rear cover - A trio of 1950s yellow ended electric multiple units at Beckenham Junction in 1981 with (right to left) 4 SUB No.4640 on a Crystal Palace to London Bridge service, 4 EPB No.5142 on an Orpington to Victoria service and, berthed in the down bay, sister unit No.5146; the hoppers in the Coal Concentration Depot can be seen on the left hand side. (Terry McCarthy)

Introduction

Lying on the south eastern fringe of London, Beckenham and West Wickham are often dismissed as being part of the seemingly dull and endless suburbs of the capital and, as such, possessing little to interest either the social historian or the railway enthusiast. To so regard them, however, would be a pity since together they provide a fascinating, if complex, story of railway rivalry, success and failure interwoven with the tale of how these two small villages metamorphosed into a prosperous community that in due course became the second largest municipality in Kent. In this book, completed in the centenary year of the publication of Robert Borrowman's classic *Beckenham Past and Present*, the present author has attempted to trace the construction, development and fate of the various railways which passed through and served the area, their impact upon those who lived there and the fate of the twelve stations that served, and continue to serve, its inhabitants to the present day - Birkbeck, Clock House, Eden Park, Elmers End, Kent House, Lower Sydenham, New Beckenham, Penge East, Ravensbourne, Shortlands, West Wickham and the earliest and most important station of them all, Beckenham Junction. To those who are primarily interested in the study of railway history this is a tale of a battle between two deadly rivals, how a line operated by a single tank engine and a clutch of four carriages became part of the main route to the Channel Tunnel and of how the Borough of Beckenham acquired an impressive total of thirteen miles of busy lines within its borders and, with the exception of a third of a mile lost more than a century ago, retains them all. To those whose interest is in the Beckenham and West Wickham of the past (and they add up to quite a formidable number) then this book may perhaps answer at least some of their questions and help to explain why the railway was, and indeed remains, of such importance to the locality and its residents. And, to those who make their daily or occasional journeys from any of the above stations, the author can only hope that these jaded travellers, being a little better informed, may hopefully now find their time on the train or tram slightly more bearable and that, while waiting for it, they may take a few minutes to consider the truth of the old adage that "God made the country, Man made the towns but the Railways made the suburbs."

By way of explanation, throughout this work the term "Beckenham" is used to describe the 3,890 or so acres which form the parish of Beckenham and was governed by the vestry and later the local board and the urban district council of that name. In 1932 the Beckenham UDC was joined with part of West Wickham into what later became the Municipal Borough of Beckenham. In 1965 the Beckenham Council area became part of the London Borough of Bromley.

Edinburgh, January 2011

Dedication

*In memory of my father, a reluctant commuter on the Mid Kent,
my mother, a regular traveller on the Palace Line and our dog Sara,
who was well acquainted with both Beckenham and its railways.*

Contents

THE RAILWAYS OF BECKENHAM

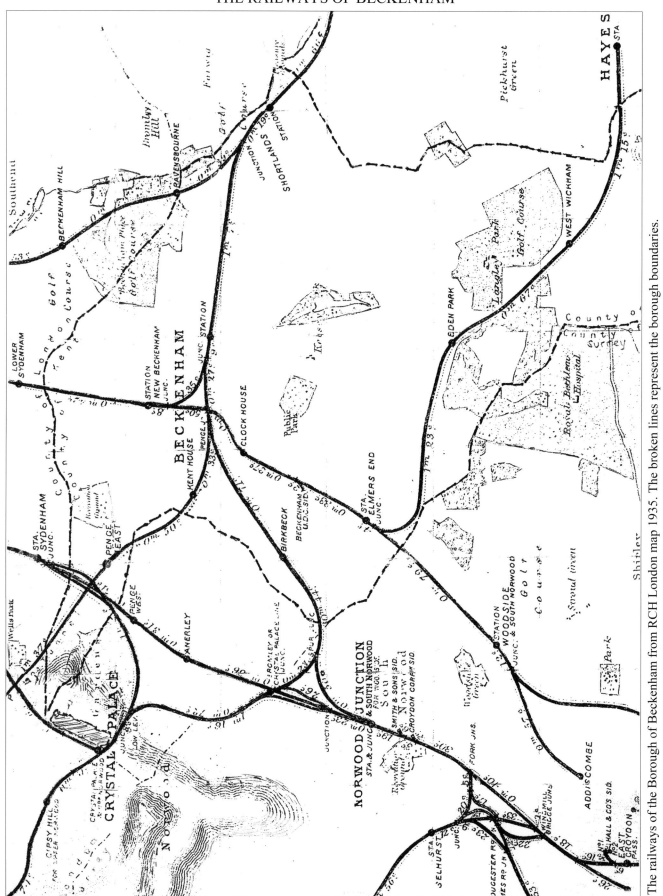

The railways of the Borough of Beckenham from RCH London map 1935. The broken lines represent the borough boundaries.

Chapter 1
THE COMING OF THE MID KENT

"The country around is of true Kentish scenery, and the walks are both charming and numerous"
Stanford's Tourist Guide to Kent

Beckenham before the railway

At the beginning of the nineteenth century Beckenham, supposedly named after Beohha, an early Saxon settler in those parts, was still a small and relatively unimportant rural community situated some ten miles from the centre of London and yet barely part of it[1]. Surrounded on all sides by open countryside and untraversed by any main road, the situation of the parish was said to be *"as delightful as it is salubrious being beautifully varied by alternative elevations and depressions, interspersed with magnificent seats and extensive woods and the landscape perfected in the distance by the majestic hills of Surrey and Kent ... and in consequence Beckenham has long been distinguished as the retirement of opulent merchants and persons of fashion."* A combination of these undoubted natural attractions and the proximity of the area to the capital city accounted for the presence of several large estates and well-to-do local landowners including the Goodharts of Lagley, the Hoare family of Kelsey and, pre-eminently, the Cators, a family of Quaker origin who came to the area in 1773 when they acquired the Manor of Beckenham including the lands of Clock House, Foxgrove and Copers Cope. The Cator family fortunes flourished and, in building their large and imposing mansion house at Beckenham Place on the northern boundary of the parish, it would have seemed as though they were well and truly here to stay.

In contrast to the landed estates, the village of Beckenham was an altogether humbler affair. Situated at the centre of the parish and dominated by the venerable parish church of St George, the village was a haphazard but picturesque collection of brick, half-timbered and weatherboarded buildings which accounted for the majority of the 159 dwelling houses existing in the parish in 1801 while the remainder of the population were scattered in small hamlets, on isolated farms and amidst the fields and woods. The economy of the local area was, at this time, still largely based on agriculture and what the villagers could not have obtained from their neighbours they could almost certainly have found in the nearby market towns of Bromley and Croydon. Indeed such was the comparative isolation of Beckenham from the world before the coming of the railway that it could still in 1850 have been said that there were people living there then who had still never set foot outside of their native parish.

The ordinary inhabitants of Beckenham at this now far-off time were said to have had *"unpretentious habits and simple tastes ... reflected in the character of their abodes which, in many cases, were sheltered from the* weather by straw-thatched roofs and surrounded by gardens in which the husbandman managed to produce vegetables and fruit for his own table, and to find amusement for his leisure hours".[2] This view might, however, have been a slightly idealised one for in contrast the Area Relieving Officer in the 1853 cholera epidemic found Beckenham to be "the most dirty of the parishes" within his range. What all were agreed on, however, was that notwithstanding any unsatisfactory sanitary arrangements, the village of Beckenham and its surroundings were a most pleasant place to live and, as yet, largely immune from the depredations of the speculative builder.

A pastoral scene in Beckenham at the start of the nineteenth century as cattle are driven past the parish church of St George. The building shown here was replaced by the present confident town church in the 1880s but what was reputed to be the oldest lychgate in Kent was restored and is happily still with us. (From a drawing by Birket Forster)

A Place of Neat Villas

Barely a couple of miles to the south of Beckenham lay the ancient settlement of West Wickham whose name denoted its Romano-British origins and whose prefix served to distinguish it from East Wickham some ten miles distant. Mentioned in Domesday, the parish had, by the start of the nineteenth century, a resident population of only 436 who lived mainly in the collection of cottages and farm buildings which made up the small hamlets of Wickham Green and Wickham Street while, some distance to the south and situated on a gentle hillside leading up to the North Downs, the fifteenth century parish church and adjacent manor house of Wickham Court lay together in rural isolation. The parish of West Wickham, fertile and undulating, stretched out from Beckenham to the Surrey border and encompassed more than 2,000 acres of well-cultivated land while a sprinkling of what were described as "neat villas" catered for its more affluent inhabitants. Undoubtedly West Wickham had much to offer those who could afford to live there and it was probably little exaggeration to say that "the beauty of the situation and the high cleanliness of the cultivation render the parish one of the most picturesque in the Kingdom."[3]

The parish managed to retain its Arcadian charms until a comparatively late date and although the village grew steadily throughout the nineteenth century there was little in the way of residential development until well after the arrival of the railway in 1882 and, even then, it could still be said that *"few parts of even the distant suburbs of London ... are prettier or more sylvan than the country between Hayes and Croydon and probably few rural villages are more sequestered than West Wickham. The district is delightfully undulating consisting of hills and dales ... which are plentifully overgrown by ferns."*[4] By the time that the railway was electrified in the 1920s the position had been drastically altered and West Wickham was taking on its present aspect with a rapidity that dismayed many of its life-long inhabitants.

Cockneys and Cators

Back in 1820 suburban development south of the Thames had only reached as far as Bermondsey and Camberwell and anything beyond this was associated with existing settlements such as Norwood and Dulwich with a few stretches of ribbon development along the main highways

Clock House, the Cator property which gave its name to a railway station. This substantial red brick mansion seen in a print of 1791 survived for another century and was so called because of the large clock fixed over the stables; the clock was later moved to the stable buildings in Beckenham Place Park where it remains. (from Robert Borrowman, "Beckenham Past and Present")

Part of Old Village, Beckenham

A postcard view of Beckenham High Street at the turn of the twentieth century showing the Old Wood House which, despite dating from medieval times, was demolished a few years after the photograph was taken, Gordon House (the one time residence of Julius Kressman, reputedly the sole passenger who used the short-lived Penge station in Beckenham Road) and the Manor House with its glass covered way leading from the road to the front door; on the right of the picture is another venerable building which, however, still survives – the George Inn - while an early roadsign warns of the hazardous bend ahead. (Nancy Tonkin collection)

and the odd pocket of industrial growth closer to the capital. However, although Beckenham and West Wickham were still relatively far out from the spreading conurbation of London, it is perhaps significant that William Cobbett in his celebrated *Rural Rides* could comment that "when you get to Beckenham … the country begins to assume a cockney-like appearance, all is artificial and you no longer feel any interest in it" and it was at least foreseeable that the rural idyll much lauded by others could not escape the rapacious grasp of the builder much longer. The first significant step towards the modern development of Beckenham was that taken in 1825 when John Cator, the tenant for life of the Cator estate and described as "a man of reckless extravagance and great eccentricity", obtained Parliamentary approval for the granting of building leases over certain of his lands in Beckenham and elsewhere.[5] Managed by his brother Peter, a lawyer to whom the subsequent development of the estate owes much, the Cator landholdings in Beckenham were however to remain relatively untouched for another generation until the arrival of the railway which was to provide the catalyst for transforming an area of woods, fields and parklands into a residential area fit for the

newly emergent middle class families of Victorian England.

But all this is to anticipate the future for, in the first half of the nineteenth century, communications between the two parishes and the city were somewhat primitive and the local roads were little more than narrow and unpaved country lanes bordered by hedges, trees and a handful of cottages. To the west of Beckenham journeys were hampered by the steep sylvan slopes of Sydenham Hill, whose high wild woods were haunted by gypsies and charcoal burners and whose bulk largely concealed the sights and sounds of the capital from the villagers. In almost every other direction the heavy clay soil, the poorly drained gravel and the ever persistent mud together with the perennial threat of widespread flooding bedevilled the efforts of even the most determined of travellers and, given the relative unimportance of the area to outsiders, there was little commercial impetus in even trying to improve the road system of the two parishes. Nevertheless, a daily coach, *The Accommodation*, left Beckenham for London "each weekday morning at 8.30 sharp" and returned from the city in the early evening while a local mail cart made two daily collections and deliveries round and about the area. West Wickham was served by a carriers' wagon owned by the Harman family for everyday needs while a daily coach ran from the Ship Inn at Charing Cross to the Swan public house in the middle of the village where, according to a contemporary source, the landlord "could give a visitor a good bed, good cheer, good information and, if need be, put a good horse into a good stable."[6] Visitors to either village were, however, uncommon and there were few, if any, regular travellers bound for London on these coaches and wagons for the journey took two or more gruelling hours and, despite the moderate fares, the cost was well beyond the financial means of all but the comparatively wealthy.

Penge Wharf and the Croydon Canal

In 1801 parliamentary approval was obtained for a canal to run from a junction with the Grand Surrey Canal at New Cross Gate to a terminus at Croydon, a distance of some 9¼ miles. Constructed to a width of 34 foot, the Croydon Canal was suitable for craft larger than those which could use the contemporary narrow canals of the north and midlands, a legacy of the fact that it had originally been suggested that it could form part of an inland waterway stretching between London and Portsmouth; its promoters, however, eventually had to settle for the canal being merely a facility to serve the immediate neighbourhood of a charming tract of still unspoilt countryside. The route of the canal was through the undulating woods and farmlands of Brockley, Forest Hill and Sydenham and, for a distance of a quarter of a mile or so, it traversed the north-western tip of the parish of Beckenham[7] in the vicinity of where Venner and Crampton Roads now stand before crossing over a tract of soon-to-be enclosed common land lying to the north of the hamlet of Penge, at that time a small and humble detached part of the parish of Battersea in the county of Surrey. At the point where the Dulwich to Beckenham road crossed over the canal, a goods facility named Penge Wharf and situated. Designed to serve the needs of the surrounding area the wharf was provided at the expense of a local landowner, John Scott of Penge Place, a large estate to the north. From here the canal continued through the common towards South Norwood eventually reaching a terminus close to where the present West Croydon station is now situated.

On 22nd October 1809 the Croydon Canal was ceremoniously opened for traffic and a contemporary newspaper described part of the inaugural journey in the following terms:

"After passing a wharf erected at Penge Common ... by means of which the towns of Beckenham and Bromley and a considerable part of Kent are accommodated with coals, manure and all articles of merchandise at a greatly reduced rate of carriage, the gay fleet of barges entered Penge Forest; the canal passes through this forest in a part so elevated that it affords the most extensive prospects, comprehending Beckenham and several beautiful villages and seats ..."[8]

Notwithstanding such sentiments the Croydon Canal

was, however, not a great commercial success and, although it was initially well-used for the carriage of bulk merchandise intended for Beckenham and elsewhere as well as being patronised by a stream of pleasure trippers eager to enjoy its undoubted scenic delights for picnics, fishing and other bucolic pastimes, the initial outlay on its construction and the continuing expense of maintaining and operating its 28 locks and numerous bridges, together with the very real competition for goods traffic from the pioneer Surrey Iron Railway between Wandsworth and Croydon, led to its early demise; the fact that the canal company's £100 shares became worth a mere two shillings by 1830 said it all. Bowing to the inevitable, the canal was closed to all traffic on 22nd August 1836 and its assets were promptly sold to the nascent London & Croydon Railway company for £40,250 in respect of the lands acquired and one shilling in respect of the illusory lost profits of the canal company.

A railway for Croydon

All was not lost, however, for the new railway was to closely follow, and indeed in places actually use, the bed of the former canal and, after crossing and re-crossing the Beckenham parish boundary on a route slightly to the east of the original canal formation,[9] the Dulwich to Beckenham road was met at the same point as the canal had passed under it. Here, a gated level crossing over the public road was provided and, on the site of the wharf, a passenger station with two platforms and a small booking office was built.[10] The London & Croydon Railway was opened to the public on June 5th 1839 but the station at Penge, which no doubt would have been well sited and convenient for the inhabitants of Beckenham being a mere hour's walk away, was extremely short-lived because of an apparent lack of patronage – perhaps not surprising since the surrounding area was still largely undeveloped and the hamlet of Penge was small and relatively inconsequential. By 13th May 1840 Penge had been omitted from the list of stations and fares appearing in an advertisement published in the *Times* newspaper and, there being no further mention of Penge station in print, it can probably be safely assumed that the station had been by then permanently closed. By 1841 the level crossing at Penge was replaced by a bridge[11] and the disused platforms appear to have been removed in connection with subsequent track alterations three years later.

For Beckenham residents, however, an alternative to Penge station was readily available in the form of Sydenham station, three-quarters of a mile to the north. At some point after 1840 a local entrepreneur named Legg, who lived at Elm Cottage in Beckenham, started up a regular horse bus service between the White Post House in Wickham Road and Sydenham station "for the convenience of those who went to town every day" – a category of persons who almost certainly formed Beckenham's first daily commuters in the modern sense.[12] In due course Legg's bus and its horses were taken over by William Ovenden, licensee of the Three Tuns public house in Beckenham, and it is recorded that Ovenden personally drove the vehicle until it is said that he met with an unspecified accident;[13] the service, with the bus presumably driven by others, appears to have survived until the Mid-Kent Railway eventually reached Beckenham in 1857.

The London & Croydon Railway itself flourished and in 1844 an experimental and rather short-lived additional line was built between Dartmouth Arms (Forest Hill), the Jolly Sailor (later Norwood Junction) and Croydon. This was operated on the so-called "atmospheric" principle whereby no locomotives were used and trains were propelled by atmospheric pressure acting on the rear of a piston in a tube as a result of a vacuum being created in front of it. In 1846 the London & Croydon Railway was taken over by the London, Brighton & South Coast Railway (LBSCR) and the atmospheric line was soon abandoned as a result, perhaps, of both technical problems such as rats gnawing through the leather pipe connections and also a perceived reluctance to part of contemporary engineers to countenance the use any alternative to the steam engine. The original line, however, prospered, and in due course was electrified and it survives to this day both as part of the Southern and Thameslink line from London Bridge to Brighton, and as part of the London Overground East London Line extension from New Cross.

Railway Mania

In 1846, as part of an unprecedented wave of financial speculation that was sweeping the country, there were a rush of proposals to construct new railways in to the northwestern part of Kent and two of these proposed lines were to play an important part in the subsequent railway history of Beckenham. The first of the lines to be promoted was that of a Mid Kent Railway which was to leave the projected North Kent line of the South Eastern Railway (SER) from London Bridge to Strood, near Chatham by a junction at Lewisham and was then to run southwards to Tonbridge with separate branch lines proposed to serve Bromley and Maidstone. The primary object of this proposed line was to open up extensive areas in the mid part of the county which were, as yet, unserved by any railway and, by increasing the sphere of influence of the SER in those districts, thus prevent the rival LBSCR from obtaining a foothold there. The Mid Kent scheme was almost immediately followed by another proposed line to run from Lewisham to Bromley and Croydon via Beckenham and whose main purpose, apart from serving the communities en-route, was apparently to serve as a warning to the Brighton company to stop them from blocking any attempt by the South Eastern to acquire the proposed Mid-Kent line. When the financial bubble burst both the Mid-Kent and the Lewisham & Bromley schemes were summarily abandoned but the South Eastern was still apparently obsessed by the thought of a challenge being made to their jealously-guarded monopoly of railway traffic between Kent and London and at the beginning of 1853 they were in negotiations with Peter Cator with a view to acquiring land in Beckenham in order to revive the Lewisham & Bromley scheme.

The Palace on the Hill

An important event which was to have an enduring impact on the parish of Beckenham and its railway system occurred in 1851 when the decision was taken to re-erect the main hall of the Hyde Park Great Exhibition, Joseph Paxton's renowned "Crystal Palace", on the crest of Sydenham Hill some three miles from Beckenham village. Situated within the parishes of Lewisham, Camberwell and Beckenham, the Crystal Palace in its new home was destined to be "a place of entertainment and a centre for the arts, manufactures and sciences." The project was enthusiastically supported by the LBSCR whose Board of Directors had members in common with the Board of the Crystal Palace Company. Eventually some 200 acres of land, including the Penge Place estate which was by that time owned by Brighton director Leo Schuster, were laid out to accommodate the vast glass-and-iron building and its surrounding pleasure grounds with their fountains, dinosaur statues and other notable attractions. As one of the most diverse engineering feats of its time the Palace required a huge army of navvies to be employed on the construction works and about two hundred of these came to seek temporary lodgings in Beckenham parish and their activities were vividly documented in a number of evangelical tracts by Catherine Marsh, sister-in-law of Frederick Chalmers, the Rector of Beckenham. Ultimately, however, it was not the spiritual redemption of these workers but the railways which they built that was to have its greatest enduring effect upon the parish.

In order for the transplanted Crystal Palace to be a commercial success a direct railway communication with London was badly needed and in 1853 the LBSCR obtained powers for a branch line a mile and a quarter long, which was to leave the former London & Croydon line at Sydenham station and terminate at a large brick-built terminus on Anerley Hill close to the proposed southern entrance of the Palace. This branch line, which included a flying junction over the original London & Croydon line at the very point where it entered Beckenham parish, was opened to the public on 27th March 1854 and, less than three months later, the Palace itself threw open its doors to the eagerly-awaiting masses. Notwithstanding the commercial and educational benefits the Palace was to confer there were nevertheless many who perhaps had reservations about the despoiling of the natural beauty of the area, and these feelings were perhaps summed up by the contemporary remark that "it is but a few summers since the sun shone upon the woody heights of the Sydenham and Norwood hills and now his rays may be seen gleaming from the roof of that vast temple to the arts of peace which has suddenly displaced the oaks and elms of the green woodland."[14] Others of a less romantic and more business-minded inclination welcomed the new venture as a harbinger of the new age of profit and progress allied to the scientific, decorative and financially rewarding arts and within weeks of the opening date the Brighton shareholders were being told that their company was " having a 'Derby Day' every day by carrying more than 10,000 passengers."[15]

The West End of London line.

The LBSCR line was, however, not destined to be the only line to serve the area and even before construction work had begun upon their Crystal Palace branch, proposals were being put forward for an entirely separate line from the branch from Sydenham. This scheme, to be known as the West End of London & Crystal Palace Railway (WEL&CPR), caused from the outset much local interest and in the evidence given to the Parliamentary Select Committee considering the WEL&CPR Bill, it was said that local roads "gave cause for concern by reason of being soft and yielding under heavy traffic and sloppy in wet weather and furrowed by the wheels of heavy conveyances" while the Chairman of the Crystal Palace Company optimistically stated that the proposed line "would be necessary because the [LBSCR] branch line from Sydenham would be incapable of dealing with the 100,000 or so persons who might be expected to resort to the Palace on fete days".[16] Running from a London terminus to be called Pimlico but described as "a point in Battersea, close to the south end of Chelsea Bridge", the new line was to be routed via Wandsworth Common, Balham, Streatham Hill and West Norwood to the romantically-named Gipsy Hill before tunnelling under the southern end of the Palace itself and reaching a new station at Crystal Palace which adjoined the LBSCR branch terminus.[17] From here the line was to continue south-eastwards to what was to become Norwood Junction, where it joined up with the former London & Croydon Railway which now formed part of the main-line of the LBSCR. The West End of London & Crystal Palace Railway Act received the royal assent in 1853 but it was to be more than three years before any of the WEL&CPR line was open to the public.

The Farnborough Extension

In the spring of 1854 several landowners living near the village of Farnborough, then a rather remote rural settlement some four miles to the south of Bromley, put forward their own scheme for a line from Lewisham to their village via Catford, Beckenham and Bromley Common. Speculation about railway construction in the area was rife and, by the time that the Lewisham & Farnborough Railway Bill had been drafted, there were two further railway proposals with a local content on the table, that of a West Kent & Crystal Palace Railway and, more importantly, that of an eastwards extension of the as-yet unbuilt West End of London & Crystal Palace Railway which was to run from Norwood to Farnborough via Beckenham and Shortlands. This latter scheme, officially known as the WEL&CPR (Extension to Farnborough) Line, but more popularly simply referred to as "The Farnborough Extension", unsurprisingly received support from the LBSCR who, seeking their own entry in to the county of Kent despite the obstructions placed in their way by the South Eastern, offered the promoters a financial incentive in the form of a guaranteed annual return of £8,000 and a promise that they would fully back the proposal and meet any objections to it which might be raised by the latter company. The opposition from the latter, however, never came for in one of the many quirks of local railway politics, the South Eastern were at that time engaged in certain internal boardroom disputes and these difficulties apparently led both to a lack of any expressed opposition by that company to the Farnborough Extension scheme as well as causing them to abandon their previously announced Mid-Kent Railway scheme from Lewisham.

The route of the proposed Farnborough Extension was to be nine miles in length and leaving the parent WEL&CPR line at the confusingly named Bromley Junction,[18] some 72 chains[19] south east of Crystal Palace station. It then proceeded in an easterly sweep through open farmland before crossing Clay Lane[20] and turned northeastwards in a shallow cutting before crossing a footpath and then a private road leading to a brickfield on the east side of the railway.[21] The line was then to run on an embankment and to cross over the main road from Beckenham to Penge on a girder bridge before swinging to the east and bridging two small tributaries of the Pool River, namely the Chaffinch Brook followed by the Beck or Rusher Brook. The line was then to run due east, through the site of the projected station at Beckenham before passing under Southend Road some 200 yards to the north of the parish church of St George. From here the line was to continue on its easterly path in a cutting before, passing under the future Westgate and Downs Bridge Roads and over the main Beckenham to Bromley road at Shortlands, a small settlement in the valley of the Ravensbourne river which consisted of a few houses and a name derived from the medieval field patterns prevalent there. Immediately following the bridge a station, provisionally named "Bromley", was to be provided to serve the nearby town of that name which was situated a mere half-mile away albeit only reached after climbing a steep hill. After this station the line was to leave Beckenham parish and, turning southwards to cross Bromley Common and thus avoiding the centre of Bromley itself, terminated "at or near the junction of the lane from Farnborough to Worley Hole with the turnpike road from Farnborough to Sevenoaks", i.e. close to the present Tubbenden Road South. The plans for the Farnborough Extension were drawn up by the WEL&CPR company's consulting engineer, the celebrated John Fowler, but could, at best, be summed up as providing a necessarily cheaply built line which followed a circuitous route and which effectively bypassed one of the only two places of any real significance on the way (Bromley) before ending at a place which, by any account, was of little importance in itself or of any general strategic importance.

Sundays Excepted

Before Parliamentary sanction could be given to the Farnborough Extension, there were two influential local landowners with whom the Company had to treat, since it was largely over their lands that the line was to pass. The first of these was George Ward Norman of Bromley, and an agreement was rapidly reached with him in regard to a number of matters affecting the Shortlands to Bromley Common section, although, as subsequent events were to show, these agreements were to be of little practical consequence. The other landowner with whom the company had to treat was John Cator and negotiations with his lawyer brother Peter became so protracted that it was only some two weeks before the enabling Act was finally passed that a full consensus was reached. The agreement, (which is set out in full in an Appendix to this work), was entered into on 15th July 1854 and was similar in content to all of the subsequent agreements between the Cators and the other companies who wished to serve Beckenham, provided in essence that in return for the Cator Estates conveying 25 acres of land to the WEL&CPR for railway purposes at an annual rentcharge of £375 and John Cator dropping all opposition to the Bill, they would in turn undertake certain obligations including that of observing a "Sunday Traffic Agreement" which would prohibit goods trains from loading or unloading at Beckenham stations on Sundays, prohibit passenger trains from calling at Beckenham during specified hours each Sunday and oblige the Company to charge full weekday fares on a Sunday and not reduced fares for excursionists. An annual rentcharge of £2,000 was to be paid but this would be waived for any year in which there was no wilful non-observance of the terms of the agreement.

This curious arrangement was not imposed out of any sense of religious piety on the part of the Cator family but rather because "fears were expressed lest because of the accommodation provided by the railway, the parish of Beckenham would be inundated by excursionists on Sundays and that thereby there would be a great detriment done to Mr Cator's estates."[22] This view was not, perhaps, without some foundation for as late as 1877 an amateur birdwatcher could complain to the *Times* newspaper that even at that comparatively late date in Beckenham "every road, country lane and footpath in the area is tenanted by an unwashed and dirty race in violation of the Wild Birds Protection Act"; unsurprisingly, similar sentiments were later expressed a few years later in relation to the opening up of the countryside in the vicinity of West Wickham station.

Notwithstanding these fears the Cator agreements stand out even in their contemporary setting as being somewhat eccentric and it is possible that the railway companies involved assumed that the Estate would not enforce the Sunday traffic provisions – in this respect they were soon disabused and within a short period of time proceedings arising out of a breach of the terms of the agreement were threatened and the railway had to give way and adhere to their promises or suffer stringent financial consequences.

Somewhat ironically, given that it was they who were most active in destroying the natural attractions and tranquillity of the Beckenham area, the various agreements which the Cators had imposed upon the railways continued in force until the end of the century by which time the day-trippers had virtually disappeared with the abolition of the open countryside they had once sought for their pleasures while those who lived on the houses built in and around the Cator estates were becoming increasingly frustrated by the restrictions placed on their Sabbath travels.

On 31 July 1854 the Farnborough Extension Act[23] was finally passed but within a matter of months its promoters were clearly having second thoughts as to the viability of the whole scheme. The West End board now approached those same local landowners who had been so vociferous in their demands for the Farnborough line in the first place and suggested that the only basis upon which the project could now go ahead would be if those landowners would donate the necessary land for the railway free of charge in addition to contributing one-half of the estimated £20,000 construction costs of the line. This plea for help was ignored, even by the Cators, and had it not been for subsequent developments it is unlikely that any part of the Farnborough Extension scheme would ever have seen the light of day.

Mid Kent revived

While the West End Board were still deliberating about the economics of their extension line, the South Eastern made a move. In April 1855 a prospectus was issued for a new scheme with the impressive title of the North Kent and Mid Kent Junction Railway which was to take a route from Lewisham to Beckenham similar to that of the abortive Lewisham & Farnborough line and thus form a strategic link between the South Eastern's North Kent line (opened to traffic in 1849) and the still to be constructed Farnborough Extension, thereby directly connecting the South Eastern with the LBSCR. This new company, afterwards better known by its shortened title of the Mid Kent Railway, was to be incorporated with a share capital of £80,000 made up of 3,200 £25 shares and with powers to borrow a further £25,000 if necessary. The original promoters included William Wilkinson, a wealthy local landowner and property speculator, John Cator, John Fletcher Hargrave, Alexander Beattie (who was also a Director of the South Eastern) and Sir John Lubbock of High Elms, an estate to the south of Farnborough village. The Chief Engineer was, once again, to be John Fowler.

The line being promoted was to commence at Lewisham Junction, some 4¼ miles from London Bridge station and between those points running powers over the South Eastern line were sought. From Lewisham the line would run through its own platforms at the junction station, adjacent to the re-sited North Kent platforms, before turning southwards and, following the western bank of the Ravensbourne and Pool Rivers, Ladywell station (0m 58ch from Lewisham) was reached. Crossing on to the east bank of the

The station frontage at Beckenham Junction in about 1885, showing the booking office, the train shed roof and main entrance and the brick porch provided to allow passengers arriving by coach some protection from the elements. The busy scene includes a coachman about to depart, a porter, what appears to be a passenger going in, a clerk, and standing with an air of authority, Robert Blackborrow, the stationmaster who sued a local cheesmonger for libel. (Bromley Libraries)

A similar view nearly eighty years later with the station still clearly displaying its Mid Kent origins, this represents how Beckenham Junction has now looked for the last 120 years or so, but the period charm supplied by the Austin and Morris cars of yesteryear has gone and an accumulation of clutter has since taken place. Now one of the town's oldest and best known buildings, it is about time that the structure is listed and given a plaque to celebrate it's century and a half of service to the public. (Lens of Sutton Collection)

Beckenham Junction looking down the approach road and entrance gates from the High Street in about 1875 with the booking hall, train shed roof and long platform canopies in evidence and, clearly visible in the background, "the tall and yellow ... earnest and stodgy" Cator Estate houses in Copers Cope Road. (Bromley Libraries)

river Catford Bridge station (1m 38ch) was reached and the line now followed the Pool River before entering the Cator estate and, in the shadow of the Sydenham or Crystal Palace gas works, a station (2m 40ch) at Bell Green which was re-christened a more socially acceptable "Lower Sydenham". Quarter of a mile to the south the line entered the parish of Beckenham and proceeded southwards through a tract of open farmland to a point close to where the later New Beck-enham station was to stand before swinging eastwards to join up with the Farnborough Extension line some 9 chains to the west of the proposed Beckenham station on the Farnborough Extension line. Such was the rural state of the district at that time that in the section between Lower Sydenham and Beckenham stations there were said to be only three inhabited houses and thus even the most optimistic proposer could not say that there was much prospect of any real intermediate traffic then although it was obviously hoped that suburban expansion would follow.

The South Eastern were at first undecided as to whether or not they would support this new Mid Kent Railway scheme but, eventually realising that the construction of a line along the proposed route was probably inevitable, they withdrew their opposition to the Bill and, on 24th May 1855, entered into an agreement with the Mid Kent company whereby in return for the latter completing "a double line of railway with proper stations, signals, sidings & c." and they or their contractors maintaining the permanent way

for the first two years after the opening, the South Eastern would staff the intermediate stations, provide the stock and also operate the trains on the line, in return for a forty per cent of the gross receipts for the first two years and thereafter (once the maintenance obligation had shifted to the South Eastern) fifty per cent. In addition to their share of the gross receipts, the South Eastern would additionally receive a share of the profits of the Mid Kent if, and only if, they exceeded a return of 5¼ per cent[24].

On 23rd July 1855 the Mid Kent Railway Act was passed and thereafter the fledgling company continued with their negotiations with the Cator Estates culminating in two separate Sunday traffic agreements dated 18th September 1855 and 23rd February 1856; these were similar in content to the earlier agreement between the Estate and the WEL&CPR. The contractors responsible for the construction of the Mid Kent were Messrs Smith & Knight, a well regarded local civil engineering firm who had a reputation for the humane and often philanthropic treatment of their employees[25]. The works appear to have begun promptly and to have encountered few difficulties of an engineering nature, having no costly major structures to build, while manpower was also not a problem, there being in the area a surplus of navvies looking for further employment thanks to the recent completion of the Crystal Palace building and grounds. By April 1856 the formation of the new line was progressing well in Beckenham parish and by the late summer of that year virtually all of the earthworks on the line had been completed and the laying of the track had commenced when bad weather now intervened and the Pool River flooded the site in an unfortunate portent of what was to be experienced in later years. To avoid any further disruption to progress, the contractor's men now required to work a great deal of apparently well-paid overtime in order to complete the contract according to schedule and to have the line ready for opening by the end of that year.

The Beckenham Agreement

A problem now arose. The Mid Kent had assumed that, by the time they had reached Beckenham, the Farnborough Extension would have been in place and the 1855 Act had indeed contained provisions for "the mode of effecting communications" between the two lines. However, by the autumn of 1856, the WEL&CPR had not even made a physical entry into the parish and therefore there was, in reality, no line with which the Mid Kent could effect any communication. As a consequence the Mid Kent and West End companies entered into a contract known as the Beckenham Agreement[26] which provided for the construction of a physical link between the two companies and the building of a station at Beckenham (the future Beckenham Junction), the station itself to be owned jointly and administered in perpetuity by a body known as the Beckenham Station Joint Committee. Tenders were accepted from Smith & Knight of £1,000 for the connecting line, and of £4,825 13s 4d for the station and all other ancillary works, the West End company being responsible for paying the whole cost of the connecting line while the cost of the station and other works was to be split between them and Mid Kent companies in the sums of £2,250 and £2,575 13s 4d respectively. The Mid Kent were to pay the contractors the whole sum due in full and upon payment to them by the West End company of their share, the Mid Kent would deliver up to the latter company the line between the junction of the lines and the station in return for the necessary running powers and the payment by them of an annual commuted rentcharge of £50 for the privilege of running over those tracks. It was further agreed that the Joint Committee should be set up as soon as necessary and that it should be composed of two nominated Board members from each company, three of whom would constitute a quorum with powers to fill vacancies and otherwise regulate their affairs. The Agreement further provided that "all clerks, porters or other servants as shall be deemed by them necessary for the traffic of the said station" would be appointed by the Joint Committee who would have the power to fix their salaries or wages. Despite the subsequent differences between the railway companies which succeeded the original partners[27], the Beckenham Agreement remained in force until 1899 when the then parent companies effectively merged their systems and effectively superseded the need for the joint arrangement.

Red, White and Blue

By Christmas 1856 the Mid Kent line was complete and the station at Beckenham had been constructed. Approached through wooden gates and over a gravel driveway, the main station buildings were generally considered to be handsome and befitting the dignity of a village that held itself in high esteem. A neat single-storey booking hall was provided; this structure was in a plain debased Italianate style similar to the other Mid Kent stations at Ladywell and Lower Sydenham and boasted an open brick porch to provide a covered entrance for passengers. Passing through the booking hall, a passenger would find himself standing on the up platform underneath a glass and iron gabled train shed roof - a pleasing structure with decorative end screens supported by sturdy brick retaining walls. On the down platform, which had its own separate entrance from Southend Road, was a small waiting room with accommodation for twelve persons and a separate goods office. The station surroundings were well planted with shrubs from the Cator Estates nursery and the whole effect was enhanced by a rather elaborate colour scheme whereby the woodwork of the train shed was painted white and the iron work red with the nuts and bolts being picked out in blue[28]. A small locomotive turntable was placed near to the Southend Road overbridge and a small engine shed, carriage siding and rudimentary goods facilities were also provided.

Public train services to Beckenham over the Mid Kent line commenced on New Year's Day 1857 with the departure of the 8.40 a.m. passenger train to London Bridge and one might presume that there were local celebrations to mark this event; unfortunately, there being no local newspaper in existence at that time, no account of that auspicious day has survived. An initial weekday service of eleven down and ten up trains was provided, the 8¼ miles from town being covered in between 25 and 30 minutes at a single fare of 1s., 9d. and 6d. respectively for first, second and third class passengers. The service appears to have been a success for within the first year it was augmented by the running of additional trains. Passengers were initially drawn from a wide and rail-less hinterland and connecting road services were provided from Beckenham station to West Wickham, Bromley, Keston, Hayes and Sevenoaks.[29] Sir John Lubbock and his sons were seen daily driving to Beckenham station in an open carriage with two horses, a postillion riding on one, and their return home at 5 p.m. was, according to Walter Mathew, a local resident, "so regular that we set our clocks by him." With such an impressive endorsement, the future of the Mid Kent Railway appeared to be assured.

Chapter 2

THE BATTLE FOR BECKENHAM

"You are no longer a local line, but a great trunk railway from London, via Chatham, to Dover."
Herapath's Journal, August 1859

A Direct and Independent Route

With the Mid Kent barely opened and the Farnborough Extension still to be constructed, Beckenham was now destined to become the battle ground for two rival railway companies. It all began in July 1852 when a small independent concern, the East Kent Railway, promoted a branch line from Canterbury to Strood, where a connection was to be made to the South Eastern Railway's North Kent line. In the following year the East Kent received parliamentary approval for their scheme and in 1855 further powers were obtained to extend their line eastwards from Canterbury to Dover but the company was seriously undercapitalised and progress was, in consequence, slow.

Matters, however, now took a somewhat surprising turn of events. The South Eastern, without warning, announced that they would not carry the trains of the East Kent company over their line from Strood to London Bridge, notwithstanding the facilitation clauses to that effect in the East Kent Railway Act which had specifically provided for the same. The East Kent, having no wish to see their own services relegated to a mere shuttle between Strood and Dover, began to have second thoughts about using the SER line and announced that "The hostile attitude assumed by the South Eastern company, and their apparent determination, if possible, to obstruct the traffic on this line, even to their own injury, has occupied the attention of the Board and in consequence they have resolved to secure a direct and independent route (to London) entirely independent of any hostile company."[1]

The opportunity of the East Kent to hit back at the South Eastern soon presented itself when an independent company, the Mid Kent (Bromley to St Mary Cray) Railway was promoted to build a line in a westwards direction from St Mary Cray and Bickley to Shortlands where it was to join up with the West End of London & Crystal Palace Railway Farnborough Extension. The new company, popularly known as "the Crays", was, despite its full name, nominally independent of both the existing Mid Kent and West End companies, although it was intended that it should connect up with and carry the traffic of both. The South Eastern were, however, also interested in reaching a working agreement with the Crays since on any view a service from Lewisham to Beckenham and Bickley had a certain commercial attraction and in particular the link from Bromley to London that it would afford was an obvious prize to say nothing of any eastwards extension into Kent from St Mary Cray. On 10th April 1856 the South Eastern accordingly proposed to

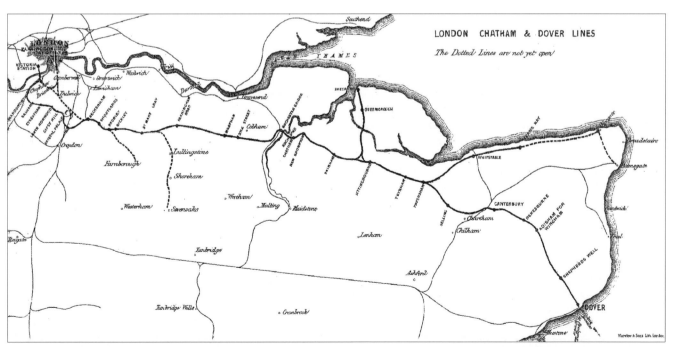

From the LCDR timetable 1862. Note that the Farnborough Extension is still marked and the Metropolitan Extensions are under construction.

the Crays that they would operate the service over the new line in return for one-half of the gross receipts. No such agreement was, however, concluded and on 21st July of that year the Crays' enabling Act[2] was passed with no arrangements for through workings by the South Eastern or indeed any other company having been made.

Under pressure

The WEL&CPR also regarded the Crays with some interest for it now made the construction of the Farnborough Extension, at least so far as the proposed junction with the Crays' line at Shortlands, a much more attractive financial proposition. Times were, however, changing fast and in the same month as the Crays Act was passed, the West End and Brighton Companies entered into an agreement whereby the latter was to work the services of the former between London and Norwood Junction but not any services which were to run over the Farnborough Extension and it became clear that the days of the WEL&CPR as an independent concern, at least insofar as their line from Battersea to Norwood was concerned, was in doubt. The South Eastern now entered the fray and in October 1856 made a proposal to purchase part of the still to be completed Farnborough Extension, namely the section between Beckenham and Shortlands, and to acquire through running powers over the West End company's line between London, Crystal Palace and Beckenham. Once again the South Eastern found its proposals rejected and in the spring of the following year the Brighton and WEL&CPR companies entered into a further agreement and sought parliamentary powers to sanction the sale of the West End Company's line "or any part thereof" to the LBSCR.

The Crays, under pressure from the South Eastern as their still would-be suitor, now formally opposed the WEL&CPR (Traffic and Leasing Arrangements) Bill and further negotiations then took place between the and the South Eastern which resulted in the first of the so-called "Bromley Traffic Agreements" whereby, in return for the Crays dropping their opposition to the Bill, the SER were in turn "entitled to run and pass over and to work and use with their engines and carriages, or with the engines and carriages of any company which might work the traffic of the line from Beckenham to Shortlands, on terms to be settled by arbitration." The Agreement, which the South Eastern regarded as being of some practical importance in that if the Farnborough Extension were to pass into "unfriendly" hands then the essential link between the Mid Kent and Crays line would be preserved, was concluded on 23rd June 1857 and in August of that year the Act authorising the transfer of the WEL&CPR to the LBSCR was passed[3]. Subsequently the Brighton company used the powers given to it in the Act when they entered into a formal lease of the West End line from Pimlico to Norwood and began negotiating for the eventual sale of tha part of the line to them.

The East Kent, seeing the prospect of an independent entry to London via the Crays and Farnborough Extension, now proposed to construct a new line of their own from Strood to St Mary Cray to connect end-on with the Crays at the latter point. The South Eastern, although nominally hostile, adopted a somewhat ambivalent attitude towards the East Kent Railway (Westward Extension) Bill, on the one hand opposing it vigorously but on the other making conciliatory gestures to the promoters of the Bill and attempting to win the East Kent over to the idea of either a merger or the abandonment of their scheme. It was clear that the South Eastern now fully appreciated the threat which the East Kent posed to them for, if their plans came to fruition, it would compromise the South Eastern's lucrative monopoly of boat train and mail traffic from Dover as well as opening up a large area of Kent to their young rival. It was, however, perhaps inevitable that the South Eastern would eventually lose the battle in an age when laissez-faire capitalism frowned upon the discouragement of entrepreneurs and when competition between railways was still seen as desirable but the outcome of the war was not yet a foregone conclusion and the Commons Select Committee, after much deliberation, rejected the East Kent Bill. The battle nevertheless continued with the East Kent refusing to accept defeat at any stage.

Four carriages but few passengers

On 1st October 1857 the WEL&CPR line from Crystal Palace to Norwood Junction was opened to all traffic and Messrs. Peto & Brassey[4], now turned their attentions to the building of the Farnborough Extension line. Within months two separate sections had been completed, the first being a double-track section 2m 5ch in length between the West End line at Bromley Junction and the physical junction with the Mid Kent at Beckenham, and the other a single line 1m 26ch in length from the eastern end of Beckenham station to Shortlands station, the latter being referred to by the WEL&CPR as "Bromley".

The position of the Crays was by now a curious but unenviable one in that they could not ignore the claims of the South Eastern, their natural ally, while at the same time they had to consider the fact that the through traffic to be provided by that company might not be as great as had been originally envisaged. More to the point, the East Kent were now threatening the Crays that if they refused to grant them the necessary running powers over their line then the East Kent would build a parallel line of their own from Shortlands to St Mary Cray. Further pressure came when, on 12 April 1858, the East Kent was granted limited running powers over the WEL&CPR between Pimlico and Shortlands despite bitter protests from the South Eastern who suspected that the LBSCR was deliberately set on a course of trespassing on what they regarded as being properly their own territory. On the 28th of the same month Colonel Yolland of the Board of Trade made his formal inspection of the line from Bromley Junction to Shortlands and was satisfied that it was generally well constructed and virtually complete but he added that he wished to see the bridge over the Brighton line at Bromley Junction widened to take double track within three months, noting in addition that the Beckenham to Shortlands section was a single line built on a double track formation and that the absence of a turntable at Shortlands meant that only a tank engine could be used on this section.

On Monday 3rd May 1858 the first (and, as it turned out, the only) part of the Farnborough Extension was duly opened to traffic and it was reported that

"The first railway train for passengers and goods, left the Shortlands station at 8.40 am. Those who expected the line to be opened with the sound of trumpets and such like ceremony, were disappointed; no intimation of its opening was given until the day previous. A goodly number of the inhabitants were on Martin's Hill to witness the starting of the first train which consisted of four carriages and but few passengers. The station, though progressing rapidly, is far from complete but, when finished, we hope to see a building which shall be an ornament to the neighbourhood as well as useful to the travelling public."[5]

It seems that the station never, in fact, lived up to this promise of being an ornament to the neighbourhood, being a simple single platform on the down side approached from a small and modestly-appointed building at street level via a long passageway and flight of stairs. When the line eastwards from Beckenham was doubled in May of the following year a second platform was added on the up side and

additional station offices in the form of a long two-storey building alongside that platform. The station facilities remained spartan, however, having neither a subway or a footbridge, and prior to its complete reconstruction some thirty-five years later, the station remained the subject of much adverse criticism in the local press.

The Shortlands Shuttle

The LBSCR, having no interest in running any service over the Farnborough Extension themselves, effectively forced the hand of the West End company into operating the service in their own right pending any further developments. Having no stock, for they had never intended to be an operating company, the WEL&CPR were nevertheless under a contractual obligation to run a minimum of five return services per day and accordingly

"Under the resolution of the Board of 19th February (the secretary) had arranged for the purchase of a Tank engine and two First two Second and Two third class carriages of the Brighton Co., for the purpose of working the Bromley line, at the price of £2,624; and that the necessary staff of men recommended by the Brighton Co., had been engaged, being as follows: At Penge station, stationmaster at 25s per week, porter at 16s per week: At Beckenham Junction a signalman at 25s per week: At Bromley station, stationmaster (who also acted as superintendent of the line)

A romanticised view of the Shortlands Estate in about 1870, showing in the foreground Shortlands station, the bridge over the main road to Beckenham and a London-bound train, in the background is the outline of the Crystal Palace. (Bromley Library)

at 30s per week, an assistant clerk at 15s per week, a porter (who also relieved the signalman one day per week) at 18s per week. Two guards at 27s and 24s respectively. One engine driver at 52/6d; one fireman at 28s and one engine cleaner at 21s per week."[6]

The locomotive referred to was an elderly Hawthorn 2-2-2 well tank LBSCR No. 15 of 1845 vintage which was, it is thought, must have been shedded at Beckenham station in the small wooden building lying to the north of the down platform. It would appear that the company seems to have secured something of a bargain for themselves for in 1860, when they ceased to run the service, they were able to sell the stock back to the LBSCR for the same sum that they had originally paid for it even though the stock was by then well past its best and the locomotive, already hopelessly antiquated in design, was in such a state that only two years later it was regarded by the Brighton company as being only fit for scrapping.

With this stock the WEL&CPR ran a daily service of nine up and eight down trains every weekday between Shortlands, Beckenham and Crystal Palace at which point London-bound passengers were required to change trains for all stations to Pimlico while in the case of the 8.31 a.m. up train from Shortlands, an additional connection was advertised with an excursion train bound for Brighton. On Sundays there were six down and five up journeys with the 4.05 amd 5.50 from Shortlands omitting the Beckenham stop. The journey on the Shortlands to Crystal Palace shuttle took between 13 and 15 minutes and was completed at an average speed of about 15 miles per hour, including stops, with the cost of a single ticket being 8d, 6d and 4d for first, second and third class passengers respectively. It was notable that the through passenger fares between Beckenham and Pimlico were appreciably higher than those between Beckenham and London Bridge via the Mid Kent, even though the former route was not only some two miles longer but also involved the need to change trains en-route and these factors did not help to encourage patronage over the West End line so that loadings on the shuttle service were light in comparison with those on the Mid Kent line.

A small station in ancient days

Robert Borrowman, the noted historian of Beckenham a century ago, asserted that that "there was for many years a station on the (Crystal Palace Railway) where the line crosses the Beckenham Road"[7] while Walter Mathew added to local lore by asserting that this small station was known as "Beckenham Road or Birkbeck Halt"[8]. Some may have doubted the accuracy of these accounts, particularly as no mention of a station here ever appeared in the official timetables or in Bradshaw's guide, but both Borrowman and Mathew were correct in that a station did once exist here but it was called neither Beckenham Road nor Birkbeck Halt but, somewhat misleadingly, was named "Penge", despite being a good distance from the settlement of that name[9]. The station appears to have been planned to fulfil a per-

ceived local need for additional railway accommodation in the district although in retrospect the perception seems to have been misconceived as in the vicinity of the station there were few buildings apart from Elm Farm, Thayers Farm and a few detached houses standing in their own grounds while the villages of Beckenham and Penge were both a good walk away and already served by their own stations, Beckenham, in the case of the former and Sydenham and Anerley in the case of the latter.

The plans for Penge station were drawn up by John Fowler and were approved by the WEL&CPR Board on 20 January 1858; they show two platforms with a small station building complete with a clock on the up side with access and a bare platform on the down side with access provided by stairs to the up platform from the north side of Beckenham Road. There were no goods facilities or sidings but the station presumably handled parcels traffic. When Colonel Yolland inspected the line for the Board of Trade prior to its opening he noted that at Penge station the Company still had to provide sloped ramps at the platform ends, that the clock was missing and that "the handles of the distant signals were to be brought together." One can only surmise that this work was carried out expeditiously and that the station was duly opened with the rest of the line on May 3rd 1858 although there is no contemporary account of this. What is perhaps even more curious is that, apart from a reference to the station in an Act of August 1860,[10] Penge is not mentioned again in any extant written records and comparatively little is known about it although Walter Mathew did comment that *"in connection with [the station] I must tell you who was the first, and I might say the only passenger use this station: he was not an Englishman, but in those far-off days a German, viz. Julius Kressman who lived in the High Street. He afterwards became Chairman of the first Beckenham School Board by reason of his knowledge of 'Kultur", I suppose."*

Irrespective of whether Julius Kressman of Gordon House was in fact the only passenger to ever use Penge station, he was in all probability one of the few[11] and it was clear that the station cannot have been a commercial success for although it seems to have survived, possibly as a request or flag stop, up to the cessation of the local passenger services between Beckenham and Crystal Palace in December 1860 there is no evidence of the station having been open after this date. The 1861 Ordnance Survey map, although physically showing the outline of the buildings and platforms omits any mention of it ever having been a station although later editions of OS maps do mark it as "Station (Disused)."[12] In 1911, when consideration was being given to opening on the same site a new halt for the steam railcars then being used on the Crystal Palace to Beckenham Junction service, a local paper noted that at Beckenham Road "at one time stood an old wooden building with a wooden platform which looked as if it might have been used as a small station in ancient days of the line"[13] and, although there would still have been local residents alive at that time who remembered Penge station, no subsequent comment was

Elm Farm from a photograph taken in the 1860s – this inhabitants of this house, immediately adjacent to the WEL&CPR's Penge station, may well have provided it with some passengers although obviously not enough to justify keeping the station open. (from Robert Borrowman, Beckenham Past and Present)

made in the following issues of the paper; that passage seems to have been the first and last description of the station to have appeared in print.

Mr Cator intervenes

The WEL&CPR shuttle from Crystal Palace to Shortlands settled into a quiet and unassuming existence and it is doubtful if it ever carried a great deal of traffic or, ever made any money for the company. Within a short time, however. both the West End and Mid Kent companies managed to fall foul of the Cator estates for apparently blatantly ignoring the Sunday traffic agreements with the result that on 5th August 1858 Edward Bellamy, Secretary of the WEL&CPR, had to issue the following notice to the public:

"In consequence of the restrictions placed upon the Traffic on this line, and of the Mid Kent line, on Sundays, by Mr Cator of Beckenham, the Mid Kent trains marked in the Company's Time Bills for the present month, as stopping on SUNDAYS (in connection with Trains on the West End of London & Crystal Palace Railway) at BECKENHAM in the hours of 1.56 DOWN and 2.30 and 4.30 UP, and at LOWER SYDENHAM at the hours of 1.53 DOWN and 2.34 and 4.34 UP, will NOT stop as advertised."

Regretfully, it was not to be long before there was another skirmish between the Cators and the railways that served Beckenham. In July 1862 a proposed injunction was sought by the estate against both the South Eastern and Mid Kent Railways in relation to the unauthorised stopping of passenger trains at Lower Sydenham[14] and Beckenham stations during the prohibited hours and, once again wisely deciding that legally they did not have a leg to stand on, the companies reluctantly concluded that they had to adhere to their agreements with the Cators however much they may have wished to do otherwise.

Battle Lines Drawn

In the summer of 1858 The Crays line was approaching completion and although at their May 1858 Board meeting the South Eastern had been offered the chance to fund that company, they failed to respond possibly fearing reprisals from the East Kent with whom the South Eastern still one day hoped to merge. In the following month a proposal was made to the South Eastern Board that they should seek to acquire the East Kent outright but, perhaps surprisingly given the unequal bargaining powers of the two companies, while the South Eastern accepted the proposal in principle, the East Kent wholly rejected it. On Monday 5th July 1858 the first section of the Crays opened to all traffic, being the single line from Shortlands (officially renamed as such on that day) to Southborough Road with an intermediate station at Bromley.[15]

On 24 July 1858 the Crays entered into a ten year working agreement with the South Eastern whereby the latter company agreed to work the former in return for a guaranteed initial dividend of £2,250 rising to a maximum of £3,280 per annum on an agreed formula. This working agreement was a direct result of the East Kent having drawn the Crays into their prolonged battle with the South Eastern "at a cost disproportionate to the length of their line" and in consequence then putting pressure on the Crays' Directors to "perfect their relations with their original allies (the SER) and to secured to the proprietors the advantage of a fixed income"[16] Without delay the South Eastern sought to exercise these powers and from 1st August 1858 commenced running their own through services from London Bridge to Southborough Road via Lower Sydenham and Beckenham, using the provision in the 1857 WEL&CPR - Crays agreement which allowed them to run trains over the Beckenham to Shortlands section. The new through services were, however, not run without interruption as, once again, the Pool River intervened and in October 1857 caused a suspension of all trains on the Mid Kent when it burst its banks and washed away part of the formation of the line between Catford and Beckenham.

On 28 July 1858 the East Kent Railway gained parliamentary approval for their Western Extension[17] and the immediate effect of this was to cause a 2% fall in the shares of the South Eastern. Among the provisions of this Act the East Kent was given the power to run its own trains over the Crays line or, if the Crays did not consent to this, over a parallel line constructed by the East Kent thus forcing the smaller company to agree not only to the running powers but also to physically double the whole of their line between Shortlands and Bickley "so as not to impede the expresses of the East Kent". In the following month, August 1858, the line from Bickley to St Mary Cray was opened and from then onwards through trains ran from St Mary Cray to London Bridge via Beckenham and the Mid Kent line. In the same month the Directors of the Mid Kent company, as if to emphasise their independence from the South Eastern, duly reported to their shareholders that "Traffic has improved especially with the opening of the Crays and that they regard with satisfaction the passing of the Act in the present session for the East Kent extension … which cannot but be the means of throwing a considerable additional traffic upon this line."

Local opinion was, however, less positive and the *Bromley Record* reported that, in connection with the announcement that 40 trains per day would run over the Crays, "Not a little alarm was occasioned … as they would have to work on a single-line of rails between Shortlands and Beckenham while to make the matter still more alarming at that time no means of telegraphic communication had been provided, so that if the utmost care was not exercised, numerous accidents must be the result." They were not and, notwithstanding the heavy snowfalls in the spring, the line from Beckenham to Southborough Road was doubled by June 1859 and the telegraph satisfactorily installed, the contractors for the work again being Smith & Knight. At the same time work was progressing satisfactorily on the East Kent's Western Extension from Strood to St Mary Cray and in the following month the doubling of the Shortlands to Bickley section of line was reported as having been completed.

Farnborough unextended

In the spring of 1859 the tripartite negotiations between the West End, Brighton and East Kent companies were progressing in relation to the sale of the West End line and on 2nd April the East Kent entered into an agreement with the WEL&CPR to purchase from them the Farnborough Extension from Norwood to Shortlands, together with (a) running powers over the now-LBSCR line to Pimlico and (b) the right to build the line from Shortlands to Farnborough all for an agreed sum of £100,200 with interest[18]. Clause (III) of the agreement provided that the West End company would, if so desired by the East Kent, work the line from Crystal Palace to Shortlands until such time as the East Kent were in a position to operate their own trains via the Crays line. The East Kent did so desire and accordingly the Shortlands to Crystal Palace shuttle service by then worked by the WEL&CPR continued as before and on 23rd July 1860 the WEL&CPR (Transfer of Farnborough Extension and Dissolution of Company) Act[19] was duly passed. The power to build the extension onwards from Shortlands

Right - Bradshaw's Timetable for August 1858.

to Farnborough had been kept alive by the WEL&CPR (Extension of Time) Act[20] of the previous year but the East Kent as the new owners of the line, having rather more pressing concerns to deal with, showed no real interest in completing the extension to the eponymous village, despite the lobbying of those who lived along its proposed route but were still unwilling to contribute towards its construction cost. The last mention of the ill-fated extension line from Shortlands to Farnborough seems to have been in the spring of 1863 when the *Bromley Record* reported that an attempt was being made to stake out the course of the line over Bromley Common but local opposition caused the statutory powers to construct the line to be finally abandoned in 1865 and Farnborough was destined not to have its railway.

The Beckenham & Sydenham Railway

In 1859 proposals were advanced for a new line to be called the Beckenham & Sydenham Junction Railway, a nominally independent concern backed by Sir Morton Peto, the contractor, and several East Kent directors including their engineer, Thomas Russel Crampton. The purpose of this short line was, ostensibly, to provide a link between Beckenham and the ex-London & Croydon line at Sydenham but in reality was designed to allow the East Kent direct access to London Bridge station and thus give that company a gateway to the City without having to use the Mid Kent and South Eastern Lines. Opposition was put up by the LBSCR who objected on the somewhat spurious ground that "the proposed junction at Sydenham is unsuitable for the intended service and that in consequence the company would be unable to handle the extra traffic which the proposed railway might be expected to generate"; in reality the Brighton had no desire to help the East Kent whom they regarded as being an opportunistic venture and a potential threat to both the South Eastern and themselves and the clause in the Bill that required the LBSCR to forward East Kent traffic through to London Bridge was seen as being particularly offensive. The Brighton company made it clear that they would do their utmost to obstruct the passage through Parliament of the Beckenham & Sydenham Bill and thus the Bill was swiftly defeated by its opponents but its spectre lived on in the further proposals of a similar nature, none of which were to ever reach fruition.

London, Chatham and Dover

On 1st August 1859 the East Kent, in a bold and provocative gesture, changed its title to that of the London, Chatham and Dover Railway - a title which was not only more geographically correct but made the intentions of the Company abundantly clear even if it lent itself to later alteration by a less respectful general public into the *"Land 'em, Smash 'em and Turn 'em over Railway"* or, more concisely, the *"Bash 'em and Over"*. By the autumn of 1859, however, and still long before the completion of their Western Extension, the newly-named LCDR were beginning to

have serious doubts about the suitability of their recently purchased Farnborough Extension from the WEL&CPR to serve as a proper main line with which to reach London. These doubts were crystallised after the subsequent opening of the main-line when the shareholders were told that "The present line to the West End is an extremely bad one and much longer than is necessary, and in addition we have not the command of our trains that we should have for we are obliged to fix our times to suit those of the London and Brighton Railway, which are very numerous and a prime source of inconvenience"

The LCDR therefore announced that they were to seek approval for the construction of an entirely new and independent route from Beckenham to London and, despite the fact that as late as November 1859 secret negotiations towards a possible merger between the two companies were still progressing, the South Eastern committed themselves to strongly opposing the LCDR proposal realising that, if granted, their rival would be in a position to compete with them on equal terms and prosper in a way that they did not wish to see. When it became obvious that opposition to the LCDR Bill was unlikely to be successful, the South Eastern resorted to blackening the already unhealthy credit of the LCDR by spreading rumours of impending bankruptcy on the basis, as noted by the *Railway Times*, that "when the Chatham company is reduced to beggary, then the South Eastern may buy up the concern for about one-tenth of its actual cost." On 6th August 1860 the LCDR (Metropolitan Extensions) Act[22] was passed although one of the more controversial provisions, a direct branch to Crystal Palace on a gradient of 1 in 20 to be worked by rope or three locomotives[23] had by now been abandoned. Construction of the Metropolitan Extensions was not to begin until the Company had opened the main-line eastwards from St Mary Cray but there was, however, not long to wait and the East Kent Western Extension line was completed and physically joined up with the Crays within three months of that date.

On 31st October 1860 the first (unofficial) through train ran from Canterbury to the new LBSCR London Victoria station on the north side of the Thames via the Farnborough Extension, the former WEL&CPR "main" line and the recently opened short line of the Victoria Station & Pimlico Railway[24]. Then, after completing the finishing touches and having obtained approval from the Board of Trade, on 3rd December of that year the public service of the LCDR was inaugurated between London and Canterbury although the initial down service, hauled by a Stephenson 4-4-0 locomotive named "Aeolus"[25] inauspiciously failed to live up to its mythological title as "the ruler of the winds" and contrived to break down. Despite this public relations setback services were soon running in their normal intended pattern of eight weekday trains, six of which ran to from Chatham and Canterbury and two to and from St Mary Cray, all trains stopping at Shortlands and Beckenham with the exception of the 7.55 am and 7.15 pm up departures and their corresponding return workings from Victoria. On Sundays there were only four trains and the 2.45 pm and 4.47 pm depar-

The elevated Saxby signalbox at Beckenham Junction seen towards the end of its life. Looking westwards we can see the West End of London line and the LCDR up main line in the left foreground with the Mid Kent (upon which the carriages are standing) to the middle right. Clearly visible in this view is the additional bracing and added panelling dating from about 1870 together with the ungainly roof-mounted SER signals and the scene is completed by the signal men and a signal lad posing at the entrance to their box. (C.B.Walker, Photographer, Upper Norwood)

through trains although tickets were still sold to and from Crystal Palace via Beckenham to all stations to Canterbury.

An early signalbox

Signalling was required to be installed at Beckenham station in compliance with the provisions of the Mid Kent Railway Act of 1855 and it is likely that some form of signalbox was provided for the opening of the WEL&CPR line in May 1858 when a signalman was first employed here. Although there is no mention of a signalbox in Colonel Yolland's inspection report or indeed in the Minutes of any of the relevant railway companies, the 1861 Ordnance Survey map does show a small structure labelled "S.B." to the west of the down platform and it can be presumed that this was the original 1858 box.[26] By the time that the LCDR through trains were running through to London via the WEL&CPR line in December 1860 it seems that a replacement signalbox had been built on the up side close to the junction of what was now the Chatham main-line and the Mid Kent and this box, a photograph of which survives, was of the notoriously draughty Saxby type 1a, a gaunt wooden structure elevated on stilts with everything below the operating floor open to the elements.[27] The building was in later years modified with additional bracing and new panelling and was made even more ungainly by the placing of signals on the roof. These signals were of standard South Eastern pattern the arms of which were painted with white dots instead of stripes and at night lamps, containing revolving coloured lenses, were shown although the same lamp served both up and down lines simultaneously. Beckenham was said to have been the second location in the country to have had the new Saxby patent interlocking signalling installed "which, at the time, was looked upon as somewhat of a marvel" and if this reference by Walter Mathew is indeed correct then it presumably concerned the patent for Saxby's new interlocking frame taken out in 1860 and first installed at Victoria station in November of that year with Beckenham as the second example.

In 1863 Charles Walker, in a paper on contemporary signalling practice[28], stated that at Beckenham "although the signalman was somewhat removed from the station, the station master heard by a platform-bell all the signalling that was going on in the signalbox and had all the information required of the various kinds of train." Another account of the Beckenham box[29] stated that

"There were 36 levers and the points had to be set right before the signal levers could be pulled over, but even this was not enough to guard against accidents so that ten minutes before the morning and evening boat trains were due, the signalman had to put a bolt through the tongue facing the points and screw on a nut. The stationmaster, Mr Moore, had to see it done and wait until the train had passed."

The reason for such extraordinary prudence appears to have been that the intense competition between the LCDR and the South Eastern for the tidal ferry traffic from

tures from Shortlands omitted the Beckenham stop on account of the Cator Sunday Traffic Agreement. The public timetable warned passengers entraining at stations between Bickley and Beckenham that they could not book with the LCDR for stations wholly within that local area or between there and London and that they should use the Mid Kent services to London Bridge instead. On the same day that the LCDR through service was inaugurated the local train service between Crystal Palace and Beckenham was discontinued and both places were then only calling points on the

A busy scene at Beckenham Junction - the first in a series of three views probably taken in the early 1880s - showing the down platform with workmen attending to various tasks but not, apparently, including repairs to the glazing of the trainshed roof or a much-needed general sprucing up – the suggestion that the station was by this time a "dirty and disreputable structure" seems to have some foundation in fact! (Tony Harden collection)

the Channel ports led to a desire to avoid any unnecessary delays to the boat trains which would, had the points not been so secured, have been subject to a severe speed limit over them and thus would loose a couple of valuable minutes from their already-tight schedule at Beckenham.

The Beckenham section

Despite the very real concern that the London, Chatham and Dover Railway had over-extended itself financially and was on the verge of financial collapse, construction of the Metropolitan Extensions went ahead. The works were to consist of three separate sections, namely (1) the Beckenham section between Beckenham and Herne Hill, (2) the West End Section from Herne Hill to Brixton and Battersea where trains would then travel over the LBSCR to Victoria and (3) the City section from Herne Hill to Elephant and Castle and Blackfriars. Despite the considerable expense that the new lines would involve (£1.1 million), largely as a result of major engineering works such as the building of

extensive sections of the line on brick viaducts, the end result would be to shorten the distance to Victoria by some three miles on an easier and less congested route than the WEL&CPR line, give the LCDR direct access to the City and to open up potential new middle-class suburbs for development at Brixton, Loughborough, Camberwell and, especially, on the extensive Dulwich College estates.

The Beckenham section was originally to include two separate connections to the LBSCR in Penge, similar to the earlier Beckenham & Sydenham Junction scheme, but these where deleted when a slight deviation to the west was sanctioned and the final route of the section agreed. Preliminary costings suggested that the tunnel required to pass under the formidable barrier of Sydenham Hill would be more than 2,200 yards long and would cost more than £200,000 or, more prosaically, £90 for every yard of track and in addition it was said that the boring of the tunnel would inevitably delay the opening of the line. In January 1861 the LCDR Board were said to have discussed the possibility of diverting the line around Sydenham Hill so as to avoid the expense of the tunnel but the desire for the most direct route possible apparently overcame this objection.[30]

On 6 August 1861 the LCDR (Works) Act was passed[31] and the final route of the 4m 20ch Beckenham section was now clear. Diverting from the former Farnborough Extension line at Penge Junction, 36 chains west of Beckenham station, the line was to swing to the north-west, crossing Kent House Lane on a three-arch viaduct and passing to the north of Penge village before crossing on the level the Penge to Sydenham road. On the west side of the crossing was situated Penge station, 1m 39ch from Beckenham. The line then passed through the Penge tunnel[32], the first 150 yards of which was a covered way under both the LBSCR Crystal Palace branch and the former London & Croydon line and was provided to preserve the amenities of the Lawrie Park estate; this covered way was removed in 1902 when the LBSCR lines were then provided with separate bridges over the LCDR line. Seven shafts were to be built to ventilate the tunnel, one of which required to be modified so that it blended into the surrounding scenery better, but it soon became apparent that the shafts could not cope well with the effusions of smoke from passing engines and the tunnel was, until the time of the suburban electrification of the 1920s said to be "notorious for its unwholesome atmosphere."[33] About half way through the Penge Tunnel the new line left the parish of Beckenham and entered the parish of Camberwell where two further stations were to be provided, Sydenham Hill and Dulwich (the present West Dulwich) before Herne Hill was reached.

Unexampled vigour

Construction of the Metropolitan Extensions began in early 1861 and in August of that year the LCDR minutes contain a commendation of the contractors, Peto and Betts, who were said to be carrying on the works "with unexampled vigour". Much of the materials used by the contractors was landed at Angerstein Wharf on the Thames and carried over the Mid Kent line, bringing a welcome boost in revenues to that company. What is perhaps surprising, given the

Beckenham Junction - The view from the footbridge looking in the opposite direction with the up bay platform for Norwood and Crystal Palace trains visible on the left and the down Mid Kent bay on the right; notice the clutter of Victorian advertisements vying for the attention of travellers and the door leading to the down side exit from the station. (Tony Harden collection)

Beckenham Junction - this time looking east towards Southend Road bridge and showing the narrow and steep stairs to the footbridge over which passengers had to hurry to change trains (with, on one occasion, a fatal result)and the apparently well -stocked bookstall on the up platform. (Tony Harden collection)

now largely built-up nature of the area, is that on the whole of the Beckenham section only three houses in total required to be demolished, a good illustration of how what are now the suburbs of London had yet to be developed. The total cost of the lands acquired to build the Beckenham section amounted to £83,512, of which sum £21,800 was paid to the Dulwich College estate governors.[34]

By mid-1861 work was progressing well on the Penge Tunnel, a project of great difficulty given its length and the fact that the bore had to pass through the London clay which was described by experts as being both "treacherous" and "liable to slip". One by-product of the clay, however, was that it proved most suitable for brick making – the result was that of the 200,000 cubic yards of clay excavated, a total of 29 million bricks were made on site and these were used not only to line the tunnel but also to build the viaducts needed to carry the City section over the crowded streets of South London. At one time 2,000 men and 250 horses were employed on the project and both day and night shifts were being worked in order that completion of the line was not delayed. At Penge the construction site covered 16 acres and, after the works were completed, the area was used for housing, the name of the LCDR engineer and their general manager being com-

memorated in the names of Crampton Road and Forbes Road[36]. The tunnel itself was lined with twelve courses of brick for the first 60 feet and thereafter eight to ten courses sufficed but unfortunately economies were made which resulted in sub-standard dimensions occurring; though the tunnel was not seriously undersized it was said that the reduced bore subsequently placed restrictions on the dimensions of LCDR passenger stock.[37]

By the end of October 1861 the LCDR line from Canterbury to Dover Harbour was complete and from 1 November boat trains commenced running to Victoria via Beckenham and Crystal Palace[38]. The position of the Crays company was now virtually untenable and as a result the Directors entered into negotiations with the LCDR leading, on 7th August 1862, to the passing of the Mid Kent Railway (Bromley to St Mary Cray) (Leasing and Transfer) Act[39]. This provided that, with effect from 1st August 1863, the LCDR would be granted a 999-year lease over the Crays in return for specified payments and, somewhat surprisingly, the latter company survived as an independent concern up to 1923. A specific section of the same Act allowed for the "facilitating [of] transmission of other companies' traffic" over the Crays line and over the Farnborough Extension between Beckenham and Shortlands "on equal terms with

Penge East station from a postcard of 1900 showing the fine LCDR building designed by company architect John Taylor and roofed with his patent tiles; the bridge which replaced the level crossing is seen on the right. (Nancy Tonkin collection)

Penge East station 2009, showing that the original building, now listed, continues to do service after almost a century and a half. Although the front canopy and patent the tiles have gone the station still has a dignified presence. (A M Hajducki)

A postcard view of Penge East in about 1905 with railway staff and passengers having their picture taken; the plethora of advertising material is very typical of the period. (Nancy Tonkin collection)

and as if it were their own proper traffic and without preference and in order to provide for the due and punctual correspondence of trains at Beckenham, all trains timed to stop at Shortlands were to stop at Beckenham … and the South Eastern shall arrange their trains so as to meet the service of the [LCDR] at Beckenham." As subsequent events were to show, neither the LCDR or the South Eastern made any effort to keep to the spirit of this second "Bromley Traffic Agreement", particularly as it affected the due and punctual correspondence at Beckenham.

Management, care and skill

Construction of the Beckenham section proceeded rapidly and on 19th August 1862 the contractors informed the Board that "commencing at Penge, a bridge has been built and the embankment between there and the Penge viaduct is nearly completed." In February 1863 the company's engineer reported that "all the bridges between the junction at Beckenham and the tunnel are built with the exception of a small stream arch near the commencement of the line and the embankment has advanced to within half a mile of that point. The station at Penge was now under construction and was to be a substantial gabled structure on the up side of the line and designed by the company's architect John Taylor. Built of yellow brick with red brick horizontal bands and pointed window arches and springers in Portland stone, the building was roofed with Taylor's patent tiles and is now

regarded as one of the LCDR's most impressive medium, sized stations. Over the platforms there were long canopies to protect passengers from the elements and adjacent to the up platform there was a large two-road goods shed while the main building itself housed the usual station offices together with the stationmaster's home. Although the company's timetables always referred to the station simply as Penge, Bradshaw's guide insisted until 1869 upon the title of Penge Lane although this was strictly unofficial; occasionally Penge (LCDR) was used thereafter until, in 1923, the station was officially re-named by the Southern Railway as Penge East.

At Beckenham station the turntable and locomotive shed were removed and both the up and down platforms were extended in length and provided with plain canopies above each to run westwards from the train shed roof. By the spring of 1863 the line was said to be almost complete and although a proposal to add a third line between Beckenham and Bickley was mooted at this time, this idea was rejected and the Board decided instead to bring the former Crays line up to acceptable main-line standard "at considerable cost." Much praise was given to the way in which the line between Herne Hill and Beckenham had been constructed so as to have reduced disruption to other lines to a minimum and in particular "The efficiency of the [Penge] tunnel contractors in the building of the tunnel was greatly admired and at the eastern end of the tunnel the new line passes under nine lines of rails belonging to the Brighton

Penge East on a wet and dreary day in the winter of 1964 – the station was (and still is) in much the same state as when it was built although the footbridge is a replacement for the former level crossing; in the background is the Penge Tunnel. (John Minnis collection)

and South Eastern companies and when it is considered that 360 trains per day passed over these lines and that not one of these lines was obstructed for a single day in the process of carrying out the new line under them, the management, care and skill of accomplishing such a work must be apparent."[40]

The Board of Trade inspection having been carried out, the Company now announced that the great day had arrived and on 1st July 1863 trains began running over the new route from Beckenham to Victoria via Herne Hill. The new services proved to be a success from the outset and at the LCDR half-yearly meeting on 28th August the Directors reported that "since the opening to Beckenham, the receipts have averaged about £133 per mile per week and last week they reached nearly £150 per mile per week." There were, however, two local casualties associated with the new line. On 1 July 1863 the LCDR running powers over the LBSCR line between Crystal Palace and Victoria were terminated although running powers still remained between the former point and Beckenham Junction[41]. Notwithstanding this all passenger services between Beckenham and Crystal Palace were immediately withdrawn, presumably on the basis that they would have been unable to pay their way, and thereafter the LCDR public timetable informed passengers that "Sydenham Hill and Penge are the nearest stations to the

Crystal Palace" without mentioning the fact that both involved a bracing uphill walk.

On the same day the LBSCR opened a new station at Penge on the site of the previous London & Croydon establishment and this station, referred to by Bradshaw until 1879 as Penge Bridges and thereafter as Penge (LBSCR) until being re-named Penge West in 1923 to differentiate it from the LCDR East station, survives to the present day. The LBSCR station was to provide competition for the LCDR line insofar as traffic from the Penge area was concerned but, since the area was now being rapidly developed as a London suburb, it was felt that there was apparently plenty of goods and passenger traffic for both even if in the event it was the LCDR who took the lion's share of the business. The second local service casualty occurred exactly three months later when, on October 1st 1863 (the date upon which the LCDR lease over the Crays took effect), the South Eastern discontinued running their own Mid Kent services beyond Beckenham although they still attached carriages from London Bridge trains to a limited number of LCDR trains at the junction but, for all intents and purposes, the Battle for Beckenham was effectively over.

Chapter 3
NEW LINES, NEW LANDSCAPES

*"The area which the railway would run through is very countrified and would be
an attractive outlet for persons living in London."*
Evidence to Select Committee on Addiscombe Extension Bill 1862

Croydon by the back door

The Mid Kent had, from the very beginning, ambitions to extend their line to Croydon, an important and growing centre for traffic which, until then, was served only by the LBSCR. At the Half-yearly Meeting of the MKR shareholders held in February 1857 it was recorded that "the Directors congratulated the shareholders on the completion of their line" at a total cost of some £68,409 and added that they were now in a position to go ahead with a line from Beckenham to the Fair Field, Croydon at an estimated cost of £100,000. Though the shareholders appear to have agreed in principle to the suggestion of an extension to Croydon there were those who thought that the financial aspects of the scheme would lead to ruin – in the words of one shareholder, Mr Brockman, "no doubt it will be a profitable undertaking for the lawyers, engineers, contractors and landowners and an expensive one for the shareholders" while John Cator, one of the MKR directors who also represented the Cator estates, said that "although he believed that the extension would be a valuable adjunct to their line" he objected to it on the basis that the proposed cost of this extension was too great. The other shareholders, however, won the day and voted 6:1 for the proposed new line to Croydon and in consequence Mr Cator, as a sole dissenter amongst the directors, was promptly and ignominiously voted off the Board by the enraged shareholders.

The LBSCR were, needless to say, hostile to the whole idea of a MKR branch to Croydon, believing it to be a ploy of the South Eastern (as the company responsible for the operation of the Mid Kent on a day-to-day basis) to allow them to effectively enter that town by the back door while at the same time the South Eastern were worried that the Brighton company might themselves acquire the Mid Kent, particularly as the LBSCR already had had discussions about a possible link between the two systems and would thus literally be in a position to challenge the SER for traffic to the heartlands of Kent.

The Norwood Spur

In April 1858 two separate but interconnected proposals were put forward, the first for a short spur line from the Brighton line at Norwood Junction to the Farnborough Extension line east of Bromley Junction and second for a west-facing spur from the Mid Kent to the Farnborough Extension line which would allow trains to by-pass Beckenham station and thus giving a direct connection between the

Mid Kent line and the LBSCR without the necessity for a reversal of direction at Beckenham. The Mid Kent were enthusiastic about both of these proposals and, as the Board reported to the shareholders in July 1858, "direct access will thus be given to all places on the Brighton line's system, which will undoubtedly bring a large accession to the Mid Kent Line." The Brighton company, initially in favour, became less enthusiastic when the Beckenham & Sydenham Junction project (referred to in the previous chapter), was floated since this would place city-bound traffic from the East Kent directly on to their line rather than over the Mid Kent. Then, in a complex series of negotiations between all of the companies concerned, the LBSCR and Mid Kent dropped all opposition to the important South Eastern London Bridge to Charing Cross extension scheme in return for not opposing the proposed link between the WEL&CPR and Brighton line. The Mid Kent Beckenham spur line proposals, after opposition from the LBSCR, were then quietly abandoned for the time being and on 1st August 1859 the latter company obtained powers for a 50-chain double track railway known as the Norwood Spur line which was to leave the former Farnborough Extension line in an easterly direction at Norwood Spur Junction (1m 70ch west of Beckenham station) and end a point just north of Norwood Junction where it physically connected with the Brighton down main-line[1]. The enabling Act contained provisions for through running of trains from the East Kent and it was envisaged that the Norwood Spur would carry transfer freight and passenger traffic between the two systems as well as a local passenger service.

However reaching any agreement between the LBSCR and the LCDR, as the new owners of the Farnborough Extension, proved problematic and, after recourse to counsel and arbitration proceedings, a new agreement was drawn up which provided that

"The LCDR shall at all times run between the Beckenham and Norwood junction stations ... such a number of trains as, having regard to the convenience of the public shall be reasonable for the interchange of traffic between the stations and the railways of the Dover and Mid-Kent Railway Companies respectively and the Norwood Junction station ... and stations southward and all profits and losses accrued in working the trains between Beckenham and the said Norwood Junction stations for the local traffic shall be borne in equal shares between the Company and the Dover Company ..."[2]

A new bay platform was built next to the down line at Norwood Junction and a small eleven-lever frame signalbox was provided at Norwood Spur Junction to control entry to and from the spur and, on 18th June 1862, the line was opened to all traffic. Passenger services over the Norwood Spur were provided by a Norwood to Beckenham shuttle service of ten weekday trains; there was no Sunday service. It seems, however, as though the anticipated interchange of traffic between the two systems never materialised despite publicity efforts on the part of both the Brighton and Chatham companies and business always remained light perhaps as a result of all local traffic being served only by the shuttle between Norwood Junction and Beckenham and, if it the local service had been extended at both ends so as to run between Bromley and Croydon, it might have fared a little better in respect of the number of passengers carried and the fares collected. Notwithstanding this, the basic Norwood to Beckenham passenger service continued virtually unaltered throughout its life and the unremarkable five-minute journey with its sparse loadings and antiquated carriages, provided a useful, if under-used, link in the Beckenham railway network.

The Addiscombe Extension

The South Eastern were, however, unsatisfied in their own ambitions to serve Croydon via the Mid Kent and still harboured thoughts of a direct line to the centre of that town even if they were, understandably, wary of taking on the Brighton company. At the end of 1861 a new scheme was floated to build a line 3m 20ch in length between Beckenham and Addiscombe Road, about half-a-mile east of Croydon town centre, and in the middle of an area which was thought to be ripe for residential development particularly in relation to a parcel of land formerly owned by the East India Company. The impetus behind the Addiscombe scheme was that the Mid Kent, having clearly been frustrated in its attempts to form a useful through route to the middle and eastern part of Kent by the opening of the LCDR main line, saw a lucrative future for itself as a suburban line and they were keen to extend their operations and open up further areas to the speculative builder – hardly surprising when one considers that the Chairman of the Mid Kent was William Wilkinson, who was not only also deputy chairman of the National Land Company but, in his own right, owned much land suitable for housebuilding in the Beckenham and Croydon areas including the grounds of his own residence at Shortlands. The proposed line to Addiscombe was not, however, quite the end of the South Eastern designs upon the middle of Croydon for, in opposition to the not dissimilar LBSCR Croydon Central scheme for a short branch to serve the very centre of the town (itself a reaction to the Addiscombe proposals), the SER supported a proposal to extend the MKR Addiscombe line right up to a terminus at Croydon Town Hall; when this was rejected by Parliament, a further scheme, this time for a line between Addiscombe and the South Eastern's Caterham branch, was briefly put forward. The outcome of all of these proposals and counter-proposals was that the Mid Kent branch to Ad-

discombe (but not beyond) became a reality.

The Addiscombe Extension, as the proposed line was now known, received almost immediate unqualified local support and in the evidence given at the House of Lords Select Committee on Railway Bills Hearings in June 1862 it was said that "many local people travelled to the market at Croydon on market days and the Norwood Spur service was unsatisfactory owing to the delays in obtaining a connection for Croydon at Norwood Junction." Hopes were also expressed that the new line would bring about the development of the areas around the stations and a local magistrate and landowner, E. R. Adams of Elmers End, summed up the position when he informed the committee that "The area through which the line would run was very countrified and would become an attractive outlet for persons from London. The [Elmers End] station would be very convenient for persons living in West Wickham, whose population has not increased lately but here are several good houses whose gentlemen go backwards and forwards to London every day. This would probably lead to an increase in building about West Wickham." John Fowler, the engineer of the proposed line, then expressed with great prescience the view that the land towards West Wickham was eminently suitable for building on and confidently stated that a branch to there from the Addiscombe line would eventually be built. On 13th June 1862 the Mid Kent company concluded a Sunday travel agreement with Albemarle Cator, by now the life tenant of the Cator estates in terms similar to the earlier agreements, and on 17th July of that year the Mid Kent (Extension to Addiscombe) Act received the Royal assent[3].

The new double-track line was to leave the Mid Kent 26 chains north-west of Beckenham station and a new station, subsidised by the Cator estates and on land gifted by them, was to be built immediately south of the junction with the original line with platforms on both the original and Extension routes. This station, which was intended for passenger and parcels traffic only, was given the invented name of "New Beckenham", there being no habitation in the immediate area although a start had been made on the Cator's Beckenham Park estate at Copers Cope Road. The main platform of New Beckenham station, with a plain yellow brick-built building housing the station offices and adjoining two-storey gabled station master's home with a bay window encroaching on to the platform, was situated on the up side of the Extension line; on the down platform a small shelter was provided while to the south a small signal box was built. No platforms were provided to serve the original line from the junction to Beckenham station.

From New Beckenham the new line travelled south, passing under the LCDR line just east of Penge Junction, where it then took a south-westerly arc through Thayer's Farm, the farm road being crossed on the level at Chaffinch or Clock House Crossing. The line then crossed the Chaffinch Brook, a prettily-named tributary of the Pool River, and close to the 18th century Clock House which was owned by the Cators, passed under Beckenham Road, a

The main building of the first New Beckenham station which was closed in 1866 and only recently demolished; this view dates from August 1988 and was taken from Bridge Road. The junction at New Beckenham and the third (1904) station are visible in the background where a Charing Cross-bound service is about to depart from the up platform (Andrew Hajducki)

bridge being substituted for the original planned level crossing on the insistence of the Beckenham Local Board. In order to keep the road gradients as gentle as possible (an important consideration in the days of horse-drawn traffic)[4] the railway line dipped at this point and in consequence the deck of the girder bridge over the Chaffinch Brook was only a few feet above water level - a fact that subsequently caused the Company and its successors endless trouble with flooding on the line at this location. The curious change in direction of the line south of New Beckenham may have been caused by a desire not to affect adversely the grounds of the Clock House but may also have been influenced with the fact that it was at the proposed junction with the Beckenham, Lewes & Brighton Railway referred to later.

Elmer's End and beyond

From the Beckenham Road bridge the line passed through open farmland and under Clay Lane to the site of the next station, Elmer's End, 1m 17ch south of New Beckenham. Here the station, whose name reflected the Aylmour family who had once lived in the vicinity (the apostrophe was later dropped) was a simple affair with up and down platforms. The station building, similar to that at New Beckenham, was on the down side at the end of a short approach road from the east and contained accommodation for the stationmaster and his family as well as a booking office. No footbridge or up platform shelter was provided and little

traffic was expected for the area was largely devoid of houses although the Free Trade Freehold Land Company had just bought up a parcel of land for the development of what became Dorset, Gwydor, Ancaster and Maberley Roads. The new line then passed into Surrey and continued in an unencumbered course to the terminus at Croydon (Addiscombe Road).[5]

On 27th March 1863 Smith & Knight were appointed as contractors on a tender of £75,000 inclusive of £5,000 in respect of the three stations. Work progressed rapidly and although delays were caused by inclement weather, there were few serious problems encountered. An agreement was then reached between the South Eastern and the LBSCR to the effect that each company would charge a similar fare for journeys between London and East Croydon and London and Addiscombe in order to prevent any ruinous fare-cutting between them and the new line was then formally inspected by Captain Rich of the Board of Trade who, on 2nd March 1864, found it to be a solidly built double track line with five overbridges and all stations completed to a satisfactory standard "except for clocks which will be provided immediately". The line opened on schedule to the public on 1st April 1864 and without ceremony the initial weekday service between London Bridge and Addiscombe consisted of eleven up and down weekday trains with four trains on a Sunday. Between London Bridge and Beckenham via the original line there were seventeen weekday and eight Sunday trains, with the majority of the week-

Elmers End looking from the road bridge to the south in about 1900 – the houses in the background are in St Margarets Road and were a casualty of the Blitz. (Nancy Tonkin collection)

The war damaged down side of Elmers End seen from the approach road with the site of the back gardens of the largely flattened St Margarets Road on the left and, on the right, the original Mid Kent booking office and stationmaster's house looking partly derelict while the only entry appears to be via a gate next to the ticket collectors wooden hut. (John Minnis collection)

day trains conveying through coaches to Shortlands, Bromley and Bickley. From the same date and for the avoidance of doubt the station at Beckenham was officially renamed "Beckenham Junction" although for many years afterwards the suffix was often omitted in timetables and railway compan documents.

A foolish bargain

By this time the Mid Kent was in its last days of independence. In February 1863 the South Eastern expressed an interest in buying out the smaller company and in August of that year the formal proposal that they should buy out the Mid Kent for £200,000 was put to the SER shareholders; eventually it was agreed that the Mid Kent stock was to be exchanged for £116,000 of South Eastern stock at an agreed guaranteed annual return of 7½%. The Mid Kent shareholders were pleased, the South Eastern's rather less so and Coles Child, a director of the LBSCR and Lord of the Manor of Bromley[6], spoke out strongly at a shareholder's meeting and said of the Mid Kent

"On this short line there is only one station of any significance whatever, viz. Beckenham ... On 1st September the Crays passes into the hands of the Chatham and ... it is only reasonable to suppose that this will prejudicially affect the receipts. When the Metropolitan Extension ... is opened to Blackfriars a further abstraction will take place. My own opinion is that the line will only then barely pay its working expenses. Our Directors press upon the fortunate proprietors of the Mid Kent a premium of £40,000, or £30 for each £20 share! I cannot understand it and must say that I have never heard of anything more reckless or outrageous. Of the Addiscombe extension I think nothing; there are scarcely any houses between Beckenham and Addiscombe; the line too between these points runs through a cold wet clay district not adapted for building and its only prospective value is an extension to Croydon (defeated this session) and a means of annoyance to the Brighton"

At the following South Eastern half-yearly meeting in July 1864 Coles Child repeated his sentiments and added that the purchase was "one of the most foolish bargains that the South Eastern Board has ever made" although given that the Mid Kent had consistently declared dividends only of between 2 and 6½% annually this was perhaps not a totally unfair comment. The contrary view presumably prevailed amongst the shareholders of the MKR and, with the passing of the South Eastern Railway (Mid Kent) Act[7] on 29th July 1864, the Mid Kent was formally absorbed in to the SER and thus the light of the last of the small railway companies to have served Beckenham in its early days was extinguished. Curiously the name "Mid Kent line" survived until modern times and within recent memory the station announcers at London Bridge and Charing Cross still referred to the "Mid Kent service to Hayes" – not bad for a company which only had a brief independent existence, never served the area named in its title and in any event ceased to be a separate entity nearly a century and a half ago!

Brighton direct

The local railway map was by now assuming much of its present shape but, had the Beckenham, Lewes and Brighton Railway had been built things might have been very different. At the end of 1862 plans were announced for a railway of this name to run southwards from an end-on junction with the Mid Kent at New Beckenham with two junctions, one facing east and one west, with the LCDR close to Beckenham Junction - the original plan was for a crossing on the level with the main-line but a "flying junction" was later substituted at the insistence of the LCDR. From this junction the new line was to pass through Langley Park, West Wickham, Biggin Hill and East Grinstead, continuing there to a terminus at Brighton; construction costs were estimated at £2.25m

In the course of a 25-day hearing before the House of Commons Select Committee on Railway Bills in July 1863 many extravagant claims were put forward for the scheme, including an unlikely proposal that trains would be able to cover the 56 miles from Cannon Street to Brighton "in less than an hour". According to James Staats Forbes, the newly appointed general manager of the Chatham company, Beckenham was to be "the great place of exchange" on the line and a basic service was to be provided by stopping trains from both Blackfriars and Victoria in addition to trains from the Mid Kent line at Beckenham. At the junction the coaches "would be formed into one train, which would go through without a change of carriage as express trains to Brighton." Geography presumably having defeated the promoters, it was proposed that there would be two separate stations at Beckenham – the existing station at Beckenham Junction (described as being "a very good station") and a new station at the junction between the proposed line and that of the Mid Kent. Traffic prospects were said to be good and Forbes stated that the route between London and East Grinstead

"traversed a beautiful district which we look with a great deal of anxiety for creating traffic. All this dense population is migrating; they are moving out of town in every direction, and upon our own line we find in the neighbourhood of Beckenham ... large new towns [which] have sprung up within a few years and the same thing is going on at Beckenham to a great degree. Below Beckenham you get to Shortlands and they are building houses there which are inhabited the moment they are finished."

Perhaps fortunately for Beckenham and the whole of this "beautiful district" the BL&B Bill was rejected by parliament, this "crude piece of Chatham and South Eastern connivance" having been strongly opposed by the LBSCR who did not relish the prospect of having to share the lucrative Brighton market with any other company.

In the following year a similar scheme, re-named the London, Lewes & Brighton Railway, with junctions at both Beckenham and Penge and following a route to Kemp Town via a roughly similar route and with separate branches to both Edenbridge and Westerham was promoted successfully and on 6th August 1866 the required enabling Act passed[8]. The new line was to be a joint venture between the South Eastern and LCDR and was to be financed by a share capital of £2.25m and £750,000 in loans. This time a financial crisis defeated the scheme by forcing the near-bankrupt LCDR to pull out and the South Eastern delayed making a decision until 1867 when the scheme was abruptly dropped, being formally abandoned in July 1868[9]. This was not quite the end of the story for in 1876 a Metropolitan & Brighton Railway was again being promoted with a similar starting point but following a more easterly route to a terminus at Brighton Pavilion and in 1883 the Beckenham Local Board petitioned against a proposed London to Eastbourne scheme that would have passed through the town. Both of these schemes were later dropped after failing to attract enough support and a direct line from Beckenham to the Sussex coast remained an unfulfilled dream.

Ill-used travellers

From 1864 onwards fresh conflict arose between the Chatham and South Eastern companies at Beckenham Junction, notwithstanding the two Bromley Traffic Agreements. Following upon the withdrawal of the South Eastern services beyond Beckenham Junction passengers from the Mid Kent to Shortlands, Bromley and Bickley were required either to change at Beckenham or to travel in one of the few through carriages "attached at their pleasure" by the LCDR

to their own trains. In theory it would have been easy for the two companies to have co-ordinated services at that station and had the will existed on the part of both the "expeditious interchange of trains" required by the Act could have been effected. There was, however, no such attempt made and on 15th January 1864 a letter was published in the *Times* and this graphic account of everyday travel on the Mid Kent caused an immediate local stir.

"Sir – In line, with hundreds of others, down the Mid Kent Railway, below Beckenham ... all of us requiring to be in town more or less punctually every morning. The recent "facilities of new lines" as the phrase goes, have only woefully obstructed our business journeyings, and have made our homes now 20 miles off London. I arrived at the London Bridge station this evening to go home by the train which is appointed in the railway bills to start at 6.15, and found that our train had taken a trip to Charing Cross leaving 200 or 300 of us waiting about 15 to 20 minutes on a very unsafe cold exposed narrow platform kicking our heels about while engines and trains passed to and fro like Cheapside omnibuses, in dangerous proximity; and after undergoing this ordeal, we arrived at Bromley precisely at 7.20, just 1 hour and 5 minutes from the time our train should have started, in making this journey of ten miles. And this is no solitary insistence, as far from being one of our worst Mid Kent grievances.

In the course of our 10 miles of railway journey leading to our homes, we ill-used travellers undergo an-

Connections provided by the Norwood Spur and Crystal Palace lines from the L.C.D.R. public timetable for 1878.

other purgatory at Beckenham ... There that "enterprising concern", the London, Chatham & Dover Railway, pushing itself about here there and almost everywhere, stops our Mid Kent way, and will not allow its neighbour's engines to move us one bit further; and here often we city folks sit shivering in our carriages or pace the cold station till it pleases our West End magnate to arrive from Victoria, and to drag us our two or three miles to Bromley and Bickley, while many of us might better have walked, were it not for cold and wet weather, over dark roads.

The morning up journey to town brings little, if any, comfort with it. Our West End magnate usurps again his obstructive dominion, and we are "taken on behind" so far as Beckenham and left there until some mysterious shunting of trains and half-trains from main-lines and "sidings" take place; and also to wait often till one and sometimes two of the trains of our Chatham and Dover masters release us from our siding, and allowed the poor snubbed Mid Kent to sneak up to the City with us – often afraid, too, one would think from its snail-like motion as it nears its quarters, to show its humbled face in its own station ..

Yours etc., "ILL USED – TRAVELLER"

Apart from these particular local difficulties, there was in addition a more general concern as to the timekeeping of trains on both the Mid Kent and the main-line sections and the Bromley Record of the same month commenting that "the Chatham time tables profess to tell us when they start, and when they arrive, and only surprise the public when they do either correctly" while, of the South Eastern, *Herepath's Railway Journal* commented that the company was "profoundly philosophical – its time table is the only instance of the human mind fully defining eternity." This was barely an exaggeration as the South Eastern "official lateness tables" of the time showed that passenger trains on the system were, on average, 16½ minutes late; the LCDR was little better.[10]

An intolerable nuisance

The inconvenience caused by changing trains at Beckenham was further exacerbated when on 1st October 1866 the LCDR ceased to attach any through carriages from the Mid Kent at Beckenham Junction and from this date onwards public pressure grew for a Bromley Direct Railway avoiding changing at Beckenham altogether. This was presumably at the behest of the South Eastern who were almost certainly making a loss on the through services in the face of competition for Shortlands, Bromley and Bickley traffic from the direct services from Blackfriars and Victoria via the LCDR. In April 1868 the South Eastern opened their new main-line from Tonbridge to London, passing only a mile or so to the north of Bromley town centre and proposals were put forward for a short branch line from Grove Park to Bromley with a possible extension to Beckenham Junction, thus obviating "the intolerable nuisance of changing trains at Beckenham which ruffles the tempers of the mildest, terrifies aged and infirm people and drives the busi-

ness man away from Bromley."[11]

The pressure for the Bromley Direct branch line grew in November 1873 after a lady from Reading collapsed and died on the Beckenham Junction footbridge while hurrying across it to change trains and although the coroner refused an inquest on the basis that she had a pre-existing heart condition, the Bromley Record suggested that

"a jury should have been summoned to return a verdict of death from natural causes accelerated by the present arrangements at the station ... Either the bridge over the line should be brought to the London end of the platforms [it being situated at the country end and under the overall roof] or that the South Eastern train should stand, as it formerly did, close by the side, when passengers had only to get out of one company's carriage into one of the other's without walking more than a few steps."

At a public meeting held some five months later in favour of the Bromley Direct Railway Bill a speaker was cheered for saying that "the railway authorities have not studied their passengers' comfort and convenience, but had treated men more like cattle than Christians."[12] The branch from Grove Park to Bromley North[13] was finally opened in January 1878 and thereafter few passengers changed from the Mid Kent to the main-line trains at Beckenham Junction and the complaints died away only to have a curious echo in the public timetables as late as 1922 when intending passengers were still warned that "The connection from the Main Line to the Mid Kent is not guaranteed when there is an interval of less than 10 minutes at Beckenham Junction and vice versa."

Problems at Penge

When the LCDR main-line was opened there were two other signal boxes in the Beckenham area in addition to the box at Beckenham Junction, namely Penge Junction, situated on the north side of the junction of the Farnborough Extension and the new main line, and Penge Station, situated on the down line immediately east of the level crossing and station. An interesting account of the practices of the signalman at the Penge station box appears in a Board of Trade report in 1868[14] in connection with the failure of the signalman to acknowledge certain urgent messages relating to an accident on the line and the report highlighted both the problems encountered by having level crossings in suburban areas and the perceived problem with the early telegraphic system in use.

"The man is constantly engaged in working the gates of his road crossing and his signal levers, which are also outside of his box, and it cannot therefore be expected that his attention should be obtained at any moment by the mere working of his telegraph instruments in the case of emergency. The Penge station is the termination of the telegraph block-system on this railway. The speaking system, from box to box, as from Herne Hill to Dulwich, from Dulwich to Sydenham Hill and from Sydenham Hill to Penge, are connected with bells but there are no bells connected with the

A curious survivor in the form of the Penge crossing keeper's house seen in June 2009 and still extant more than 130 years after the abolition of the level crossing itself. (Andrew Hajducki)

The brick abutments at Barnmead Road which once supported the girder bridge carrying the ill-fated Penge Loop line and, later on, a single carriage siding; the railway embankment adjoining it is now so overgrown that a good photograph of it is now almost impossible. June 2009. (Andrew Hajducki)

Sunshine and shadow at Kent House, looking eastwards in July 1990. The truncated buildings on the platforms are still in use and to the right can be seen the upper storey of the main entrance building in Plawsfield Road while the tall trees in the middle background mark the site of Penge Loop North Junction. (John Scrace)

speaking instruments from box to box on the continuous wire between these stations. Bells would indeed do more harm than good in such a case, because any one signalman wanting to communicate with another signalman would ring the bell in every signalman's box. But no signalman can attend properly to instruments inside his box when he is at the same time required to attend to duties outside his box, such as those which are required by the Penge signalman.

The road which thus crosses the railway at Penge is said to be a private road but it is one which is much frequented, and which, as buildings go up in the neighbourhood, will become more and more important. It is desirable that either the signalman should have an assistant to work the gates under his orders or that he should be provided with the means of working them from the interior of his cabin. And all his levers should be under cover and so arranged that he may always be within sight and hearing of his telegraph instruments."

The road in question was named Penge Lane and formed part of the Penge to Sydenham road, the southern part of it supplanting the original route from the Crooked Billet at Penge Green which was then renamed Old Penge Lane. The problems highlighted in the report were partially alleviated within a short period of time by the employment of a crossing keeper at Penge Station and the building of a suitable house to accommodate him and by the provision of a footbridge to the immediate west of the crossing, the latter removing the necessity of opening the double gates at the crossing unless road traffic, as opposed to pedestrians, dictated it. Eventually increasing traffic on both the railway and the road led to delays to rail and road traffic rendered the continuance of the crossing impossible and in about 1876 the crossing was closed, Penge Lane being renamed St John's Road and the original public road route being reinstated and improved[15] and, although this removed the problems associated with the crossing, there were those who regretted the move and some sixty years later it was commented upon that the road over the crossing "must have been very convenient for drivers of vehicles; today it is necessary to make a very circuitous journey in order to reach the other side of the track."[16]

Crystal Palace revived; Crayfish frustrated

On 1st July 1864, exactly one year from the discontinuance of all passenger trains over the old WEL&CPR line to Beckenham, the LCDR inaugurated a replacement Beckenham Junction to Crystal Palace service of five trains a day although the Penge station on the Beckenham Road was not re-opened and no Sunday service was provided. For the next half-century or so the modest shuttle provided between these two points remained remarkably consistent and, almost certainly, totally unremunerative since loadings were light, a single composite carriage often sufficing for all the traffic despite the best efforts to publicise the trains as providing a useful link between the main-line, the attractions of the Palace and the link to the LBSCR services from the latter point. The attraction of the service to the travelling public was not enhanced by the failure of the LCDR to properly connect the shuttle service with its other trains at Beckenham Junction and in March 1866 the *Bromley Record*, anticipating a recurring complaint of the next century, published the following letter:

"Sir – The spirit of perversity seems to have overshadowed the directors of the L.C.& D. Railway. After being closed for a length of time, the link between Beckenham and the Crystal Palace was opened, to the great convenience of the residents, down the main line as far probably as Sevenoaks and Rochester, who could, by its aid, be rapidly be set down at the Crystal Palace doors. Any sensible person would have supposed that the sole object of the Directors was to induce the public to take advantage of this, and accordingly the trains were arranged to start at Beckenham immediately after the arrival of the main line trains. By a peculiar obliquity of vision the Directors do not seem to have seen the accommodation thus given, for now they start the 1pm train immediately before the arrival of the main-line train at Beckenham, so that I, wishing to enjoy a sight of the Crystal Palace, upon stepping out upon the platform at Beckenham, am met by a sight I don't at all enjoy – that of the tail board of the Crystal Palace train in the distance, and I may wait (if I like) two or three hours for the next. The Directors may say "go to Sydenham Hill"; yes, and walk a mile in such weather as we have had of late! My title may make you think I am fond of water - but I am not fond of rain. The arrangement sees simply ridiculous; and I hope that the insertion of this in your forthcoming number may lead to something better, if all the wise heads of the LCDR company can comprehend it all.

Yours obediently, A "CRAY"FISH"

New Beckenham renewed

In October 1866, and in connection with the withdrawal of the Mid Kent through carriages beyond Beckenham, the arrangements at New Beckenham were revised so that the separate trains from Addiscombe and Beckenham Junction were now combined at New Beckenham and from there proceeded as a common train up to London. The existing layout of new Beckenham station did not, however, permit such workings and in consequence a new two platform station was built some 8 chains to the north of the junction between the two lines and the original station, barely thirty months old, was then closed. The original station building, however, was spared and became for many years the residence of successive New Beckenham station masters before becoming a private house in railway ownership and surviving in domestic use, somewhat remarkably, until 2003 by which time it was reputedly the oldest surviving closed station in the London area. The new station seems to have been fairly basic in nature and the subject of continual complaint for in 1870 the Board of the South Eastern, never keen to spend money unnecessarily, were actively considering whether or not better facilities were

required for passengers at New Beckenham and although they do not appear to have addressed the issues raised they did in 1874 authorise the expenditure of £140 to provide an additional siding to the south of the station on the up side of the line so that a spare set of carriages could be stabled there overnight. That the second station at New Beckenham was unsatisfactory was perhaps shown by the fact that it was again completely rebuilt barely forty years later.

The Penge Loop

In 1865 the independent Crystal Palace & South London Junction Railway opened its branch line from Nunhead to a new High Level station at Crystal Palace via Honor Oak and Upper Sydenham. This new service, although always operated on behalf of the South London Junction company by the LCDR, was a bone of contention and relations between them deteriorated to such an extent that the latter now proposed to have their own independent access route from Victoria and Blackfriars to the LBSCR Low Level station at Crystal Palace via a short east-facing connection from the main-line between Penge and Beckenham with a west-facing junction with the old Farnborough Extension line close to the site of the old WELCPR Penge station which, it was envisaged, could be re-opened to serve the housing developments now taking part in the district. On 16th July 1874 Parliamentary authorisation was obtained[17] for what was originally referred to as "the Beckenham loop" but which became known officially as the Penge Loop and was locally called "the Barnmead spur" after the field that it crossed. The line was 16½ chain (363 yard) in length and was to be of double-track laid on an embankment with a girder bridge on brick abutments crossing the lane that in time became an extension of Barnmead Road; it was to be built at a total estimated cost, including signalling, of £11,000, a somewhat costly sum at the time equating to about £50,000 per mile.

By the time that the consent was given for the construction of the line, however, the LCDR and CP&SLJR companies had apparently resolved their differences and in the following year the former took over the latter, thus ending any conflict and thereby obviating the immediate need for the Penge Loop, if indeed there had ever been any real need for it. One would have expected his to have been the end of the story but, in order to prevent the parliamentary powers from lapsing (as they would have done within five years from authorisation if no construction was undertaken), the LCDR decided to keep its options open and decided to go went forward with the building of the Penge Loop. Works were commenced in the summer of 1878 and the line was completed by 10th July 1879 when the Board of Trade inspected it and authorised its opening to all traffic. The junction with the LCDR main-line was named Penge Loop North Junction and a 24-lever signalbox (known later as "Kent House" and, even later still, as "Kent House B") was provided; this was a standard Stevens wooden-box pattern structure similar to that at the corresponding 15-lever Penge

Loop South Junction box at the other end of the loop. It seems unlikely that the line ever carried any scheduled services or even unscheduled ones and although it is not known if the South box was ever in regular use this would seem highly improbable. The track on the Penge Loop remained physically in place for a number of years but the rusty rails must have been an embarrassment to the company and it would appear that by time that Kent House station was opened in 1884 the loop line was no longer usable as at the North junction the down line points had been removed and one of the rails on the up line was missing while the South junction signal box had been permanently switched out of use. By 1886 all of the track on the loop had been lifted and the South signal box had been abolished.[18]

The Penge Loop was, however, partially revived some twelve years for on 1st July 1899 a carriage siding was relaid on the loop formation with a simple trailing connection from the up loop line at what was now known as Kent House B signalbox. This siding was then used on occasions to stable empty passenger stock but, after the electrification of the main line in 1925, the siding was no longer used and was officially taken out of use as from 11th September 1927 and the deck and girders of the bridge subsequently removed. Although more than eighty years have now passed the remains of the Penge Loop line are still familiar to present-day residents of Beckenham and are seen by passengers on passing trains and trams while the wooded embankment and bridge abutments remain as visible reminders of the folly of Victorian railway companies and form the unique spectacle of a closed railway line in Beckenham.

Great houses and small villas

At this point in the narrative it is interesting to consider the effect that the railway was having on Beckenham itself. When the Mid Kent reached Beckenham in 1857 there were barely 350 houses and 2,000 people in the parish and initially the railway seems to have had little impact. When Sir John Lubbock told the shareholders of the Mid Kent in August 1859 that "considerable arrangements have been made for building at Beckenham and other places on the line which would tend still further to increase the business of the railway" this would seem to have been more of a pious hope that a reality. However between 1861 and 1871 the population of Beckenham tripled and in the following decade it doubled again so that by 1881 it had reached 13,000 while the number of occupied houses increased from 362 to 976 and 1,995 – a staggering increase due primarily to the catalytic effect of the railway. A local guide commented that "that moderniser revolutioniser, the railway … changed Beckenham from the quiet village to the favoured and genteel suburb" and added that "The fields which within memory of those still amongst us, had borne golden crops of corn, were marked out in building plots, and in due course villa residences were built and occupies, chiefly by

city gentlemen."[19]

In general the early residential development was a haphazard and piecemeal process with the major exception of the Cator estate, sometimes referred to in contemporary sources as the "Beckenham Park Estate". Here, following upon the opening of the Mid Kent line, two roads, Copers Cope Road and Park Road, were laid out as wide gravelled avenues lined with forest trees and building plots of either one acre or half an acre in extent – in time these roads were followed by other new roads on the east side of Beckenham Junction including Albemarle Road, The Avenue and Foxgrove Road. Although development on the estate was initially slow (there being only two houses constructed in Copers Cope Road by 1862) a more intensive programme of house building was undertaken in the next decade and by 1876 it could be said that "New Beckenham is a village of villas, mainly of a superior class", while a later assessment of the architecture of the estate described the houses as being "tall and yellow, with tentative polychromy; they are rather earnest and stodgy."[20] In order to protect the amenities of the Beckenham Park Estate prohibtions were put on the non-domestic use of the houses and no advertisements could be displayed upon them, especially those connected with "the business or occupation of school masters, school mistresses, boarding-house keepers, auctioneer or estate agents or any art or mystery of any trade or manufacture whatsoever."[21] By the end of the century much of the estate that lay within an easy walking distance of Beckenham junction or New Beckenham stations had been developed with mostly detached and substantial houses suitable for wealthy professional and City business commuters and their families, a type of first and second class traffic which the railways were only too happy to attract. Although plot sizes had by now declined to one-third of an acre and semi-detached houses of more pleasing and artistic designs were to be found on the fringes of the estate, development of the Cator lands continued well into the twentieth century particularly to the east and north of the original houses but by then many of them, being too large for modern families, devoid of modern amenities and too costly to maintain, were being divided into self-contained flats with varying degrees of success. Even after such division these houses were still prone to demolition and replacement by smaller units and, later on, by residential blocks of comparatively expensive but undistinguished design.

Other housing developments in Beckenham were of a more varied nature. The development of the eastern areas of the parish began in 1863 when William Wilkinson, by then chairman of the Mid-Kent Railway, auctioned off 130 acres of his land at Shortlands House and realised sums of up to £500 per acre – regarded as a great deal of money at that time. Thereafter houses of a similar quality to those built on the Cator estate appeared sporadically for the next thirty years or so while elsewhere in Shortlands "rows of newly erected cottages have sprung up like mushrooms, threatening to destroy entirely the rural aspect of the place."[22] In central Beckenham the developments varied from the villas of Hayne, Cedars and Rectory Roads to smaller artisan dwellings in cottage style off the High Street and elsewhere but much of the rural nature of the village would survive for at least another generation. At Penge the British Land Society carried out a development of good-quality houses at Newlands Park in the 1870s and these houses were close to and served by the LCDR station close by. At the same time the important scheme of the Birkbeck Freehold Land Society was inaugurated when they commenced building an estate of smaller houses to the west of the Crystal Palace line between Beckenham and Elmers End Roads[23] and nearby the Churchfields estate was constructed on adjoining land owned by the parish. Although the majority of the smaller new houses in the west of Beckenham were designed for what was referred to at the time as the lower middle classes or better-off artisans, there were few concessions to the less well off in the form of humbler terrace houses at affordable rents; a notable exception to this was the Alexandra Cottage estate close to Penge station where small semi-detached cottages with gardens were built from 1866 onwards on the site of the Porcupine Field by the Metropolitan Association for Improving the Dwellings of the Industrial Classes; these were intended for the tenancy of workers who required to travel to London and for labourers and gardeners serving "the great houses of Beckenham" and this was regarded as a particularly useful provision as the 1861 census showed that 41% of the employed adult employed population of the parish of Beckenham were engaged in domestic service.

The Poor we shall always have.

By 1877 the LCDR was contributing one-tenth of the entire parish rates bill in Beckenham and therefore, not unsurprisingly, were anxious to develop suburban passenger traffic, particularly that of the first class season ticket holder. The company, however, eschewed third class season ticket traffic in favour of workmen's ticket traffic from selected stations. These reduced rate tickets, available on certain specified trains only were, in effect, the only method other than by walking by which poorer people could travel to their daily work. The company, while granting "the privilege to Artisans, Mechanics and Daily Labourers" using Penge station, refused to extend the use of workmen's tickets to Beckenham station and a particularly mean-spirited development of this policy in July 1879, prompted a letter to the editor of the newly-founded *Beckenham Journal*:

"Sir, Allow me to ventilate in your columns ... a very serious grievance that the working classes of Old Beckenham have against the London, Chatham and Dover Railway Company. For many years it has been the custom at Penge station to issue "workmen's tickets", priced 2s., enabling the holder to travel by town by either of the two trains in the morning and return by any train after 4.30 pm, during the six working days of the week. Speaking as one of them, I can bear witness that this low fare has been a great boon to the working classes of the neighbourhood, and much appreci-

ated by them, many of whom like myself have walked from and to Beckenham daily in order to avail themselves of the advantage offered. On applying for the renewal of my ticket in the usual way on the first Saturday of this month I was told that I couldn't have another, as "by order" the issue of tickets to persons resident in Beckenham had been stopped. In vain I urged that as I walked to Penge station it couldn't matter to the company where I lived, and that the Birkbeck estate, and the houses near Kent House Farm (to inhabitants of which the company still issues tickets) were as much in Beckenham parish as the village where I live; the clerk said he had no option but to refuse me. Now, sir, the above "order" unless swiftly rescinded, must have the effect of driving away the few working people who do reside in Beckenham, a result which cannot be other than injurious to the interests of the place. Already it is a complaint with the rich that they cannot get sufficient servants, or work done near at hand, and should the company adhere to its determination this difficulty will of course increase, for it must be remembered that the average working man cannot afford to pay the daily third class return fare to London"

The same writer commented in the following edition of the paper that

"We have it on high authority that "the poor we shall always have with us", but the railway companies and local landowners (acting, as some maintain, in concert) seem determined that the dictum shall not apply in the case of Beckenham residents, being what with high fares, and there being no small dwellings, it is impossible for the poor man, however desirous, to become one of them."

Despite such eloquence the company was not moved.

Eden Park at the turn of the century looking towards Hayes and showing the rudimentary construction of the platforms and the general lack of pretension or aesthetic merit. (A. F Selby; John Minnis collection)

The up platform and buildings at Eden Park undergoing some much-needed renovations in 1921 before the area was transformed – the need for such upgrading works is patently clear! (H J Paterson Rutherford)

Chapter 4
ONWARD!

"There is no better and more deservedly abused line in the Kingdom as the South Eastern"
Bromley Record 1890

Carriages without a horse

Although there had been several attempts to bring the railway to West Wickham, none of these had come to fruition. In 1864 the LCDR had supported a scheme for a Penge to West Wickham via Eden Park railway and in 1865 the South Eastern Railway had proposed to build a line between Grove Park, Hayes and Farnborough with a branch between Hayes, West Wickham and Elmers End but both schemes were abandoned almost immediately. Traditional means of transport continued unabated and in August 1869 the *Bromley Record* almost incredulously reported that

"A bona fide Stage Coach, running from the White Horse Cellar, Piccadilly, down into the centre of Kent is one of the wonders of the day; almost equalling that of the first announcement of railways which reached the country villages at the annual fairs many years ago, in a song the chorus of which "So up to London we will go in a coach without any horses" is still fresh in our memory. It was then considered one of the most ridiculous and extravagantly insane mentions that ever entered the mind of mortal man to suppose that a coach would travel without any horses but now the wonder is to see a coach with horses."

The coach, operated by Charles Hoare of Kelsey Manor, continued to run to and from West Wickham and was later revived, the *Beckenham Journal* of June 1878 commenting that "this pleasant form of locomotion [is] patronised by a large number of distinguished aristocratic travellers". However the delight of these travellers, aristocratic or otherwise, was to be short-lived for two years previously a proposal had been put forward for a West Kent Railway to run from Beckenham to Oxted via West Wickham and Addington and in 1878 a scheme was advertised for a line to run from Norwood to Otford via West Wickham, Downe and Chelsfield; in July 1878 of that year the *Beckenham Journal* reported that, in connection with this scheme, surveyors had been seen in the area marking out the route and it was becoming obvious that, sooner rather than later, West Wickham would get a railway.

The West Wickham & Hayes Railway

Then, in 1879, part of the 1865 plans were again put forward, this time for a railway branch line 3¼ miles long from Elmers End to West Wickham and Hayes under the auspices of the prosaically named West Wickham & Hayes Railway. Less grandiose than previous schemes, it was claimed that "The area is well-suited for development as a good suburban building district having very pretty country

without railway accommodation."[1] Supported by the South Eastern as a foil to a similar scheme backed by the LCDR[2], one of the most prominent promoters of the proposed West Wickham & Hayes plan was Colonel John Farnaby Lennard who, in 1859, had become lord of the manor of West Wickham and was the owner of the majority of the acreage in the parish.[3] A man of great business acumen, Lennard had successfully appropriated part of West Wickham Common to his landholdings and, although he was of an acquisitive nature, he seemed to have been strangely averse to see widescale development in the area of the nature that was engulfing the neighbouring parishes of Beckenham and Bromley despite his interest in promoting local railways. Typical of those who doubted his motives was one local diarist who commented on his backing of the Beckenham & Brighton and West Kent schemes said that "at last Colonel Lennard will spoil our quiet village as he has been striving to do and make us a mere suburb of London, double-dealer that he is."[4]

Other local promoters of the West Wickham & Hayes were Alfred Watkin, son of the South Eastern Chairman Sir Edward Watkin, Charles Goodhart, owner of the Langley estate and Alexander Beattie, a shareholder in the SER and who became chairman of the new company; all lived locally and were the first and only directors of the WW&H. Francis Brady, engineer to the South Eastern served the new company in the same capacity and the two other officers appointed to the Board were John Shaw, secretary, and Alexander Stenning, surveyor.

Eden Park

The line was to traverse open country for its entire length and left the Addiscombe line some 4 chains south of Elmers End station, swinging eastwards on an embankment on a rising gradient of 1 in 76 before passing on the up side a brickworks followed by the Monks Orchard estate and on the down side some farm buildings belonging to the Eden Park estate, which eventually was to give the entire area its name[5]. In order to preserve the amenities of the estate its owner, William Rudd Mace, made the company provide accommodation bridges, to set back the line 300 feet from Elmers End Lane (now Upper Elmers End Road), "to trim, soil, plant and sow with grass seed the embankments" and to provide "continuous iron fencing" while the Beckenham Local Board insisted that where footpaths crossed the line arches or tunnels not less than 6ft 6in "with a corrugated iron roof or ceiling" be provided. Mace further insisted on the provision of a station, despite the fact that the area sur-

The simple country booking hall building at Eden Park in August 1988 – the SER's favoured wooden frame and board style persisted well in to the twentieth century by which time is was an anachronism and underlined the company's unwillingness to spend money on its passengers. (Andrew Hajducki)

rounding it was almost entirely unpopulated and accordingly Eden Park, a modest two platform wooden structure with a small booking office on the up side and staggered platforms connected by a subway, along with a small station masters house next to the main road to West Wickham. By rail it was 1m 27ch from Eden Park to Elmers End and to reach Beckenham Junction a journey of 3½ miles with a change at New Beckenham was required, whereas the distance by road from Eden Park to Beckenham village was barely half this distance. Although the station plans had been approved in June 1881 it was found that the down platform would have overlooked the grounds of a large villa called Elderslie, which the railway had been obliged to purchase from William Mace some months before, and consequently at the insistence of the new tenant of Elderslie, A.H. Baker, the platform was moved to the north; the position of the small signalbox at the station was moved in April 1882 for the same reason and a screen of shrubs was planted. Elderslie, named after the Renfrewshire birthplace of Scottish patriot Wiliam Wallace, is no more, its site being marked by the 1939-built road called Elderslie Close.

West Wickham

From Eden Park the line entered the parish of West Wickham and, passing south of Langley Park on a south-easterly course and rising gradient of 1 in 80, traversed a wholly rural route partly on an embankment and partly in cutting, to the next station, West Wickham, 67 chains from Eden Park and actually situated in the small settlement of Wickham Green about a third of a mile north of the village High Street. Here the buildings consisted of standard SER wooden-framed boarded structures with the main offices on the up side and a small shelter on the down side, both being linked by a covered iron footbridge. A small goods yard with a shed was provided on the down side and a carriage dock on the up side capable of handling horse boxes and the station also boasted a 12-lever signalbox. It was anticipated that there would be tourist traffic in the form of walkers, picnickers and excursionists at West Wickham and in anticipation a large new facility, "The Railway Hotel"[6], was built to service their needs, its licence being transferred from an existing public house "The Leather Bottel" which, along with four cottages, had been purchased by the company at a cost of £1,650 for the purpose of housing railway workers[7]. From West Wickham the railway continued south-eastwards on a rising gradient and in a deep cutting under three impressive overbridges carrying, respectively, Red Lodge Road and field footpaths linking Hawes Lane to Pickhurst Rise and Hawes Down to Hayes Hill before the railway passed out of the parish and within a quarter mile reached the branch line terminus at Hayes, 1m 15ch from West Wickham.

The "Old Leather Bottel" at Wickham Green was purchased by the railway company to house its workers and the licence was subsequently transferred to the "Railway Hotel". (Bromley Libraries)

Lucas and Aird, contractors to the West Wickham and Hayes Railway, with their small pug engine and staff near Hayes in about 1882. (R. C.Riley collection)

West Wickham station in 1921 looking towards Eden Park with the dock line for horse boxes visible behind the signal and signalbox in the background; the footbridge is the only modern survivor from this scene. (H J Paterson Rutherford)

West Wickham looking towards Eden Park in the early years of the line – the goods yard is on the right and there appears to be a barrow or contractors crossing in the foreground. (Lens of Sutton)

The official opening of the line at West Wickham station in May 1882 with company officials and other important local personages; Cudworth well tank No. 238 was the last survivor of her class and her final passenger duties were on the Hayes line between 1890 and 1892. (Bromley Libraries)

Bacon and tobacco

The West Wickham & Hayes Railway Act was passed on 9th July 1880[8] and running powers were given over the SER between the junction and Elmers End station although these were never used for on 11th August 1881 the South Eastern acquired the West Wickham & Hayes Railway for the sum of £162,000. Construction of the new line was undertaken by Lucas & Aird for the tendered sum of £69,283 (later reduced to £65,000 when the SER supplied the rails themselves) and was greatly expedited by the use of steam shovels and other automated machinery. A local schoolboy later recounted that

"They were exciting times for us lads when they were making the branch line to Hayes. I used to be out Elmers End way a good deal then and it was an experience for us to watch the navvies. Mr Wall, the sub-postmaster at Elmers End didn't mind. He ran a grocery shop and he had all the navvies' trade. They lived on fat bacon and screws of twist tobacco. Of course they were also partial to liquid

refreshment and made the "Leather Bottel" at No.6 Wickham Green their headquarters."[9]

An account of the itinerant workers who built the line speaks highly of their morals and diligence, something of a contrast to many of their contemporaries.

"A very nice woman at West Wickham who had a good many men lodging with her the whole time that the line was in the making, gave them an excellent character and said that she missed them in every way. She had always heard that railwaymen were a rough lot but that she had found them as quiet and nice a set of men as could be ... Sir John Lennard publicly thanked the men for not poaching and stated that a game keeper who had been on the estate for 50 years assured him that he had never had a better head of game."[10]

In anticipation of the opening of the Hayes branch the signalbox at New Beckenham was replaced by a new structure built immediately opposite the old while at Elmers End, where regular passengers had complained to the SER Board about the inadequate facilities provided there as far

A Hayes train waits in the up bay at Elmers End in about 1907; the rails appear to have been recently renewed and re-ballasted. (R.C.Riley collection)

A C class 0-6-0 hauls a London-bound train tender first between Hayes and West Wickham in about 1905. (A. F. Selby: John Minnis collection)

A Hayes train leaves West Wickham in the hands of a C class 0-6-0 in the early years of the twentieth century; the Red Lodge Road bridge is in the background. (A. F. Selby: John Minnis collection)

back as 1873 in relation to the poor state of the platforms, the lack of a footbridge and the absence of any proper shelter on the up side, the platforms were in consequence repaired and raised in level and, immediately opposite the 1864 building, a new brick built single storey brick booking office and waiting room was provided. Two bay platforms were added to accommodate the new service and a covered footbridge and platform canopies were installed while two new coal sidings were laid on the up side parallel to the bay platform line; at the same time a new 43-lever wooden signalbox of standard SER design was built in the angle between the Addiscombe and Hayes lines.

Mixed feelings

By January 1882 the South Eastern directors were informed that the section between Elmers End and West Wickham had been completed except for the signalling; contracts for the latter were won by signalling contractors Stevens & Sons of London who were paid £183.1.0 for Eden Park and £231 for West Wickham, including the signalboxes. The final capital construction costs of the branch were later estimated at £162,315. Progress on the remaining works was so rapid that on 23 May 1882 the official Board of Trade inspection by Colonel Hutchison was carried out. On the Whitsun bank holiday, six days later, the first train hauled by a Cudworth 4-4-0 No. 238 was run amidst celebrations presided over by Sir John Lennard; regular services began in June 1st. From the outset traffic was light and services were provided by an irregular shuttle of 13 weekday and 4 Sunday trains to and from Elmers End. The anticipated commuter traffic never materialised, despite some building development in West Wickham, and the leisure traffic was slow to build up, despite the introduction of statutory half-day and Bank holidays. Not all were happy to see West Wickham opened up to the world and in a guidebook to the area published as the line was still being built the author warned that

"It is hoped that this new branch, while supplying the means of access to the city, will not be instrumental in introducing hordes of the London "rough." In some beautiful localities it has been found that bringing of the railway right up to it and planting a commodious "Railway Inn" in close proximity has been the means of closing the locality to the lover of nature and rural scenery by the wholesome introduction of the rough aforesaid, who does not care to visit a district if it entails a walk of four or five miles."[11]

One even more unwelcome category of guest was the poacher and in 1886 a gentlemen who had poached pheasants on Sir John's land entrained at West Wickham with his booty only to be arrested by an awaiting constable when the train reached Eden Park. Travellers, welcome and unwelcome, were, however, few and in August 1899 Eden Park was abolished as a block post and the signalbox was removed for reuse elsewhere and the station was later closed on Sundays due to lack of custom. In a description of a journey at the turn of the century it was said that "the small

A delightful 1921 view of Elmers End taken from the north end of the up platform. The platform extension when the Hayes line was opened in 1882 can be seen beyond the original 1864 station building while the 1882 new booking office building can be seen on the right. This would appear to be a summer view judging by the ladies' dresses and the fact that a number of passengers are awaiting the Hayes train; the girl on the right is studying a poster map and perhaps dreaming of holidays to come. (H J Paterson Rutherford)

Elmers End signalbox from the rear – a standard SER wooden box of the 1880s with later additions and still in remarkably good condition a century later considering it's age. (John Scrace)

branch line was run by a completely antiquated engine and rolling stock. The engine was probably built in the 1860s and had been put out to grass on the small branch line"[12] and the Hayes branch was left to slumber in bucolic peace for many years more.

Mid Kent developments

On the Mid Kent line traffic was growing steadily as the various suburban districts it served were being gradually built up. In September 1866 a spur was built between Ladywell station and Parks Bridge Junction enabling Addiscombe business trains to by-pass Lewisham station. In July 1871 an intermediate station was opened between Elmers End and Addiscombe at Woodside; this station, later known as Woodside & South Norwood, was privately funded and was designed to serve both Croydon racecourse and housing development taking part in the area. Woodside was rebuilt in August 1885 to become the junction station for the 2 mile 29 chain Woodside & South Croydon line which provided a link to the Croydon and Oxted line at Selsdon Road. Operated jointly by the SER and LBSCR, the service was primarily a local one operating between Selsdon Road and Woodside and generated little income for its owners but a few through services were provided over the Mid Kent line consisting mainly of Kent coast excursions and relief trains. Local services over the line were withdrawn in 1915 and its stations closed completely in 1916 but the line was later to play a significant part in the history of the Mid Kent in the electric era.

A further Mid Kent innovation was the provision by the South Eastern of through trains between Addiscombe and Liverpool Street via New Beckenham and the East London line at New Cross. These ran from 1st April 1880 and the initial daily service was of 16 trains each way although whether the service was actually provided to reflect a genuine demand for it rather than a more political move to reflect the South Eastern's more radical designs in relation to the East London line was less clear. On 3rd March 1884 the through trains were diverted to St Mary's (Whitechapel) and, presumably failing to attract sufficient custom in the way that most radial London services had, the East London trains from Addiscombe were withdrawn altogether on 30th September of the same year.

Work in progress

On the LCDR main line the increasing traffic, both local and long distance, began to cause delays to passengers and frustration to the Board. In 1878 the company sought powers to quadruple certain sections of the line between Herne Hill and Bickley at an estimated cost of £200,000 and these were granted by parliament on 27th May in the following year[13]. These powers provided for the widening of three sections of the main line namely (1) a section one mile five furlongs and six chains from Herne Hill to Sydenham Hill stations, (2) a section one mile three furlongs and nine chains from "the southern side of the footbridge which crosses over the railway near the southern end of Penge station, in the parish of Beckenham" to the Southend Road bridge at Beckenham Junction and (3) a section three miles, five furlongs and eight chains from the latter point to the eastern end of Bickley station. Powers were also given, *inter alia* to rebuild Beckenham Junction station and the

Kent House Station in the first decade of the twentieth century (Nancy Tonkin collection)

Southend Road bridge and to replace the footpath crossings between Penge Junction and Kent House lane by subways. However before any work was undertaken the LCDR Directors reported that the line had reached its full capacity, particularly in relation to the bottleneck of Penge Tunnel and that no further traffic could be encouraged on the line until the problem of the tunnel was satisfactorily dealt with. Quadrupling would not, of course, solve the tunnel problem since a second tunnel would be out of the question due to its cost and in its place the idea of a parallel route to the existing line but avoiding the Penge Tunnel was mooted and the question of quadrupling was, temporarily, put into abeyance.

In 1879 re-signalling of the existing main line began and in November of that year the Sykes "Lock and Block" system was introduced between Sydenham Hill and St Mary Cray. At Penge station, following the closure of the level crossing there, a new wooden signalbox was built to the west of the down platform and about the same time the original Penge Junction signalbox was replaced by a new structure a hundred feet or so to the west of the existing box while at Beckenham Junction a standard SER-pattern wooden box was built at the London end on the up side immediately adjacent to Rectory Road. Further east of Beckenham Junction another new box was provided within a short time– this was Shortlands Bank, a small wooden hut structure placed on the down side a few yards east of where Downsbridge Road crossed the line. Shortlands Bank was an intermediate box provided primarily to facilitate workings at Beckenham Junction by allowing two trains at once to occupy the long section between there and Bromley South. The box was in regular but intermittent use until be-

ing finally closed at the end of the century; thereafter the box remained in position before being removed in about 1910.

Kent House

The last quarter of the nineteenth century saw not only a rapid increase in the population of Beckenham but also the completion of the railway system serving the district, with a further four stations and two new lines added to the parish network. Already by the late 1870s many of the former fields between Beckenham and Penge had been built over and although a promise had reputedly been made to reopen the old WEL&CPR Penge station at the Beckenham Road bridge nothing had come of it and there was still no intermediate station between Beckenham Junction and Penge on the main-line, between Beckenham Junction and Norwood or Crystal Palace or between New Beckenham and Elmers End on the Mid Kent, leaving a large part of the parish without easy access to any railway connection at all. Various rumours that a station was imminent were circulated and in 1879 the *Beckenham Journal* suggested that the site of the old station was being re-surveyed with a view to being re-opened. In 1880 the same paper carried an advertisement for the lease of a house in Mackenzie Road "within two minutes of a new station to be opened on the LC&DR" while in October of the following year a letter writer in the *Journal* complained that "Some time ago we heard that a station was to be opened on the Birkbeck estate, but this has not yet come to pass … I trust that it will not be long before we, in this district, are as in as favourable a position to reach London as our richer brethren in other parts of the parish. At

The down side subway entrance leading from Kings Hall Road to Kent House station in about1963. (Lens of Sutton)

An Orpington train hauled by Kirtley R1 class 0-4-4T No. 700 enters Kent House in1910; unfortunately in this picture the "A" signalbox is obscured by the train. The particular locomotive found little work after the electrification of the suburban lines but nevertheless survived until 1952 having had a spell of regularly working the Westerham branch line.(J Holdsworth)

Kirtley "Bluebell" class 2-4-0 No. 41 "Verbena", a sister of the ill-fated "Snowdrop" which came to grief at the same spot in 1864, passes Kent House "B" signalbox with a down Ashford train in about 1890; signalman James Evenden was killed here while leaving this box in 1903. The houses in the background are in Kings Hall Road. (Tony Riley collection)

A down train enters Kent House watched by stationmaster Harris, a porter, two ladies and a child who, quite sensibly, is excited by the arrival of a steam engine. (J Holdsworth)

Almost exactly 100 years later and a down train at the same spot in 2009 with another lady in view but, sadly, no station master, porter or excited child. (Andrew Hajducki)

LONDON, CHATHAM, AND DOVER RAILWAY.

NOTICE

TO

ENGINE DRIVERS, GUARDS,

AND ALL CONCERNED.

(Including the Servants of the Great Northern and Midland Companies.)

OPENING OF KENT HOUSE STATION.

(BETWEEN PENGE AND BECKENHAM.)

On **WEDNESDAY**, October 1st, at **5.0** a.m., a New Station, situated between Penge and Beckenham, to be called "Kent House," will be **opened** for Traffic.

A New Signal Box, at the Beckenham end of the Up Platform, **will be** brought into use as an independent signalling Station, and **additional Signals** will be **provided**, as under:—

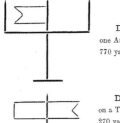

Down Distant Signal.—A new T Post, with one Arm and Light, on the Down side of the Line, about 770 yards from the Signal Box.

Down Stop Signal.—The left Arm and Light on a Two-arm Post, on the Down side of the Line, about 270 yards from the Signal Box.
    The right Arm and Light are the Penge Up Distant Signal.

Down Starting Signal.—The right Arm and Light on a new T Post, at the Beckenham end of the Down Platform.
    The left Arm and Light are the Penge Junction-new Down Distant Signal.

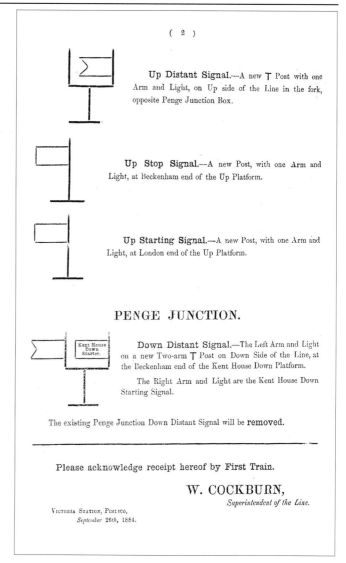

(2)

Up Distant Signal.—A new T Post with one Arm and Light, on Up side of the Line in the fork, opposite Penge Junction Box.

Up Stop Signal.—A new Post, with one Arm and Light, at Beckenham end of the Up Platform.

Up Starting Signal.—A new Post, with one Arm and Light, at London end of the Up Platform.

PENGE JUNCTION.

Down Distant Signal.—The Left Arm and Light on a new Two-arm T Post on Down Side of the Line, at the Beckenham end of the Kent House Down Platform.
    The Right Arm and Light are the Kent House Down Starting Signal.

The existing Penge Junction Down Distant Signal will be **removed**.

Please acknowledge receipt hereof by First Train.

W. COCKBURN,
Superintendent of the Line.

VICTORIA STATION, PIMLICO,
September 26th, 1884.

present we do not seem so valuable, I suppose, as we should most probably ride second class to town instead of first class, as is the case from Beckenham Junction with those living near there". Although agitation for a station on the site of the former WEL&CPR station continued sporadically until 1925, the immediate need for the same largely disappeared with the subsequent opening of two new stations in the vicinity.

The first of these new stations was at Kent House. Albemarle Cator, who had succeeded John Cator as the life tenant of the Cator estate, wished to develop the western part of his estate lying to the north of the LCDR main-line, entered into negotiations with the LCDR for the provision of a new station situated 50 chains south east of Penge station and 69 chains west of Beckenham Junction. In February 1883 Albemarle Cator gave the land to the railway company on the condition that it was to be used solely for passenger traffic and that no goods yard or facilities whatsoever be made there and a substantial two-storey station building was provided on the up side, connected to the main road by the newly formed Plawsfield Road. On 1st October

1884 the new station, Kent House (Beckenham), named after the nearby ancient farmhouse situated immediately adjacent to the Surrey and Kent county boundary, was opened. The ticket office was situated in Plawsfield Road in a plain building which gave subway access to two island platforms which were provided in anticipation of the proposed quadrupling of the line at this point – Kent House signalbox (the former "Penge Loop North Junction" renamed on the same day) occupied a position adjacent to the east end of the of platform. The station name was later modified and by the end of the century the suffix was dropped, presumably on the assumption that by then all intending passengers were aware that Kent House was a Beckenham station.

In May 1884 powers were sought to extend the time limit for the quadrupling of the track between Beckenham Junction and Shortlands[14] (those in the 1879 Act being about to lapse) but there appears to have been a change of heart on the part of the LCDR Board and instead of quadrupling 880-yard long passing loops were put in at Kent House. These loops, one on either side of the line, served the outer faces of the existing island platforms and the signalling arrangements were altered with a new 18-lever signalbox being built on the up side just south of the Green Lane bridge. This was named "Kent House A", the former Penge Loop North Junction box becoming "Kent House B" and its lever-frame being reduced to 20 levers with the 24-lever Penge Junction box in due course being renamed "Kent House C". The new works were all completed on 2nd May 1886 and brought into use eight days later.

Business at Kent House station was, initially, slow although local builders Syme and Duncan immediately began to build a development of pretty semi-detached houses in Barnmead Road around the up side of the station while a few years later housebuilding started at Aldersmead and Kings Hall Roads on the down side. Even after these developments and the provision of additional trains and workmen's ticket facilities Kent House remained a quiet station for some time until the housing developments in Mackenzie Road, Churchfields and other districts to the west brought a large amount of additional season ticket traffic.

The Catford Loop

Further developments were to follow. In 1888 the LCDR General manager, James Staats Forbes, dropped something of a bombshell to the shareholders when he told them that in his view the Penge Tunnel was in poor condition and that *"it was known locally that the whole of the Sydenham Hill was moving and that at some unspecified time in the future the tunnel would distort and collapse"* although he added that he did not expect this catastrophe to occur within his lifetime.[15] Not unsurprisingly immediate confusion was caused since it appeared that Forbes' announcement could only have a prejudicial effect on the company's finances although in hindsight he may only have intended to strengthen the growing demand for a new line to by-pass and relieve the existing main-line but it was also said Forbes had a morbid fear of tunnels. The source of his information was never disclosed and the tunnel has, of course, survived intact to this day!

The by-pass, however, was soon to become a reality and in the same year an independent company, the Shortlands and Nunhead Railway, was promoted with capital of £320,000 and John Farnaby Lennard, Viscount Lewisham and Albemarle Cator were among the directors appointed. The new line was, in the terms of its enabling Act, to be "four miles, six furlongs and six and a quarter chains or thereabouts in length commencing with a junction with the LCDR near Shortlands station on that railway and terminating by a junction with the Blackheath and Greenwich branch of the LCDR near Nunhead Junction station." The promoters swiftly entered into an agreement with the LCDR

The distinctive Nunhead and Shortlands Railway pattern booking hall building at Ravensbourne seen in the mid 1960s. Unfortunately destroyed by fire in May 1986 it has been replaced by a modern structure but the boarded footbridge still survives. (Lens of Sutton)

Ravensbourne in 1921 looking towards London – although it may now be a little busier, it is essentially little changed in its appearance and still retains the air of a small country station. (H.J.Paterson Rutherford)

in March 1889 whereby they would provide "proper and sufficient stations for passengers and goods" at least at three locations including one 39 chains north of the junction at Shortlands, the object of this station, to be named Ravensbourne after the nearby river of the same name, being to assist in the development of the eastern part of the Cator estate. The LCDR approved of the scheme, the Directors reporting in August 1889 that it would *"open up a charming suburban residential district" [as well as] "affording an alternative route into London, and relieving the existing line through the Penge Tunnel already at certain hours so crowded as seriously to interfere with the punctual running of the various Express, Local and Goods services passing over it, and which now impeded each other."*

The line was sanctioned on 12th August 1889[16] and powers were given for the company to enter into traffic agreements with LCDR. Construction of the Shortlands & Nunhead Railway, better known today as the "Catford Loop" line, began in 1891, the contractors being Lucas & Aird working on a tender of £156,862. Three "steam navvies", four light locomotives and a large number of horses were used by the 750 men employed and the line was completed within a short period of time. Certain major engineering works were involved and a total of nine million bricks were used to transform what had been, in the company's words a landscape which was "pretty, undulating and well-wooded, the timber is exceptionally fine and plentiful and the rising ground on each side of the line offers delightful sites for villa residences." To protect these "delightful sites", a number of lineside proprietors including Albemarle Cator insisted that the company planted trees and shrubs to screen the line from view and this accounts for much of the sylvan aspect of the line even today.

Ravensbourne to Shortlands

The new line crossed the Mid Kent south of Catford Bridge station and there were a further two stations before Beckenham parish was reached namely Bellingham and Beckenham Hill, the latter being half a mile north of the parish and county boundary but the name was presumably chosen to stimulate housing development in the area. The line then crossed through Beckenham Place Park, the Cator family seat which was later acquired by the London County Council as a public park and golf course, before entering Beckenham parish at Ravensbourne station. This station had a red-brick booking hall, in a similar but plainer style to Bellingham, a covered footbridge and short canopies on each platform. Two coal sidings were situated on the down side (an additional delivery siding for building materials being added in about 1893) and a small Saxby 17-lever signalbox was built at the country end of the up platform.

A Catford Loop down working passes through Ravensbourne in the 1930s with the small Saxby signalbox at the end of the up platform and the goods yard visible to the right (Lens of Sutton)

The view from Shortlands Road in about 1910 showing the gates and entrance to the booking hall with the platform canopies behind and, in the left foreground, Ivynook the house of stationmaster F. Bowles; the station buildings survive but house was demolished to provided additional car parking space. (Nancy Tonkin collection)

Shortlands on a miserable day in the 1950s, looking towards London. (R C Riley collection)

Shortlands signalbox in 1956 with a Southern Railway 4 SUB No. 4105 (one of the production models which followed the prototype "Sheba" units) on a Catford Loop working to Holborn Viaduct. (R C Riley; The Transport Treasury)

A down train enters Shortlands watched by a full compliment of station staff in an early twentieth century post card (Nancy Tonkin collection)

Shortlands station looking east in about 1955 before the modifications carried out in connection with the Kent Coast electrification, in the foreground is the deck of the bridge carrying the lines over the main road to Bromley. (R C Riley collection)

The line then continued, partly in cutting and partly on embankment, to a point 19 chains north west of Shortlands station where a physical junction was made with the main line and on the down side a 32-lever Saxby type 5 signalbox named Shortlands Junction was built. On 2nd June 1892 full signalling was brought into use at Shortlands where both the Junction box and a second box, Shortlands Station situated at the country end of the up platform, were brought into use and the box at Shortlands Bank switched out before being entirely closed in March 1898. The passenger station at Shortlands was completely rebuilt with booking facilities and an adjoining post office housed in a handsome brick building at street level together with a separate house for the station master to replace the demolished eastern side accommodation. Two island platforms each with substantial brick buildings and long canopies were constructed, the east platform dealing with down trains and the west with up trains, Catford Loop trains crossing the main lines at the junction; a subway connected the platforms with entrances from the street on both the east and west sides of the street. The opportunity was also taken of rebuilding the bridge over the main road, the Beckenham Local Board contributing £400 towards the cost.

The Shortlands & Nunhead Railway opened for traffic on 1st July 1892 and in the following year the stations at Bromley and Bickley were rebuilt, the whole section from Shortlands to Bickley being quadrupled from 1st May 1894; when the work was completed Bickley became the main outer terminal for LCDR suburban services. The S&N enjoyed only a brief independent existence, being worked from the outset by the LCDR and being absorbed by that company in 1896[17]. In the 1920s the areas surrounding the stations on the line did finally develop but Ravensbourne remained a quiet country-like station in an area of scattered low density housing.

A dirty and disreputable structure

1890 finally saw the rebuilding of Beckenham Junction. Following the withdrawal of the Mid Kent through services to the east, two bay platforms were constructed alongside the original platforms, that on the up side shared by the Crystal Palace and Norwood junction services while the down bay served the Mid Kent trains. Following the footbridge death and much local criticism, Colonel Yolland of the Board of Trade visited the station on 4th January 1876 and made certain recommendations for improvement to the station's Joint Committee. These were ignored and in January 1879 Julius Kressman, vice-chairman of the Beckenham School Board, sent to Yolland a memorandum signed by a number of local residents pointing out the dangers presented by the narrow down platform, the inadequate footbridge and the general lack of facilities. As a result Yolland revisited the station and produced a new report in which he said that the complaints were justified and that the two companies had admitted this but had failed to act. He went on to report that

"The station has been altered in an objectionable manner since it was first opened in 1856 (sic). It is true that no accident has yet occurred at it, but it was pointed out to me by one of the memorialists that he had an escape from being on the narrow part of the platform when a London, Chatham and Dover train passed. I am not aware that the question has ever been decided whether or not a railway company is legally justified in altering the original construction of a station from its state when submitted for inspection to an officer of the Board of Trade prior to its being opened for traffic in an objectionable and dangerous manner, but I cannot help thinking that the Directors and officers of this Railway would be placed in a very peculiar and uncomfortable position if a fatal accident were to occur to any persons which could be traced to the objectionable features...

The station is still increasing in importance. In the months of July and November of the year 1875 the number of tickets issued at the station were: in July 15,657; in November 14,176. While in the year 1878, the numbers in the same months: in July 19,016, in November 14,735, irrespective of those who merely use this station as an exchange station, or those who have been booked to it.

I have further to say that the station could be greatly improved at moderate cost.[18]

Despite this report nothing was done, presumably because of the possibility of quadrupling the line at this point and the only alteration carried out at the station was the provision of a cabmen's shelter, the £37 5s cost of which was met by public subscription. In 1888 the Beckenham Local Board began to complain in earnest and on 30th May 1889 a deputation met with Sir Edward Watkin, Chairman of the South Eastern, and two of his directors. Sir Edward was sympathetic stating that his Board were aware of the necessity of improving the conditions at the station and he promised to consult with the LCDR and to draw up plans for improvements. By January 1890 the Local Board felt that they had been "pigeon-holed" and agreed to seek counsel's opinion. The following month the *Beckenham Journal* delivered a blistering attack on the South Eastern, saying that their telegraphic address "Onward" had been chosen by their Manager when he was clearly in a sarcastic frame of mind and added that

"Fewer places have made greater strides as a suburban residential place than Beckenham, and we venture to assert that no place of its importance is worse off in regard to its train service, or has to put up with such a dirty, disreputable, draughty and dangerous structure, yclept a station.

There is no better and more deservedly abused line in the kingdom as the South Eastern. Sir Edward is undoubtedly a man of wonderful ability and great energy, but he has too many irons in the fire. His remarkable powers are spread over too great an area. If he were to confine them to the better working of the South Eastern line alone, instead of inventing projects for spoiling the rugged beauty of Snowdon with his "puffing Billies", boring a rabbit war-

Clock House in 1968. The canopy above the main entrance has gone and there have been minor alterations since then but the spirit of the SER still lives on. The parade of shops in the background was known as Clock House Parade and dates from the early years of the century when the area was being developed with largely terraced housing for commuters and their families; Clock House Road (from which the car is emerging) contained the childhood home of author Enid Blyton. (John Minnis)

Clock House station taken from the north side of Beckenham Road in about 1900; the station master, Traitor Reynolds, lived in an adjacent house called Himalaya, the garden wall of which is just visible to the right of the station while the tall building on the right of the picture was the start of a parade of shops devastated in a V1 attack with much loss of life in 1944. (Bromley Libraries)

Hop picker's Special enters Clock House in the summer of 1954; the signalbox here controlled entry to the goods yard on the left of the picture and the nearby Beckenham Council siding (behind by the train). (Denis Cullum; Lens of Sutton Association)

ren under the Channel and outdoing Eiffel in London, he would earn the gratitude of hundreds of thousands and be one of the most popular instead of one of the most abused Railway Directors."[19]

The Local Board, who had set up a sub-committee to deal with the matter, now applied to the Court of the Railway and Canal Commission in order to force the companies to comply and the result was a consent order made on 19th May 1890 whereby the Secretaries of the SER and LCDR agreed to execute a number of works including the building of a new footbridge half-way down the platforms, the widening of the down platform, the repair or removal of train shed roof, the erection of a new booking office on the down side and waiting rooms on both platforms, the provision of new and extended canopies over the platforms and the provision of additional sidings and better goods facilities and the cleansing and painting of the whole structure. The companies, beaten into submission, carried out the required works almost immediately, the overall roof being removed although its supporting walls were retained and incorporated into the new structure and thus Beckenham Junction assumed the form still easily recognised by present-day travellers.

Time for Clock House

In the same year as Beckenham Junction was rebuilt another station was added to the local network. This station

was Clock House, situated 58 chains south of New Beckenham and 65 chains north of Elmers End and deriving its name from an adjoining property owned by the Cators which had a stable block surmounted by a large clock – the house itself was demolished in 1896 but the district and electoral ward became known after it. Although a station at this location had been requested as far back as June 1878, at the same time that the reopening of the original Penge WEL&CPR station barely quarter of a mile away was being sought, it was not until the rising tide of housing development reached its high point that such a venture became a commercial proposition. In 22nd November 1887 the South Eastern board sought permission of the Beckenham authorities to divert a footpath which was to cross the land upon which the station was to be built and on 22nd May 1889 they authorised the construction of what was to be provisionally known as "Penge Road" station at an estimated cost of £3,873; in the following month the title was officially, and perhaps fortuitously, changed to Clock House. By May 1890 the station was virtually complete and the opening date of 1st June was being advertised.[20]

The booking hall at Clock House was a single-storey yellow stock brick structure similar to the contemporary structures at Elmers End and Woodside and situated on the south side of the road bridge. From here two covered stairways led down to the platforms where long curved canopies in typical SER style provided shelter. Above the tracks was, appropriately, a large clock fixed to the side of the booking

Postcard view of the down platform at Clock House in about 1905 – the canopy survived intact until "rationalisation" twenty years ago. The goods yard is behind the palings and part of the stock of prominent coal merchant J.Bennett can be seen while in the background is the distinctive roof of a former private school ("Beckenham High School") which later became the Wesleyan Hall. (Nancy Tonkin collection)

Clock House in more recent times with the canopies cut back and removed. This 1992 view shows a Hayes train entering the station while in the background can be seen Clock House Parade with its decorative roof tower and the now dated and distinctly undecorative 1960s office block built on the grounds of the original Clock House. (John Scrace)

Mr Reynolds and the Clock House station staff pose on the down platform in about 1900. note the remarkable similarity in expression between the passenger with the bag and the rakish dog belonging to the ticket collector (J Holdsworth; Tony Harden collection)

The scene from the down platform at Clock House on the 18th January 1967; note how the canopy has already been shortened and the remarkable signage on the up platform with SR targets alternating with BR totems (Tony Harden collection)

hall and on the down platform large doors led to a loading bay where the mails could be transhipped to road vehicles. At the end of the up platform was a small 18-lever wooden signalbox of SER design and on the down side a coal siding and staithes were laid out, an additional coal siding being added in 1910; both the sidings and the later Beckenham UDC siding were controlled by the Clock House box. In time the station became surrounded by housing and consequently was busy throughout the day and, until rationalisation a few years ago, the buildings survived remarkably intact having a rather gloomy Victorian atmosphere, especially on a cold and damp winter evening.

Clock House Station with a down train arriving in about 1910 (Terry McCarthy collection)

New Beckenham level crossing seen in about 1895. This postcard view was taken, looking north up Park Road and the large house visible was No. 63 Copers Cope Road, otherwise "Elmhurst", the residence of a distinguished surgeon Mr T.M.Young. (Bromley Libraries)

The Cator Crossing at the end of the nineteenth century – this small occupation crossing carried a private road and a foot-path between Blakeney Road and Kings Hall Road with some of the newly constructed houses in the latter seen in the background. Abolished in 1901, the crossing was replaced by the three-way bridge carrying Bridge Road over the Mid Kent. (Bromley Libraries)

Reputedly the former crossing keeper's house at New Beckenham by which time it was in residential use, seen in January 1963 when the snow had already been lying on the ground for a month and would continue to do so for another two. (G H Platt; John Minnis collection)

Chapter 5

PEACE AND WAR

*"Woe unto those who join house to house, that lay field to field,
till there be no place that they may be placed alone in the midst of the earth."*
Isiah 5, v.8

The Local Board complains

By the last decade of the nineteenth century Beckenham was very much beginning to assume the character of a prosperous suburb rather than a rural village. The 1891 edition of the *Official Guide to the South Eastern Railway* stated that "Amongst the more select residential villages within easy reach of London, Beckenham, with its fine ancestral parks, elegant villas and broad thoroughfares, possesses many attractions. Although during recent years it has vastly developed, and assumed the proportions of a small town, yet it covers so wide an area that, unlike many other places under similar conditions, it still retains several semi-rural characteristics in its well-grown timber, pretty gardens and shaded roads." Many of these semi-rural characteristics were to disappear in the quarter century before the First War when Beckenham's population increased by over 50% and a further 3,000 houses were added to the housing stock. In 1883 an ill-fated local concern, the Penge & Anerley Omnibus Company, started a horse-bus service from Crystal Palace to Beckenham Junction through increasingly built-up surroundings, but this venture failed within a short period. Two years later Thomas Tilling of Peckham commenced their own horse-bus service from Penge to Beckenham via Kent House, Beckenham and Shortlands; that service, in various guises, survives to the present day.

The question of problems at New Beckenham station and its level crossing were raised anew in November 1891 when, following upon an incident at which a runaway locomotive smashed through the crossing gates there, the Beckenham Local Board made a number of complaints to the SER Board. The crossing itself was a busy one, being the only public link between the eastern and western parts of the Cator estate and a number of "near misses" between trains and passengers added to a general feeling that the crossing was fundamentally unsafe while at the same time proposals had been put forward to upgrade the road to provide better access for traffic between Sydenham and New Beckenham. In addition to this crossing there was also in existence an occupation crossing built to carry a northwards continuation of Blakeney Road across the Mid Kent in the vicinity of the old Cator Estate stables (the Cator or Blakeney Road crossing) and permission had later been given to build a public level crossing with a crossing keeper's cottage here to replace it. A third crossing, Chaffinch or Clock House Crossing, which carried a road over the Mid Kent line seven chains to the north of the new Clock House station, was also problematic becoming it was

becoming increasingly busy with the development of the Thayers Farm estate for residential purposes. Other problems highlighted by the Local Board were the lack of a footbridge, waiting rooms and other facilities at New Beckenham station, the want of fast trains to Cannon Street, the defective carriage lighting in the Mid Kent carriages and "the inconvenience suffered by Beckenham Junction passengers owing to their carriages always being tacked on to the rear of the Croydon portion of the train."

A writer in the *Times* had already summarised the situation at New Beckenham most eloquently when in June 1886 he said that

"There is neither bridge nor subway for passengers crossing from one platform to the other or for pedestrians crossing at the station. This month's Bradshaw gives nearly 60 trains which pass over this crossing during the day; the traffic is great. This, however, is only half the danger as with but a few exceptions each of these trains passes over the crossing in two distinct portions. Each up train, consisting of two parts, one from Croydon the other from Beckenham Junction, is joined at the station and each down train is also divided there to return to the same places. Nor is this all, for if the City man in these parts has been unable to reach the platform by dodging one of these portions, he must keep a watchful eye on the light engines engaged in the portion traffic and the sausage machines rushing through the station. To the uninitiated the latter are fast trains, which usually put in an appearance as one is about to catch a train on the opposite side."

The Local Board now resolved to enter into negotiations with the SER to find an acceptable solution to all of these problems.

Little value to the public

Other matters of concern now arose. In October 1890 the question of the extension of workmen's trains to Beckenham surfaced again, the Local Board doing an about turn and now supporting the cause. Demand for these was not, however, universally approved and one member, a Mr Glenside, commented that "these trains were unmitigated nuisances to some people especially when no special provision was made for bringing men home, the carriages being filled up with their workmen" showing that even among third-class passengers there were social divisions. In the summer of 1892 the LCDR and SER abolished their joint ticket arrangements at Beckenham Junction and travellers were no longer able to travel out by one company's services and

Thomas Bingham, stationmaster at New Beckenham, and his complement of staff on the up platform at New Beckenham in about 1910; one wonders if the boy was called up a few years later and survived the conflict. (Lens of Sutton)

An Addiscombe train entering New Beckenham in about 1910. The scale of the building, complete with its tall chimneys, reflects the social status of the neighbourhood and the amount of first class traffic it generated rather than the total number of passengers in this lightly populated but "exclusive" area. (Nancy Tonkin collection)

The down side buildings of the second Lower Sydenham station seen from the approach off Worsley Bridge Road in about 1906. (Nancy Tonkin collection)

return by the other. The Local Board complained and the LCDR rather dismissively replied that in their view the issue of joint tickets "was of very little value to the public." The Local Board promptly wrote to the company that "they differ from them as to the utility of joint season tickets and request reconsideration" of the matter but their request was merely refused. Accordingly in February 1893 the Local Board, dissatisfied with the company's attitude, petitioned against a proposed Bill to amalgamate the Chatham and South Eastern companies and although the Bill came to naught the LCDR Act of 1894 introduced a "harmonisation" of the fare structures of the two companies. This move, coyly termed "a levelling exercise" by the LCDR, had the immediate effect of increasing local train fares, a first class single ticket between Victoria and Beckenham Junction leaping up by 33% from 1s 0d to 1s 4d and thus showing that the Local Board's mistrust of the LCDR was not unfounded.

In 1894, the year in which the Beckenham Local Board was superseded by the Beckenham Urban District Council, further complaints were made as to the unpunctuality of local trains and when the Board of Trade issued comparative figures in the following year showing that the percentage of "right time or up to five minutes late" suburban trains on various lines, the SER figure being 63% and the LCDR being 35%, the *Bromley Record* commented that they were not surprised to see the Chatham at the bottom of the list but supposed that the South Eastern's better position "must be due to an accident."

Continuing agitation for the extension of workmen's tickets to Kent House and Beckenham Junction resulted in 1894 in the Board of Trade holding an enquiry into Workmen's tickets from Penge and recommended that these be extended to Beckenham stations. The LCDR still refuse to act and, given that the South Eastern now provided these tickets from Clock House and Elmers End, their intransigence was now becoming increasingly anachronistic and difficult to justify. In 1906 it was finally agreed to extend the Penge workmen's ticket scheme to Kent House and in time additional peak hour third-class only services leaving from and terminating at the station were put on. In December 1913 workmen's cheap tickets were introduced at all stations throughout the South Eastern & Chatham system and on all early trains and the single fare from Beckenham Junction to London was set at 5d, compared to the ordinary third class fare of 8d. Cheap workmen's tickets continued to be issued from all Beckenham stations until the facility was finally abolished by British Railways on 1st January 1962.

New Beckenham renewed (again) and Lower Sydenham moved

In May 1897 agreement was finally reached with regard to the level crossings and New Beckenham and on the 14th of that month the Council concluded an agreement with John Farnaby Lennard as executor of the late Peter Cator and the trustee of Albemarle Cator, who by then had

The third New Beckenham station in September 1913 showing the new run-round middle road which allowed Beckenham Junction and Addiscombe trains to be divided and attached here; the course of the passenger subway joining the up and down platforms can be clearly seen in the foreground while the photographer is standing at the top of the platform ramps at the site of the former level crossing. (H.J.Paterson Rutherford; R.C.Riley collection)

been declared insane. The contract, given effect to by legislation passed on 6th August 1897[1], provided for the building of a new road and three-way bridge over the Mid Kent line (the present Bridge Road), the closing up of the New Beckenham, Cator and Chaffinch Crossings and the rebuilding of both New Beckenham and Lower Sydenham stations. The original Lower Sydenham had been built in 1857 outside of the parish boundary but it was now to be built, at the Cator trustee's expense, a quarter of a mile to the south and consequently just within the Beckenham boundary. The South Eastern were to receive contributions in respect of New Beckenham of £1,000 from the Cator funds towards the new bridge and £400 for the pedestrian subway while the Council agreed to match those contributions with equal amounts and the Cator estate was also given powers to plant and maintain trees and shrubs in the new roads and on the banks "so long as they do not interfere with the safe working of the railway." A time limit of 2½ years for completion of the works was set, June 1901 being the agreed date by which the new station and bridges would be opened. The Cator and New Beckenham crossings were closed and the new Bridge Road was opened on 14 November 1901 but the plans for New Beckenham station were only passed in No-

vember 1902 and the works were not completed until November 1904 with the new station being officially opened in the following month. The new station was, by general consent, a great improvement on the old and passengers now had long platforms backed by high brick walls and protected by canopies, a substantial booking hall and waiting room on the up side and two parallel white-tiled pedestrian subways, one for passengers and one for pedestrians walking between Park Road and Lennard Road; at the country end of the station and adjacent to the now-closed crossing a tall SECR-pattern signalbox fitted with a 50-lever Evans O'Donnell frame was built. Three tracks now passed though the station, the middle track being a run-round loop to allow for the more efficient division and combination of the Beckenham Junction portions of trains. In 1906 the new Lower Sydenham station was opened, an altogether less grand affair than New Beckenham and built in the standard and by now rather antiquated South Eastern wooden framed and boarded design with a matching 50-lever signalbox. The access roads to the station were improved so as to provide better connections with the Cator estate, the development of which, it was hoped, would continue to move northwards.

New Beckenham looking north from the site of the level crossing in October 1961 with the tall SECR signalbox prominent on the right – the height of the box was necessary to give the signalman a clear view of the junction of the Addiscombe and Beckenham Junction lines to the south; note the continuing presence of gas lighting despite the electric trains. (John Scrace)

New Beckenham looking south on a drab 15 October 1955 with the wide gap left by the abolition of the centre run-round road clearly evident. (Pamlin Prints; John Minnis collection)

Lower Sydenham with 2 EPB unit No. 5750 heading the 10.05 Charing Cross to Hayes service entering the station on 6 June 1969; the semaphore signals and wooden signalbox became history some two years later while the train itself survived for another twenty. (John Scrace)

Lower Sydenham looking south in the 1950s; note the packages awaiting collection on the down platform and, in the distance, New Beckenham station half a mile away. (Lens of Sutton)

Lower Sydenham in 1906 with a view to the south (Nancy Tonkin collection)

Lower Sydenham looking north with the gas works and signal box in the background and the signs of goods activity in the down siding, 14 October 1961. (John Scrace)

Infringing their rights

The 1894 Act also provided that the power of enforcement of the Sunday traffic agreements would be transferred from the Cator estate to the Beckenham UDC and this was perhaps inevitable for by now the restrictions were just a tiresome anomaly. Twenty years earlier it had been said that *"such an arrangement has long been felt to be entirely opposed to the interests of the public and considerable inconvenience has resulted. They often wished to attend the places of worship in the Metropolis, or to see their friends on the Sabbath-day, but owing to existing arrangements, they have no facilities for so doing ... such an agreement infringed the rights of the inhabitants and consequently ought not to be tolerated."*[2]

Despite sentiments such as these the traffic restrictions had not been lifted and trains still did not call at Beckenham Junction, New Beckenham or Lower Sydenham stations during the "prohibited hours." Eventually the railway companies decided that the time had come to deliberately breach the Sunday traffic agreements and consequently did so by stopping their trains during the prohibited hours at the relevant stations with the result that Albemarle Cator raised an action against them for their infringements and demanded the full payment of the rent-charges due. A compromise was duly reached, it being felt that the Sunday travel restrictions no longer served any useful purpose with the almost complete suburbanisation of the areas involved, and the legal proceedings were stayed pending the transfer of such rights to the Council. With the subsequent passing of the 1894 Act they were so transferred and never again enforced and it was in this way that one of the unique early features of the railway in Beckenham came to an end.

Two into one

On 1st January 1899 the LCDR and South Eastern entered into a working agreement with each other and a formal Amalgamation Act was passed on 5th August of that year; henceforth their lines were operated by the South Eastern & Chatham Railways Joint Management Committee (SECR) and, although each company still existed independent of each, other revenues were combined and split 59:41 in favour of the South Eastern and henceforth locomotives and stock were pooled and services and publicity combined. New motive power (with engines finished in an attractive lined green livery) was in due course commissioned and such perennial problems as the perceived poor coaching stock, timekeeping and publicity were at last addressed but not before time as Cosmo Bonsor, the chairman of the new Managing Committee, later commented that at the time that the SECR came into being its two constituent companies "were regarded as the standing joke with the clown at the pantomime and the comic in the musical hall".[3]

One of the first acts of the new Management Committee was to improve the line between Beckenham Junction and New Beckenham and another was to rebuild certain of the local bridges and structures which were no longer adequate. In February 1900 the bridge over Beckenham Road on the Crystal Palace line was replaced by an impressive structure which included 65ft-long girders and the *Bromley Record* commenting that "with modern appliances these massive beams were put into their respective positions in the marvellously short time of little over one and a half hours." The same year brought a suggestion from the Beckenham Council to the SECR that a new station should be built to serve the Birkbeck and Churchfields estates and that the Penge Loop at Kent House should be reinstated to carry a circular service before adding several of the usual complaints to the effect that local train services, particularly on the LCDR lines, were suffering from a lack of punctuality and poor rolling stock. The company, while ignoring the suggestions for new stations and services, replied that as a result of the amalgamation they would now be able to use more powerful locomotives, make repairs to existing stock and build more carriages to try to meet the complaints. Despite this promise little changed in the short term and in October the Council again complained of the "wretched condition of the rolling stock used on the Chatham section for suburban services." Gradually changes were made but, despite fairly substantial investment in new rolling stock from 1909 onwards, the complaints continued. On the operating side, in September 1902 the Chislehurst loops were brought into use, together with the new running sheds at Orpington, and this brought about the extension from Bickley to Orpington of many local services via both Herne Hill and the Catford Loop; at about the same time a new brick-built signalbox of Saxby & Farmer Type 5 design with a 26-lever frame was built as a replacement for the wooden box at Penge.

Offensive odours

A long-standing problem at Beckenham Junction now came to the attention of the Council. As far back as 1871 the residents of the rather superior houses in Copers Cope Road, whose gardens backed on to the goods yard, had complained of the offensive odours emanating from wagons containing household rubbish and horse manure which had been left standing there. The South Eastern refused to entertain the matter since the traffic had been conveyed to there by the Chatham company; the latter company then undertook to discontinue the traffic but, like many of the promises that they made to the inhabitants of Beckenham, they failed to keep it. By 1901 the problem had become so serious that the Beckenham UDC brought an action in the Chancery Division against the SECR in an attempt to have the nuisance abated – one particularly serious complaint being that open wagons full of manure destined for the fruit farms of Kent were left unattended in the sidings all day on Sundays before onward transmission on the following day. Finding no satisfaction here, the local authority's action proceeded further and the "Beckenham Appeal" became a cause celebre locally. The case was, however, never heard in the Court of Appeal for the company backed down at the last minute and settled the case at the door of the court by undertaking "to put or procure to be put suitable and proper coverings … over all trucks of house refuse brought on to the sidings at Beckenham Junction and not to detain any of such trucks in the said sidings or junction for more than two and a half hours from the time of arrival under normal circumstances."[4]

The shape of things to come

On 22nd November 1900 the Beckenham UDC opened an electricity generating plant at Churchfields Road immediately adjacent to the Mid Kent line between Clock House and Elmers End and a private siding with a trailing connection was provided on the up side some 27 chains south of Clock House and operated from a ground frame controlled by Clock House signalbox[5]. The venture was a success and not only was Beckenham (and from 1913, West Wickham as well)[5a] said to have virtually the cheapest cost per unit for its electricity but in addition household rubbish was mixed with coal and burnt to provide power for generation, an early example of practical environmental recycling. Electricity generation ceased after the second war but the depot remained in use and the siding continued to be used for council purposes until the mid-1950s, being finally taken out of use in 1961.

According to Robert Borrowman "during the year 1901 and the two succeeding years the principal question which attracted local attention was the provision of tramways." This was not the first time that trams had been proposed – in 1888 a scheme for a line from Crystal Palace to Beckenham had been proposed (as noted in an earlier chapter), in 1895 a Crystal Palace to Beckenham and Bromley route was floated and in 1898 plans for a more ambitious scheme for a grandly-named London Southern Light Railway from Herne Hill to Farnborough via Beckenham and Bromley was successfully opposed by the Beckenham councillors on the ground that it would constitute "an intolerable nuisance to ordinary traffic"– once again it will be noted that Farnborough was destined never to be served by rail! On 11th August 1903 the UDC obtained powers to build tram lines from Penge to the junction of Beckenham High Street and Manor Road, from Penge to the Lewisham boundary via Kent House Road and from Kent House Road to Sydenham High Street, these routes connecting up with the British Electric Traction Company's tramway route from Croydon to Penge[6]; in addition the Council had been given powers to operate horse and motor buses, the only local authority in Greater London to be given these powers. Despite the fact that a local poll had shown an overwhelming support for the scheme, the Council abandoned its plans in 1905, citing mechanical and contractual problems having made the scheme unworkable and it was to prove to be an-

The third and last signalbox at Penge East – this neat Saxby Type 5 box dating from the first decade of the twentieth century was retained after 1959 solely to work the access to the goods yard opposite and is seen here in September 1967 just four months before its complete closure. (John Scrace)

other 95 years before a tram was seen in Beckenham. The B.E.T.South Metropolitan tram line from Croydon to the Pawleyne Arms in Penge High Street was opened on 10th February 1906 and the extension from there to Thicket Road at the south entrance to Crystal Palace Park was opened on 12th April of that year along with a second line via Anerley Road to Crystal Palace Low Level Station; the Penge line was replaced by buses in 1933 and the Crystal Palace route by trolley-buses in 1936.

In the same year as the trams reached, attempts were being made to stem the losses on the poorly patronised Crystal Palace and Norwood Junction and Beckenham Junction services and in order to save the cost of traditional steam-hauled workings on these lines steam railcars (single carriages which incorporated the locomotive) were employed on the former service and motor trains (push-pull services operated with two carriages with a small tank engine sandwiched between) were employed on the latter; in the case of the Crystal Palace line, the trains over which had been extended to Bickley in late Victorian times, were again cut back to Beckenham Junction. This change of operation brought about renewed requests from the Council for the provision of an additional stopping place adjoining the Beckenham Cemetery (the site of the present Birkbeck station) and at Beckenham Road (the site of the old WEL&CPR Penge station) and although the SECR promised to give "special attention" to the proposal nothing was done. In 1911 these requests were again reported in the local press and in the following year requests were made for unstaffed halts to be opened at Beckenham Road and the cemetery were by both the Council and the local ratepayers' association but when a deputation was sent by them to them to meet with the Company, the SECR refused to meet it. Perhaps the company had no wish to see a revival of the long-lost Penge station and in any event the opening of Kent House and Clock House stations had taken away the real need for an additional station at this point and it is probable that the SECR Board were in reality contemplating a complete withdrawal of both the Crystal Palace and the Norwood Junction shuttle services on economic grounds as average passenger loadings per train appear to have been in single figures on both lines[7]. A more successful venture was that of 1907 when in response to local requests the SECR putting on additional peak hour trains from Beckenham Junction to Holborn Viaduct and Victoria, making certain alterations to the station there by lengthening the up bay and installing an extra siding next to that platform.

A large and modern town

By now Beckenham was developing into a large and modern town being linked by development to Penge, Sydenham and Bromley with only the area to the south still being open countryside. The areas close to Clock House, Elmers End and Kent House stations were still in the course of development and two and three-bedroom semi-detached and terraced houses, selling for between £350 and £500 now

tended to be the norm while a local builder advertised a more spacious four bed-roomed "well built and attractive" house in Queen's Road (rather an optimistic "three minutes from Clock House station and eight minutes from Kent House station") with the added advantages of "separate tradesman's entrance, large garden and gravel soil" (a boon in often-waterlogged Beckenham) "at prices from £420" or an annual rent of £40. On the Kelsey Park estate, advertised in 1912 by the SECR publicity department as providing "artistic detached and semi-detached houses in an area of great natural beauty", building was underway, the irony being, of course, that the very houses advertised were spoiling that same great natural beauty. To the south H & S Taylor, a building firm from Lewisham, purchased a part of the Park Langley estate, lying to the south of Beckenham town centre, from the Goodhart trustees, and began to develop a garden city suburb ("Parklangley") complete with a shopping centre, winter garden and dance-hall; these additional features were later dropped but construction of what are now regarded as highly-desirable residences continued and the estate was developed with high-class housing and the curious "Chinese" Garage (in the Road to Mandalay style) until the development was completed in the 1950s. A private motor bus service "for residents only" was inaugurated

Blakeney Road bridge looking north in late Victorian times and showing the replacement for the bridge upon which Tacita came to grief; this, in turn, was replaced by the present structure in the late 1920s. (Author's collection)

The Railway Hotel – this imposing building in the High Street dated from 1860 and was a noted social centre as well as being the meeting point of several fox and drag hunts right up until the first decade of the twentieth century. The Hotel was unfortunately destroyed by bombs in 1944 and the sad remains later demolished; the site is now part of the open amenity area known as Beckenham Green. (Nancy Tonkin collection)

on 7th October 1910, buses being advertised to meet "the principal London trains at Beckenham Junction"[8].

An abiding concern, however, was that house construction throughout the area had out-stripped demand and in 1911 a total of 612 houses were vacant in Beckenham or almost 10% of the total housing stock. This was not a new phenomenon – in Bromley in the 1860s and in Penge in the 1890s similar concerns were being expressed and blame for the large number of empty houses was attributed to the allegedly high train fares and absence of concern for ordinary working men but in truth many of the empty houses were either too large and out-dated or too expensive for potential residents of any class, and were built in a style that no longer appealed to modern families or, less palatably, were merely the result in a glut of speculative house-building. The housing surplus eventually disappeared after the First War, when returning servicemen and a desire to provide "homes for heroes" led to a shortage of houses, only to re-appear temporarily in 1941 when the dangers of bombing led to a temporary depopulation of the Beckenham area.

In July 1910 the Council proposed that late trains, including the 1.15 am from Holborn Viaduct, should call additionally at Beckenham for the convenience of newspaper employees and other late workers in the City who lived in Beckenham and this request was swiftly granted. The Council's General Purposes Committee then had circulars printed and distributed which advertised Beckenham "as a place of residence for late workers in London." Subsequently the Council, along with other local authorities, approached the company with a request that something be done to eliminate the overcrowding and dangers of train operation at Cannon Street and Charing Cross where the scene was becoming chaotic "which failing the Councils would encourage the extension of the Electric Tube Railway throughout the districts concerned so as it induce healthy competition".

Mention of motor vehicles in the area first appear in the pages of the *Beckenham Journal* around the turn of the century and the first public motor buses in the area ran on Tilling's route 75 from Woolwich to Croydon via Penge. The era of the horse was, however, not quite over and it was not until 3rd January 1914 that the last horse bus was run on the route between Penge, Beckenham, Shortlands and Bromley; on 1st June of that year the London General Omnibus Company motor buses began to run on route 112 covering the same road as the horse bus. Horse-drawn vehicles still collected and delivered goods from local railway yards and sidings until well into the 1940s and Hansom cabs continued to be available at Beckenham Junction until 1935 when the ubiquitous Austin taxi-cab finally supplanted them. Horse buses were, however, never seen again in the area except for a brief ceremonial reappearance during the 1935 Beckenham municipal charter celebrations.

The lights go out

When the lights went out all over Europe the SECR assumed a new role under the control of the war-time Railway Executive which had assumed responsibility for all of Britain's railways. The company became busy serving the Channel ports and the main line through Beckenham soon choked with a sad procession of troop, armament, ambulance and refugee trains[9] while local train services were soon altered and cancellations were made to reflect changing travelling patterns brought about by war, many regular workers having joined the forces. Such was the change that it was said that in Beckenham (if not in West Wickham) social life had come to an almost complete standstill. In August 1914 the three new motor buses that had served on route 112 were requisitioned for war use in France and the service was finally suspended in January 1915. In the following month many variety of special reduced fare railway tickets were withdrawn on the SECR but this seems to have had little effect on the number of day-trippers to West Wickham common and woods and it was recorded in April of that year that many enjoyed the spectacle of an Admiralty air balloon's forced landing in a field close to the station.

As rationing loomed and the demands of the war in France became more demanding it was announced by the Railway Executive that in common with other services throughout the country as from 1st December 1915 the Beckenham Junction to Crystal Palace shuttle service was to be withdrawn until further notice. There seems to have been

little local protest at this withdrawal, perhaps because it was seen as being part of the war effort drive to save vital coal stocks and to release men for the front or, more realistically because few people still used these trains or cared about them. Thus, for the second time in history, regular passenger services were suspended over the Beckenham to Crystal Palace line and this time the cessation was to be rather longer than that of 1863 but it was, perhaps, inevitable as patronage of the trains had always been poor and the main attraction of the line, the Crystal Palace itself, had been in commercial decline ever since a disastrous fire in 1866 and there was a growing feeling among many that the Palace was now shabby and no longer fashionable; by 1914 it was closed to the public, having been requisitioned as a naval station.

Further railway service suspensions now followed and from 3rd April 1916 the Sunday service between Beck-

enham Junction and New Beckenham was withdrawn and, although the weekday service continued, Sunday trains over this line were never restored. On the same day the Elmers End to Hayes Sunday shuttle service was also withdrawn, a loss far more deeply felt, at least in the summer months, when holiday options were curtailed by circumstances. However in August of that eventful year local transport received a boost when bus route 112 was reinstated as a re-numbered route 109 and extended to serve the munitions works at Woolwich Arsenal[10]. Then, in December 1916, a massive programme of further railway closures and cancellations throughout Britain was announced by the Railway Executive, again for the purpose of releasing manpower and conserving coal. This time the victim was to be the Norwood Junction to Beckenham Junction service which had already been cut back to three daily return trips the year before; the whole passenger service was now withdrawn

Beckenham High Street shortly before the first war with a horse bus bound for Penge standing next to Rectory Road and the approach to Beckenham Junction. All the buildings on the left side of the street survive to this day while all those on the right disappeared as a result of two V1 missiles falling here in 1944. The cart is waiting next to the Southend Road bridge over the railway while in front of it is a block of shops and houses later replaced by Albemarle House while the Railway Hotel stands back from the road and the lady with the pram is passing the premises of Welford's Surrey Dairies and may well stop to look in the windows of D. Nottle's toy and fancy goods shop - Mr Nottle who was a keen professional photographer and was probably responsible for taking this picture. (Bromley Libraries)

A postcard view of Beckenham Junction in about1910, with an Orpington train entering the down platform. A wealth of interesting detail is evident including the period dress of the two ladies standing next to the entrance of the down booking office, the milk churns awaiting collection and the stepladder used to attend to the lamps. (Nancy Tonkin collection)

Beckenham Junction looking east from a commercial postcard taken in about 1920 with, on the right, the up goods sidings still in use. (Lens of Sutton)

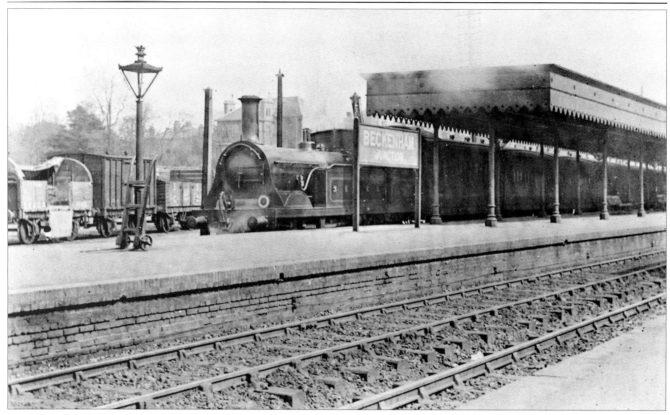

A Q class 0-4-4T stands in the down bay; the view shows the replacement canopies of 1890. Besides the SER open wagon and van in the yard is an elderly open coal wagon of the South Suburban Co-operative Society. (A. F. Selby/Lens of Sutton collection)

Beckenham Junction – a view looking along the up main platform with a selection of passengers awaiting their trains and a Norwood service waiting in the bay with a wealth of incidental detail. (Nancy Tonkin collection)

The up starting signals at Beckenham Junction with a panoramic view over the goods yard with much evidence of activity. (D Cullum: Lens of Sutton Association)

The SER signalbox at Beckenham Junction seen in 1919 with maintenance work taking place alongside and, in the left background, Dell Cottage. (SECR Society)

Beckenham Junction showing the up platform buildings and the wooden lamp room; this 1953 view includes a post-war Bulleid-pattern 4 SUB unit departing on an Orpington to Victoria working. (Lens of Sutton collection)

The gas-lit 1890 down side at Beckenham Junction seen in December 1967. The buildings not only survive in the twenty-first century but are now freshly painted and rather better looked after but where have all the Morris Minors gone and did the large enamel sign end up in someone's collection? (John Minnis)

An Austin taxi waits at the down side of Beckenham Junction in 1935. The cabmen's shelter was put up in 1879 at a cost of £37 5s and was paid for by public subscription but in time it appears to have been used as an illegal gambling den. Horse-drawn taxis survived in use here until the mid 1930s but present day minicabs now operate from the up side of the station. (H R Copeland collection)

with effect from 1st January 1917 and, as it turned out, there was to be no reprieve for the regular passenger services between Norwood and Beckenham although the spur line remained open for exchange goods trips and troop movements.

The War also brought about considerable social changes to Beckenham and West Wickham, not the least of which was the appearance in the area of Belgian and French refugees, the disappearance into war work of domestic staff, the billeting in local homes of military and naval personnel, the establishment of military hospitals in Balgowan school and elsewhere and the introduction, for virtually the first time, of female staff on the railways. In 1917 women clerks appeared at local stations while others were employed as guards on local trains and as signalwomen but, just as happened in the subsequent war, the services of these women were dispensed with at the end of hostilities when demobilised servicemen reappeared to assert their rights to employment with the SECR.

The path leading to the down side at Beckenham Junction in about 1930 with a large wooden sign drawing attention to an old established firm of estate agents in the adjacent building. (Author's collection)

The swansong of steam on the Mid Kent as H class 0-4-4T No. 328 arrives at the down bay at Beckenham Junction shortly before the introduction of a regular service of electric trains on ex-SER suburban lines in February 1926. This locomotive, although not seen again Beckenham, had a useful life post electrification and survived in British railways use until February 1961.(H C Casserley)

Shortlands station with a down goods working passing a terminating train from St Pauls on the first day of regular electric train working, 12 July 1925 with the Whitehall Laundry prominent in the background. (Rev A.V .W. .Mace; R.C.Riley collection)

Chapter 6
SOUTHERN ELECTRIC

"We congratulate the Company on the admirable way in which it carried out the change from steam to electric traction."
Beckenham U.D.C. minutes.

Enterprise and economy

At the end of the War the SECR suburban services were generally in a poor state and severe congestion was now being experienced on the approaches to the London termini with timekeeping on the Mid Kent line was particularly badly affected. The situation had deteriorated to such an extent that serious proposals were put forward in 1920 for the construction of a number of entirely new lines including one that was to run between Eden Park and Kent House so that a new Hayes to Holborn Viaduct service could be run, and a new connection was proposed between Elmers End and the LCDR line at the Beckenham Road bridge so that a direct Addiscombe to Victoria service could be provided, the object being to transfer services from the busy South Eastern lines to the relatively quieter LCDR termini.[1] The poor timekeeping endemic on the SECR suburban services was partially addressed by a new timetable in 1922 that avoided conflicting train movements, particularly at Borough Market Junction where the lines to Cannon Street and Charing Cross diverged, but this was not a total answer to the more widespread problems that the company were experiencing. A more obvious solution to the overcrowding which had been exacerbated by the short-lived post-war boom was that of the electrification of the SECR suburban lines, an idea that the Company had been toying with since 1903 and in 1918 they appointed an electrical engineer, Alfred Raworth, as their Electrical Engineer. By then the London Brighton & South Coast Railway had in place an a.c. overhead electric network ("the elevated electrics") extended over the former WEL&CPR line to Crystal Palace and Norwood Junction in 1911 while four years later the London & South Western Railway inaugurated a d.c. third rail electrification scheme of the suburban lines out of Waterloo. Raworth's plan was for a 1500V d.c. twin conductor rail system which, under its first stage, would see virtually all of the SECR lines within the Beckenham area electrified. Taking advantage of state credits for approved unemployment alleviation schemes provided by the Trade Facilities Act 1920 the scheme might well have come to fruition had it not been for the fact that the Railways Act 1921 was passed by Parliament, providing for the enforced grouping of the SECR, LBSCR and the LSWR into a new company to be known as the Southern Railway.

At the end of the pre-grouping era stringent economies had become necessary and a lack of wartime maintenance, increased wages and the rising price of coal had all had an effect on the SECR's finances so that, even though electrification would drastically reduce the running costs of local trains, it became necessary to practice some more immediate economies. Locally this meant that there was no restitution of the Norwood Junction and Crystal Palace shuttle services although the track was left in place so as not to rule this out in future even if the weeds and general neglect of the lines involved showed that there was little in the way of goods traffic in the interim. The escalation of staff costs were dealt with in July 1921 when the posts of Station Master at Clock House, Kent House and New Beckenham stations were abolished, these stations now coming under the jurisdiction of Beckenham Junction, while Ravensbourne was put within the jurisdiction of Shortlands and Eden Park, West Wickham and Hayes were placed in the care of the Elmers End stationmaster. Despite these moves the area was, nevertheless, still heavily dependent upon its railways and, in a guide to residential properties near London, the

Many residents of the area will still remember the water tower which, although long out of use, stood next to the up berthing sidings at Beckenham Junction as a last vestige of the vanished steam locomotives until 1972; its site is now occupied by the Tramlink lines. (R C Riley)

Making Ready for July 12

One of the New Southern Electric Trains.

FOR the past twelve months the carriage works of the Southern Railway at Ashford, Brighton and Lancing have been at full pressure building the trains for the new Electric Services to be opened next month and in December.

Interior of a First Class Compartment.

WHEN, on **July 12th,** the "Electrics" start to run from Holborn, St. Paul's, and Victoria to Orpington and Crystal Palace, and from Waterloo to Guildford and Dorking, many of the older steam trains now filling the gap will be withdrawn.

The travelling public has appreciated the fact that it takes time to construct 850 vehicles; next month they will have concrete evidence—and what could be better?—that the line with the greatest suburban traffic has been, and is, hard at work on its reconstruction; and will be hard at work until the "change over" is complete.

The new South-Eastern portion has cost £1,600,000 and that from Waterloo £833,000— a total of £2,433,000

SOUTHERN   ELECTRIC
More Trains ———— New Coaches
E. 21/6/5.   H. A. WALKER, General Manager.

---

rail scheme. Under the scheme, described by the Southern as "the biggest scheme of suburban electrification in the world", Stage I was to cover the former LCDR lines from Victoria and Holborn Viaduct to Orpington via Beckenham Junction together with the Catford loop and Stage II, covering the ex-SER lines from Charing Cross and Cannon Street included the Mid Kent line and its branches

The contracts for the local electrification works were let out in November 1923 and at both Shortlands and Elmers End steel-framed red brick substations of the LSWR "cathedral" pattern were erected to house static transformers, three rotary converters and the necessary switchgear for converting the public supply into the 660V direct current necessary to run the trains while a similar building at Upper Sydenham on the Crystal Palace High Level Branch fed the Penge Tunnel through cables running down one of the ventilation shafts[2]. At Shortlands, where it was intended that the Catford loop service would terminate at the east face of the down island platform, track and signalling alterations were carried out and on Sunday 20th December 1925 Shortlands Station signalbox was closed and the Junction box was extended in a style matching the original and a second-hand 53-lever LCDR frame was fitted.

Much local interest was caused in the works and in addition Beckenham UDC, in a joint approach with other local authorities, requested the SR to provide a new through electric train service from Orpington to Croydon via Beckenham Junction and Norwood. The Southern replied that "such trains would be no doubt appreciated by a small proportion of local residents but when the [pre-war] shuttle services were provided they were unremunerative and consequently withdrawn."Undaunted the Councils tried again and on 17th November 1924 met with Sir Herbert Walker, the SR General Manager, who promised that the Crystal Palace service would be revived in due course and that if passengers still wished to travel from Beckenham to Croydon then they would be able to so by changing at Crystal Palace. The deputation, needless to say, also discussed matters such as overcrowding in first-class carriages and the proposal to build a new ticket office on the Southend Road bridge at Beckenham Junction. The latter scheme never came to fruition but the explanation for the former was that since second class travel on the former SECR lines had been abolished in September of the previous year some passengers had upgraded while much of the better steam-hauled stock had been withdrawn from service pending its conversion at Ashford works into the new electric multiple units.

The living rail

By Easter 1925 the Stage I works were virtually complete and trial running of electric trains between St Paul's (Blackfriars) and Shortlands via the Catford loop commenced on 8th June. Heralded by local press announcements, a public service of electric trains commenced running between Victoria and Orpington via Beckenham Junction, Holborn Viaduct and Orpington via Beckenham Junc-

Times commented at the beginning of 1923 that Beckenham " is a convenient and pleasant suburb with the advantage of late trains and fast services to the City and West End and properties are comparatively cheap there."

Planning for the future

Before any radical change could be effected the railways in the area passed into the hands of the new Southern company and, within a short time, its new green livery on both trains and stations began to appear locally. On 9th July 1923 the LCDR station at Penge was renamed Penge East, the former LBSCR station becoming Penge West; the latter station then lost its station master and for the first time ever came under the jurisdiction of Penge East. More importantly the new administration drew up plans for immediate suburban electrification plans for its Eastern Section which corresponded to the area of the ex-SECR lines, adopting as standard the existing London & South Western d.c. third

tion and St Paul's to Shortlands via the Catford loop on Sunday 12th July and, notwithstanding teething troubles stemming from blown fuses, brake failures, traction motor problems and the breakdown of two trains in the Penge Tunnel on the following day[3], the public were generally enthusiastic and the new trains were welcomed. Compared to the old irregular and often unreliable steam trains, the initial service provided was seen as lavish – on the main line a 20-minute basic service of trains from Orpington to Holborn Viaduct and Orpington to Victoria, running five minutes apart so as to leave a gap in the timetable for steam-hauled outer suburban and express services, was provided while on the Catford Loop a 20-minute service to St Pauls was run. Additional rush-hour trains were run and on Sundays a half-hourly service was provided. Equal importance was given to the City and West End as destinations – the 1921 Census showing that of the employed population resident in Beckenham some 40% worked in the City and between 10 and 20% in the West End.

In July 1925 a deputation from the Beckenham UDC met the Southern Railway's Chief Operating Superintendent and, after congratulating the Company "on the admirable way in which it had carried out the change from steam to electric traction" matters of concern were raised including that of first-class compartments being occupied with impunity by third-class passengers and a request that some of the Kent coast trains should stop at Beckenham Junction, a practice that had prevailed prior to electrification. In relation to the latter point the Company regretted that this could not be done for "operational reasons" in that if they were to do this "it would throw the whole schedule out".

Stage II of the electrification scheme was now under way and it was announced that electric services on the Mid Kent line would commence in December 1925. From 21st September the Elmers End to Hayes shuttle service was provided by electric trains for staff training purposes but it was not until 26th February 1926 that a partial service of electric trains was provided on the Mid Kent proper while the full service was delayed until July partially due to the effects of the General Strike and also because of problems relating to the non-availability of new stock. Among track and signalling alterations carried out at that time the central run-round loop at New Beckenham was removed, having been little used since 1916, while on the Hayes branch an

---

SOUTHERN RAILWAY

Signal Instruction No. 41, 1925.

Instructions to all concerned as to the

ABOLITION OF SHORTLANDS STATION SIGNAL BOX

AND

NEW AND ALTERED SIGNALS, ETC.

SHORTLANDS JUNCTION.

To be brought into use on Sunday, 20th December.

Shortlands Station signal box will be put out of service and all signals, points, etc., at present worked therefrom will, in future, be worked from Shortlands Junction signal box.

A bracket post carrying the up fast and slow line home signals, erected between the up fast and up slow lines, about 20 yards the Bromley South side of the up platform. See diagram No. 1.

Diagram. No. 1.

No. 1. Up slow home signal.

No. 2. Up fast home signal.

A bracket post, erected outside the up slow line, 986 yards from the up home signals. See diagram No. 2.

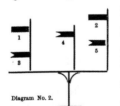

Diagram. No. 2.

No. 1. Bromley South up slow advanced starting signal.

No. 2. Bromley South up fast advanced starting signal.

No. 3. Shortlands Junction up slow distant signal.

No. 4. Shortlands Junction up fast to up main distant signal.

No. 5. Shortlands Junction up fast to up loop distant signal.

No. 5 is the new signal.

The up main advanced starting signal will be moved to a new position 212 yards nearer Beckenham Junction.

SHORTLANDS JUNCTION—*continued.*

A ground signal, situate in the down slow line at the Bromley South end of the station, controlling movements from the down slow to down fast or back on down slow line.

The undermentioned existing signals will be put out of service :—

Shortlands Station box up fast and up slow home signals.

Shortlands Junction up fast and slow to up main distant signals.

Bromley South up fast and slow advanced starting signals.

Shortlands Station up fast and slow distant signals.

Shortlands Station box down slow and fast home signals.

Shortlands Station box down slow and fast distant signals, situate on the post carrying Shortlands Junction down main and loop home signals.

The work will be in progress from 12.5 a.m. Mr. Foster to provide flagman, as required.

During the time these works are in progress drivers must look out for hand signals.

The District Inspectors to be present when the new signals, etc., are brought into use and report to the Divisional Operating Superintendent on the working.

Waterloo Station,
15th December, 1925.

EDWIN O. COX,
Chief Operating Superintendent.

(R. 10,230.)

additional live rail was laid in order to increase the capacity of the running rails to return the negative current.

The new electric Mid Kent service was a complex one, providing an hourly train from each of Cannon Street and Charing Cross to both Beckenham Junction and Addiscombe, running independently to each destination and thus providing a 15-minute service between London Bridge and New Beckenham; the Hayes branch was still served by a shuttle from Elmers End. Additional rush-hour services were run and on Sundays half-hourly trains ran from Charing Cross to Addiscombe and an hourly shuttle from Elmers End to Hayes – on the latter service Eden Park, which had been partially rebuilt after a fire in 1921, still served virtually nothing and remained closed until 2 pm. No Mid Kent trains ran beyond Beckenham Junction on weekdays and the lavish provision of trains over the spur reflected operating expediency rather than public demand; no Sunday services were run over the spur.

East London to Addiscombe

Although the East London Railway from Whitechapel had a physical connection with the Mid Kent via North Kent line at New Cross and Lewisham, no through trains had been operated since 1884. In 1924 Sir Herbert Walker conceived of the idea of acquiring the still-independent East London company, which was worked by the Metropolitan Railway, and of then using it as part of a new radial through service from Paddington to Addiscombe using the northern part of the Circle Line, the East London and the Mid Kent with services operated jointly by the Southern and the Metropolitan. The Met were, perhaps unfairly, contemptuous of the existing steam-hauled services on the Mid Kent, describing the trains in their report as being "old, dirty and in bad condition" and the stations as being "old and dingy". Despite the initial enthusiasm of both of the potential partners to bring this joint venture to reality, nothing eventually came of this as neither of them was prepared to advance the capital cost of new trains, the existing Metropolitan trains being found, after experimental runs on 17th February 1926, to be underpowered in comparison with the new Southern electric multiple units and thus unable to run alongside them and keep up with their schedules. The East London line remained SR property until nationalisation but was used solely for a shuttle service from Whitechapel to New Cross Gate and New Cross, the sight of the red train in the bay platform at the latter station being familiar to generations of Mid Kent travellers. From time to time similar schemes were mooted, such as the 1978 proposals to extend the Fleet Line to Hayes, but it was not until recent times that positive steps were taken and only in 2010 did it become possible to travel over the East London Line and south of New Cross when Overground trains began to run to Croydon and Crystal Palace via Sydenham.

A General "B" type single deck bus passes the Lych Gate of the rebuilt St Georges church in about 1925 while running to Chislehurst from Penge via Kent House, Beckenham, Shortlands and Bromley; this still familiar route was later renumbered 227 and for twenty years until 1971 was operated by the fondly remembered RF buses complete with conductors.(Bromley Libraries)

Elmers End Road looking south from its junction with Mackenzie Road, c.1935; the bridge carries the Crystal Palace line and the entrance stair to Birkbeck station is on the right. Note also the poster for the Regal Cinema in Beckenham. (Nancy Tonkin collection)

Birkbeck station looking towards Beckenham Junction in 1963. The station was at this time fully staffed with the main booking office and waiting room on the up platform and passengers intending to travel in the down direction would require to buy their tickets and then change platforms via the road. (Lens of Sutton)

The Ghost Train revived

In August 1926 it was announced that the Crystal Palace to Beckenham Junction line, unused since 1915, was to be reopened and electrified as part of the works connected with the conversion of the ex-LBSCR overhead electric lines to third rail as authorised by the Southern Railway Act 1925. This was welcomed locally since the line had fallen into such disuse that shrubs and young trees were growing between the rusting rails and the public were reminded that the line had previously been known as "the ghost line" from the fact that after closure "phantom trains would suddenly rattle down otherwise derelict line bearing troops to some unknown destination".[4]

Comprehensive works in connection with the reopening were undertaken. The Norwood Spur line was relaid as a single-track uni-directional goods line from the Beckenham direction and the signalbox at Norwood Spur Junction was permanently switched out as from 3rd February 1929 and closed on 14th April when it was replaced by a 6-lever ground frame. At Beckenham Junction the layout was altered, a new double-track crossover put in, the up bay platform lengthened to give a platform some 514 feet in length and the former up side goods sidings abolished, the site being partly used to construct two berthing sidings, an improved access road, car parking and a new bus stand; the tall brick water tower was, however, retained and remained a feature of the station for another fifty years. Further berthing facilities for electric trains were provided alongside the New Beckenham spur and to the east of the station radical improvements were made. These were said by the Company in a press release printed in the *Times* in May 1929 to have been necessary "to do away with the bottleneck which presents such difficulties in the operation of up boat expresses and stopping electric trains over the same metals" and consisted of the physical abolition of Penge Junction with the consequent closure of the Kent House C signalbox there on 16th October 1927 and the quadrupling of the line from there to Beckenham Junction at a cost of £105,000 so that the Crystal Palace line trains could be run independently of the main-line. At the same time the ramshackle Blakeney Road overbridge, which had been clumsily widened in the past so that traffic on the road had to negotiate a badly-placed central support, was replaced by the present girder bridge and the whole of the main-line between Kent House and Beckenham Junction was raised to improve the gradients on it. In addition the Mid Kent line was raised by several feet so as to try to reduce the risk of flooding, a more serious problem now in view of the electrification of the line. The line between Penge East and Shortlands was completely resignalled and at Penge East an additional lever was installed while the box at Kent House B and the former Penge loop siding at Kent House were all abolished as from 2nd December 1928; this box was later demolished along with the loop siding girder bridge. At Beckenham Junction the SER box was closed on 16th September 1928 and replaced by a new box situated on the down side and in the angle of the main and new Beckenham lines – the new box was of a Southern Railway traditional brick lower storey and timber upper design of type 11a and was fitted with an 82-lever Westinghouse frame which had been recovered from another location. Beckenham UDC benefitted financially from the works to the extent of £75 paid to them by the Southern for a strip of allotment land required for railway widening.

Brickbats and Birkbeck

On 3rd March 1929 the new electric train service from Beckenham Junction to Victoria via Crystal Palace commenced and a basic 20-minute timetable was provided. Initially the service appears to have been a success and on 2nd March 1930 a new station was opened at the point where the line crossed Elmers End Road, 1m 27ch west from Beckenham Junction. Situated on the London side of the bridge and named Birkbeck after the nearby housing estate of the same name, this was a simple station in the style of other SR halts with two platforms 520 feet long with small waiting shelters incorporating, on the down side, a ticket office. Access was by means of staircases on each side of the bridge and a large green and white enamel sign was fixed to the side of the bridge in order to attract potential travellers. The *Penge & Anerley Press* greeted the event with the comment that "the station has been foreshadowed for many years and should prove a great boon to the residents of the district" but a combination of factors including the proximity of both Elmers End and Anerley stations (both with direct services to the City) and a relatively good bus service passing by conspired against its success and Birkbeck did not (and never has) lived up to its expectations – a fact due, in no little measure, by the fact that the lack of proper connections at Beckenham Junction where, like "Cray Fish" of a previous era, passengers would see the Crystal Palace train depart from Beckenham Junction just as main-line trains were about to arrive – as one local historian put it the "lesser men" who followed SR General Manager Sir Herbert Walker destroyed his dream by such poor timetabling, remarking that "presumably any who wish to make the journey have long since been accustomed to get their car out"[5]

In March 1931 a last plea was made by the Beckenham UDC for the reopening and electrification of the Norwood Spur line and for the resumption of the Norwood Junction shuttle, possibly extended into Croydon. The Southern, however, were not enthusiastic and Walker replied that such a scheme would involve considerable expenditure and that the service between Beckenham and Norwood would provide little advantage over the new service to Victoria via Crystal Palace and that in any event it was impossible to run through trains to East Croydon "owing to the existing track occupation".

The terminus of the standard gauge siding at Bethlem Hospital with an interesting assortment of wagons in view; note the way in which the former parkland of the Monks Orchard estate gave way to the hospital development. (Elcock & Sutclife; Bethlem Art & History Collections Trust)

The Bethlem Hospital Line

In 1926 the trustees of the Bethlem Royal Hospital purchased the Monks Orchard Estate on the outskirts at Beckenham close to Eden Park station with a view to constructing there a replacement for the existing hospital in Southwark and the main contractors appointed for the project were Harold Arnold & Sons of Doncaster and the architects were Elcock & Sutcliffe of London. In order to convey materials to the site for what was to prove to be a major construction project the contractors entered in to a contract with the Southern Railway for the carriage of the same by rail and as a result a branch line 59 chains in length was built running southwards from a trailing junction a little to the south of Eden Park station. The cost of the branch, which was lightly laid across the poorly-drained fields, cost £750 to construct and was controlled from a temporary two-lever frame in the West Wickham signal box; no road crossing was required as the whole of the line lay to the south of the existing Upper Elmers End Road. On 11th August 1928 the *Beckenham Journal* reported that

"Amongst the steadily growing building operations being carried out at Elmers End and Eden Park, a rather interesting development is taking place in the grounds of the New Bethlem Hospital, once known as Monk's Orchard.

For the purpose of transporting building materials for the new hospital, a railway siding is being constructed at Eden Park. On the opposite side of the road from Eden Park station, behind the trees and therefore invisible from the road, an army of workmen are labouring on the formidable task of building up a plateau to the same height as the embankment along which the trains run to West Wickham, Hayes and Elmers End. A miniature railway has been laid through the woods and across the fields for carrying materials and cement mixers, water tanks and wells have been arranged. Huts and offices have sprung up and what was once a thickly wooded estate has been cut up and hewn about to make room for the new buildings."

Motive power on the standard-gauge branch was provided by two 0-6-0 saddle tank locomotives which had previously seen service in Nottinghamshire and elsewhere on railway and housing estate construction[6] and a small number of second-hand wagons obtained from the Southern Railway and elsewhere that were used internally on the line. The miniature railway referred to was a network of two-foot gauge temporary lines lightly laid on the surface of the ground and moved about when necessary much in the same way that narrow-gauge lines had been provided to serve the battlefield areas on the Western Front a dozen years previously. The track was made up of short sections that could be

Part of the extensive 2 ft gauge system with a wagon being tipped amongst a great deal of activity; one of the small ex-War Department tractors can be seen in evidence and also worthy of note are the seemingly uncomfortable clothes of the workmen. (Elcock & Sutclife; Bethlem Art & History Collections Trust)

slotted together in sections rather like the track on a model railway and the motive power used consisted of five diminutive twenty horsepower petrol locomotives that Arnolds had originally purchased from the War Department and a total of 80 tipper wagons to run with them.

In the first month of construction work 716 tons of ballast, 731 tons of gravel, 600 tons of sand, 42,000 Sussex bricks and 6 tons of steel bar were delivered to the site by rail and by December 1928 the number of Sussex bricks delivered had increased to 139,500 together with, amongst other materials, 43,000 facing bricks, 12,000 slates and a large quantity of earthenware drainage pipes. A visitor to the site commented that Eden Park station was, at that time, "a station almost lost in the woods" and he noted on another visit "the twisted skein of railway lines" covering the formerly pastoral land and added that "large trucks from three railways and a real locomotive belching black smoke in the woods hurried my departure."[7] By April 1930 virtually all of the work on the site had been completed and both of the railway systems were dismantled in that month and re-

moved for re-use elsewhere. The Hospital was formally opened by Queen Mary on 9th July. A new section of the Elmers End to West Wickham A214 road, known as Links Way, was built on part of the site of the connecting line and transfer sidings and there are now no remains of either system to be seen in the landscaped hospital grounds or in the gardens of the houses built on its periphery.

A good investment

By the 1920s Beckenham was again enjoying a residential building boom as the outward expansion of the London suburbs, which had been put on hold during the duration of the war, recommenced with vigour. New houses appeared in areas which had still been farmland and the demand for smaller and more affordable houses coupled with cheaper building methods and the availability of affordable mortgages through building societies and, under the provisions of the Housing Act 1925, from the Beckenham UDC helped to satisfy would-be home owners to realise their dreams. The breaking up of large private estates due to changing economic conditions helped to make the Eden Park area ripe for development and the semi-detached house with its distinctive bay windows, large gables and stuck-on half-timbering and other "Tudor" accessories[8] became a familiar feature of the "new" Beckenham, whether replacing virgin farmland or the grounds of by now lost Georgian and Victorian mansions. By 1934, when Beckenham UDC, somewhat controversially absorbed its smaller and more rural neighbour West Wickham, both the population of the area and its housing stock had increased by almost 50%. In the following year Beckenham became a Municipal Borough, the second largest in Kent by population and the wealthiest in terms of rate income and, as the Charter Handbook issued at that time commented, "Beckenham has grown up."

Much of this development had taken place when the railways were being electrified and the Southern Railway helped by its publications such as *Country Homes at London's Door* which went through three editions between 1927 and 1929 and extolled the virtues of Beckenham, Eden Park and West Wickham as places to live, saying in 1929 that in respect of the last-mentioned "nowhere is a small country village being converted into a rising township under more favourable conditions" rather in contrast to a statement published elsewhere only two years earlier to the effect that "West Wickham … is still a real country village and not a camouflaged suburb."[9] The railway company was anxious to get across the message that "A Southern home is a good investment and property is increasing in value year by year in the Districts served by the Southern" and in an attempt to entice prospective house-hunters the SR also mentioned the availability of "Go-As-You-Please" Cheap Tickets so that the districts mentioned in their publications could be easily visited and, in order to appeal to the whole family, it was noted that "Cheap Tickets for Dogs (accompanying passengers) are also issued." In *Country*

Homes local estate agents sung the praises of the area, examples being "Live in Beckenham – London's Premier Residential Suburb" and, in respect of West Wickham, they advertised the availability of "well-built labour-saving houses in lovely rural settings."

An interesting question was that of from where the inhabitants of these new houses came and the answer seems to be that although many were newcomers from the north and midlands attracted by new employment opportunities others came from nearer at hand including other districts of Beckenham itself. Alan Jackson, in *Semi-detached London*, postulates that "most of these new suburbans originated in the Victorian and Edwardian suburbs, making place as they moved outwards for regional immigrants and less fortunate Londoners coming from even older and more crowded property nearer the centre" and he noted a typical radial migration pattern along the railway routes with which the new house-buyers were already familiar.[10] Thus in Beckenham migrants in all probability came from Brixton, Herne

Spirit of the twenties – the extraordinary (and now listed) Road to Mandalay style "Chinese Garage" at Park Langley where uniformed attendants would meet your needs. If only all of suburbia was quite this eccentric! (Bromley Libraries)

Hill, Norwood, Crystal Palace and Catford along the ex-LCDR lines to the new developments served by Beckenham Junction, Ravensbourne and Shortlands station while the new householders of the Mid-Kent suburbs of New Beckenham, Elmers End, Eden Park and West Wickham, who were already familiar with the line from their weekend excursions to the commons and woodlands of West Wickham and Hayes, were attractive to former residents of New Cross, Lewisham, Catford and Sydenham[11]. These families, whilst often maintaining their employment and travel patterns based on the Southern termini which they knew well, gave new off-peak business to the local lines as they frequently visited their former neighbours, friends and relations and invited them back for Sunday tea and tours of the garden as few saddled with a mortgage could, in those economically uncertain times, afford to pay both the building society and the hire purchase companies for a car, however modest.

Content in Kent

In Beckenham itself new development was now mainly in the area south of the town centre with Village Way and Stone Park Avenue and the areas to the east and the areas surrounding them completed by the mid-1930s although the Park Langley development continued and on the Cator estate and elsewhere some infilling of semi-detached and smaller detached houses took place. In the Elmers End area, housing now extended along Upper Elmers End Road in an almost continual development between Elmers End and Eden Park stations and onwards towards Monks Orchard and West Wickham while smaller developments took place in Shortlands and other parts of the Borough where building land was available. However it was in West Wickham that the most incredible expansion of all took place, the population rising in the decade from 1921 from 1,501 to 6,229, to 10,080 in 1934 before virtually doubling again within five years. Much of the development was again of the type familiar in suburban areas throughout Greater London but in the case of West Wickham redeemed by the extensive tree-planting carried out by the council and by local residents. West Wickham High Street metamorphosed into its modern aspect and new roads were laid out in the vicinity where formerly cattle had grazed and children had played. Much of this change bewildered the original villagers – as the *Beckenham Times* commented in 1932 "the old inhabitants view with amazement the transformation scenes enacted from day to day" and two years later the same paper stated that "West Wickham is no longer a village; the last traces of rural life are disappearing."

The development of West Wickham was no doubt helped by the provision of frequent electric trains to London but the effect of electrification should not be over-emphasised as the dividing line between cause and effect is far from clear and Beckenham and West Wickham would, no doubt, have undergone the development that they did irrespective of whether or not the railway had been electrified. In the 1920s the motor bus arrived in West Wickham

By 1930 there were few vestiges of West Wickham's rural past but Yew Tree Cottage was an exception and this picture shows both the antiquity of the building and its ability to adapt to serve a new generation of country ramblers and excursionists who travelled there by train; such charm was not to last and in August 1939 the cottage was swept away for road construction. (Bromley Libraries)

and by 1930 a network of services to Croydon, Bromley and even central London existed although, perhaps surprisingly in view of their municipal link, a direct bus between West Wickham and central Beckenham did not materialise until 1953. On Sundays in the late 1920s so many buses carrying day-trippers were seen in West Wickham that that there were complaints in the press of insufferable local traffic congestion: the Southern Railway in response to this competition cut some of its excursion fares to try to stem the flow of traffic away from the motor coach although in later years it was the private car which caused this congestion and began to make an inroad into both local rail and bus journeys. Nevertheless the transformation of the Hayes line from a rural branch-line into a commuter line was well under way and in 1929 the newly-formed West Wickham Residents' Association asked the Southern to improve the weekday service on the Hayes branch; in 1932 eight-coach trains were introduced on the branch, causing the platforms

at Eden Park and West Wickham to be lengthened.

By this time much of the grounds of the older large properties in West Wickham had been divided up into plots for building on – examples were the Wickham House estate sold for building in 1925, Ravenswood and its 40 acre grounds sold for the same purpose in 1922 and the Wickham Hall estate sold in 1929. Following the completion of a major drainage scheme carried out by the Bromley Rural District Council farmland was being covered by houses at a rapid rate ably abetted by the Southern Railway with alluring slogans such as "Live in Kent and Be Content" and publicity that extolled the rural beauties of the area promising that "various estates are planned out in a tasteful manner" all of which added to the pressure on the remaining open countryside. The advertising campaign was relentless and in 1936 the Southern Railway's *Homes in Kent* publication said of West Wickham

"With so many estates being developed in the

From "Homes at London's Door" 1929 edition

Figures adding up

In the decade after electrification the railways of Beckenham flourished as never before, and examples of the growth of traffic were provided at Beckenham Junction where there was a 42% increase in ticket sales between 1927 and 1934 (from 277,338 ordinary and 5,345 season tickets to 394,804 and 14,680 respectively), at Ravensbourne where there was a 271% increase (9,151 to 24,887 ordinary and 145 to 882 seasons) and, especially, at Eden Park where ticket sales increased ten-fold between 1925 and 1934 (8,358 and 61 seasons to 75,841 and 4,188 – in the case of Eden Park the figures may have been artificially low because of the fact that a quarterly season ticket from there to London cost £4 3s 6d whereas the short walk to Elmers End would result in an quarterly season of only £3 3s, a considerable saving at a time when a typical office worker might be earning between £2 10s and £4 per week. In December 1935 the SR General Manager's Office gave the following comparative figures for the total number of season ticket holders at various stations[13]:

neighbourhood, it is not possible to mention all, but prices range from £645 to £1500 and upwards, a good average figure for the area being £900 ... There are many estates (some of them as convenient to Eden Park or Hayes stations as to West Wickham) all in very beautiful surroundings and the newcomer can choose either an elevated or valley site according to his particular desire."

But even though Pevsner dismisses West Wickham architecturally with the line that "Little comment is called for on the efforts of the twentieth century", it was, and with the passage of time increasingly remains, a pleasant tree-lined environment where people wanted to live and to realised their suburban dreams.[12] By 1939 there was little empty land left to infill in Beckenham and West Wickham and that which remained was either destined for other uses or considered to be too remote from a convenient station; in any event the economic drive behind the housing boom in the south-east was beginning to flag and in September of that year Herr Hitler put paid to any further development for the time being.

Eden Park shopping parade and station entrance in a postcard of 1935 by which time the transformation of open country to suburb was almost complete although the council's favoured renaming of the area as "South Beckenham" was never put into effect. (Nancy Tonkin collection)

The Southern Electric sign at Eden Park which displayed an interesting set of destinations, presumably chosen to reflect the most popular destinations of the day. (Lens of Sutton)

Anerley	290	Beckenham Jn	1,490
Birkbeck	118	Bromley South	1,023
Clock House	787	Eden Park	300
Elmers End	1,458	Hayes	746
Kent House	794	Lower Sydenham	128
New Beckenham	381	Penge East	1,044
Penge West	101	Ravensbourne	101
Shortlands	560	West Wickham	1,586

The figures show the predominance, locally, of Beckenham Junction (where connecting bus services and the availability of taxis assisted onward travellers), West Wickham (where housing developments had transformed the formerly rural station), Elmers End and Penge East, the continuing pattern of sparse traffic at New Beckenham and Ravensbourne and and the failure of Birkbeck to attract much traffic in its first five years of operation.

Trains for travellers

During the 1930s there were several changes to local train services, particularly on the Mid Kent line where changing employment patterns and housing development led to radical alterations. The Hayes branch gained through services from Cannon Street and Charing Cross and, in time, eclipsed the former importance of Addiscombe and Beckenham Junction as termini. On 30th September 1935 the Woodside to Selsdon line, closed to all local traffic since 1916, was reopened as an electrified passenger line and the provision of through trains to London from Sanderstead via Selsdon, Coombe Road, Bingham Road, Woodside and Elmers End. A 30-minute off-peak service on this line, provided in anticipation that the area served would see rapid suburban development, led to a huge reduction in the Mid Kent service to Beckenham Junction, the spur being left with a mere eight daily trains and becoming so forgotten that barely a year later the *Beckenham Journal* could report somewhat incredulously that there were now less trains serving the line in 1936 than there had been in 1857, overlooking the fact that the same could not have been said twelve months previously. In 1935 the Catford Loop trains which terminated at Shortlands were extended via Swanley to Sevenoaks. By then off-peak local traffic was beginning to decline caused by the extension of motor bus routes through the Borough and the rise of private motoring. The Southern, however, were aware of this and tried to counter the effects by issuing day returns and weekend reduced fare tickets to London, to the seaside and to country stations as well as offering fares suited to local conditions an a particularly intriguing example was provided with the opening of the Regal cinema in Beckenham in September 1930 when the Southern Railway promised "support in the form of cheap fares to Beckenham Junction and Clock House", a move that was no longer so attractive when West Wickham, Bromley and Elmers End all obtained their own cinemas.

By 1938 the electric train service to Beckenham consisted of weekday up departures on Mondays to Fridays (figures in brackets trains timed to leave Beckenham stations before 9.30 am) totalled 372 (86) made up as follows: *Main Line*, Orpington to Holborn Viaduct 70 (19), Orpington to Victoria 58 (9), *Catford Loop*, Sevenoaks to St Pauls 56 (14), *Palace Line*, Beckenham Junction to Victoria 31 (10), *Mid Kent*, Addiscombe to Charing Cross 28 (3), Addiscombe to Cannon Street 31 (11), Sanderstead to Charing Cross 28 (3), Sanderstead to Cannon Street 5 (2), Hayes to Charing Cross 30 (9), Hayes to Cannon Street 28 (3), Beckenham Junction to Charing Cross 2 (1), Beckenham Junction to Cannon Street 5 (2). In addition there were certain additional local shuttle services to and from Elmers End to connect with London services. A total of 146 (41) trains ran on the New Beckenham to Ladywell section of the Mid Kent. In general Saturday services were every 30 minutes with the exception of the Catford Loop and Victoria to Orpington services which ran every 20 minutes. There were no Sunday services between Orpington and Holborn Viaduct or

Beckenham Junction and New Beckenham.

On 30th November 1936 the Crystal Palace burnt down, the fiery spectacle being watched by the inhabitants of Beckenham – a portent of more fiery spectacles some four years later. This was the last spectacle that the public responded to at the Palace whose fortunes had by then had sunk to an all-time low and, as a result of the amount of water poured on the smouldering wreckage by firemen's hoses, subsequent repairs had to be carried out in the tunnel at Gypsy Hill so that from September 1937 to April 1938 the service from Beckenham Junction was reduced to a shuttle to Crystal Palace only.

Despite the electric trains and lengthened platforms, local stations were little altered and at this period were mostly gas-lit with the exception of one or two which were lit by feeble electric bulbs and, outside of the rush hour, many of Beckenham's stations often still possessed the aura of sleepy country halts rather than busy suburban centres. The new electric services were well patronised and although local first-class traffic was in decline due to competition from the private car, bus competition was largely limited to local journeys and it was in many ways a heyday for the Southern. On the Mid Kent traffic was now so heavy that in June 1939 the Elmers End signalmen feeling overwhelmed by the number of trains passing their box had to request that further safety equipment be installed there and the Company responded by installing a closed three-position block system at a cost of £2,500. Local passenger services had by then reached their absolute zenith and the Borough of Beckenham was, indeed, enjoying peace, progress and prosperity and was by now the richest and possibly the most progressive local authority in Kent.

For the duration

The dream came to an abrupt end in the summer of 1939 when the spectre of war was imminent and plans were drawn up for air-raid precautions in the Borough. A tentative scheme was proposed to evacuate all local children living to the north and west of the Mid-Kent line between Lower Sydenham and Elmers End although it was not put into immediate effect[14]. On September 1st, three days before the declaration of war on Germany, the Defence Regulations were introduced and the night time black out came into force immediately with restricted station lighting and trains running without any lighting at all. Soon carriages were fitted with blinds, dimmed lighting and notices stating that

DURING BLACK OUT –
BLINDS MUST BE KEPT DOWN

BEFORE YOU ALIGHT – make certain the train
Is at the platform and that you alight
on the platform side

Ironically the first civilian casualty of war in Beckenham occured in the following month when, in the gloom of the black out at Shortlands station, a male passenger failed to alight from an evening Catford Loop train on the platform side and fell to his death in the street below.

Severe reductions in local train services were now made and from 11th September 1939 the few remaining Mid Kent trains to Beckenham Junction were withdrawn along with the Orpington to Holborn Viaduct through service, although a minimal peak-hour service was later reintroduced on that route following complaints from the public. On 16th October the through Victoria to Crystal Palace and Beckenham Junction service was withdrawn and for the rest of the war a shuttle service was in operation between the two latter points while on the same day through trains between London and Addiscombe were withdrawn and replaced by a shuttle service to and from Elmers End while the Mid Kent off-peak service was reduced to two trains per hour, one from Sanderstead and one from Hayes giving between them a half-hourly service north of Elmers End, the subject of adverse comment from the West Wickham Residents' Association. Another development was the withdrawal of many types of cheap ticket and, from 6th October 1941, the withdrawal of first-class accommodation on all London area local services – this was less of a shock than might have been thought since fare increases had tended to alienate the former first-class commuters from West Wickham and Beckenham and, as a letter sent out to all first-class season ticket holders pointed out that, given wartime overcrowding and blackout confusion, there was little point in paying a premium when the accommodation was being occupied by passengers irrespective of what class of ticket was being held. The former first class compartments were thereafter popular with "the democratic element" who favoured them to the extent that these compartments suffered a rapid deterioration from over-use and misuse.

Raiders overhead

Beckenham was particularly unfortunate in that although it had few strategic industrial targets with the exception of a few factories (most notably Muirheads electrical works at Elmers End and factories in Kent House Lane and the area towards Lower Sydenham and elsewhere) it lay on the direct path to London from the south and consequently the Borough received more than its fair shares of bombs both from conventional aircraft (with over 500 recorded incidents), pilotless V1 missiles (73 incidents) and the V2 rockets (5 incidents) resulting in over 300 civilian deaths and a total of 10% of the housing stock in the borough was either completely destroyed or severely damaged. Over a five year period there were many direct hits and near misses on the railways of Beckenham to say nothing of unexploded and delayed action bombs which caused additional problems to the bomb disposal teams. In consequence local train services were often delayed and subject to cancellation particularly when the approaches to the London termini were

Beckenham from the air, 1946. The busy goods yard of the Junction station is in the foreground while the war-ravaged site of the Railway Hotel and the vanished Church Road and St. Georges Road stand in front of the parish church; in the background is the 1930s Town Hall needlessly sacrificed to build a supermarket car park in 1992. (Beckenham History)

Above is West Wickham after a bombing raid on 1 November 1940 with the up platform buildings wrecked and (below) shows the station patched-up for further service a few weeks later. Due to post-war shortages the station was not rebuilt for another eighteen years. (John Minnis collection)

also under attack and it was estimated that on the Herne Hill to Holborn Viaduct section of line there were 62 separately documented incidents while between New Cross and Charing Cross there were double this number of enemy attacks[15].

On a lighter note, the demoralised soldiers returning by train from Dunkirk in June 1940 made an impact on the Borough. At Beckenham Junction they threw letters and cards out of passing trains in the hope that local inhabitants would pick them up and forward them on to their families while an enterprising young amateur cine-camera owner made a record of these troop trains[16]. At Penge East returning British Expeditionary Force veterans were given chocolate, fruit and cigarettes by local residents and they were entertained by the Salvation Army band assisted by the stationmaster on his clarinet. The magazine of the Beckenham & Penge County School for Boys, situated close to Kent House station, recorded in 1940 that

"The memorable week was that of the evacuation from Dunkirk, when eyes were increasingly turned railwaywards as more and more troop trains came through. The signalman who held up these trains full of French soldiers right opposite the school earned our ever-lasting gratitude. We broke bounds and wire fences, and, unfortunately, marrow and asparagus beds, in our zeal to welcome our allies and give them water and all we could raise from the tuckshop. Ten cents or a cap badge was ample recompense and there must be many a photograph of an unknown French child lying in an equally unknown English boy's pocket."[17]

At about the same time precautions were taken to foil potential invaders and these included the removal or obscuring of local station nameboards, the placing of anti-tank traps near to West Wickham station and the installation of concrete "pill-box" defence posts at various vulnerable rail-side locations including the three-way bridge close to New Beckenham. It was not long before the first enemy bomb to directly affect the Borough of Beckenham fell, when a sports ground close to Lower Sydenham station was hit at 1.40 am on 26th August 1940, damaging both the station itself and the brake van of a passing goods train. Major incidents were to follow rapidly and in that year these included damage to Beckenham Junction goods yard by an HE (High Explosive) bomb on 13th September and a delayed action bomb falling on the Crystal Palace line on the 15th, the latter causing the suspension of the service on that line for two weeks. On the same day a cluster of incidents at Penge East caused damage to the platforms and the goods shed, the tunnel mouth and, crucially, the tunnel itself. A contemporary report stated that

"A heavy bomb fell within 60 ft from the centre line of the Penge Tunnel where there was only 20ft of cover. The concussion from the explosion caused the crown of the arch to collapse over a length of 35ft and a width of 16 ft. Soil continued to fall through into the tunnel until a hole showed above ground level above. Unable to commence restoration work for several days by a delayed action bomb in the vicinity. When this was disposed of a mechanical excavator was taken to the site and about 2,000 cubic yards of soil was

removed from above the tunnel. A new arch was then constructed, then soil was removed from the tunnel and the line was re-opened for traffic on 9th October, 24 days after the damage."[18]

During this time the main-line was closed between Herne Hill and Kent House and a substitute bus service provided while from Kent House to Orpington a railway shuttle service was inaugurated with through trains from London being diverted via the Catford Loop. On 3rd October 1940 Beckenham Junction was hit again and two coaches badly damaged by an HE bomb while the cattle dock there was damaged in a separate incident some three weeks later. On 8th October the 7.47 am Hayes to Charing Cross train was damaged when a bomb fell during the morning rush hour on the river bridge at the terminus and a number of casualties occurred. The year ended with another HE bomb falling between Penge East station and the tunnel mouth two days after Christmas, displacing the sidings, breaking windows over an extensive area, wrecking signalling in the vicinity and damaging the just completed repair work to the eastern end of the goods shed which had been necessitated by the incidents two months earlier.

Bombs over the borough.

Of all the local stations, West Wickham was, considering its semi-rural position, incredibly unlucky. In the evening of 1st November 1940 an HE bomb fell on the platforms and track demolishing a section of the brick-built up side building and badly damaging the down; two staff members and four passengers were injured in the incident. Then on the third and last great night raid on London, which occurred on November 5th 1941, another similar bomb fell in virtually the same location as the first, smashing the replacement windows in the patched-up down building and severing the electricity supply. Elmers End fared little better. Several near incidents caused lines in the area to be blocked on several occasions but on Sunday 19th January 1941 an attack on the nearby Twinlock factory devastated the houses in St Margarets Road, blocked the running lines and caused some damage to the down side of the station while exactly three months later another attack on St Margarets Road further damaged the down side of the station as well as the adjacent SR electrical sub-station, derailed several wagons in the coal siding and injured a member of the staff. On May 11th, in the last great attack of the blitz on London, a train stabled in the down bay received a direct hit[19] and part of the platform canopy was demolished; the nearby substation was also damaged and the stationmaster, who was in residence at the time, suffered from severe shock and required hospital treatment.

The night of 16th to 17th April 1941 saw both the worst attacks to date on the London area and the worst ever attack on Beckenham itself where, in the whole area of the Borough, there were upwards of 200 incidents with 40 people killed outright including Shortlands resident Sir Josiah Stamp, the then chairman of the London Midland & Scot-

Elmers End from the footbridge, looking south in December 1956 showing the missing section of platform canopy and the bedraggled nature of the original station house enlivened only by some of the colourful BR travel posters of the era; the SR electrical sub-station can be seen on the left. (Pamlin Prints)

tish Railway. At 9.44 pm on the 16th the Mid Kent line was blocked between Lower Sydenham and New Beckenham by a portion of a crashed plane falling upon it and by midnight the line between Beckenham Junction and Kent House was closed by an HE bomb, Kent House station had been damaged and coaching stock in the Mid Kent sidings at Beckenham Junction was wrecked; on the Hayes branch the lines between Eden Park and West Wickham were severed at two points and between the latter station and Hayes the line was blocked for a whole week after an HE bomb landed on it. This momentous night ended with the stations at Holborn Viaduct, Blackfriars, Cannon Street, Charing Cross, London Bridge and Victoria all being closed because of bomb damage and the following day commuters from local stations found it well nigh impossible to get to their work.

The beginning of the end

For the railways of the Borough it was largely business as usual during 1942 and 1943 but in the following year Beckenham Junction was once again damaged several times including an occasion on 23rd February 1944 when an anti-aircraft shell exploded in the goods yard severing the tracks and damaging both the signalbox and goods shed while in a similar incident on 25th March windows of empty coaching stock stabled nearby were broken. On 30th

June the nearby landing of a V1 damaged the station buildings, stationmaster's house and the signalbox and on 10th November of that year a similar weapon landed in the vicinity and caused the goods lamp room to be burnt out, two wagons in the yard to be destroyed, the windows of the signalbox and various carriages to be broken and six Southern road vehicles parked in the yard to be badly damaged.

Other stations also received damage in this year – West Wickham was once again a prime target and on 21st February 1944 the signal box and already damaged station buildings were again wrecked while on 16th June of that year a flying bomb removed the replaced windows of the waiting room and badly smashed the roof. The final attack on the station happened on 10th July 1944 when the blast from a V1 which landed on the nearby Langley Park golf course caused extensive damage to both the station and the signalbox. The station was eventually patched-up but the inhabitants of West Wickham had to wait a further 14 years before they acquired a proper replacement. At Penge East on 22nd June windows in the station and signalbox were blown out and the signalman was injured while at Clock House the booking office was partly wrecked on 21st June 1944 but luckily spared on August 2nd when a V1 fell on buildings between the station and the Beckenham Road bridge killing 42 people and laying waste to a large area. In one of the worst incidents of the war a V1 fell on Elmers

West Country class 21C134 (later 34134) "Honiton" with the recently revived "Golden Arrow" passes through Beckenham Junction in the last year before nationalisation with, in the down bay, a SUB unit with a Bulleid trailer. (R C Riley collection)

End bus garage on 18th July 1944, destroying it and its complement of buses and causing much loss of life while twelve days later a similar device landed 100 yards from the down platform of Shortlands damaging the station buildings and blasting out the windows of the 12.31 Holborn Viaduct to Sevenoaks service injuring one passenger. At the beginning of 1945 a V1 landing on the Midland Bank sports ground blasted New Beckenham station and signalbox and a V2 falling a week later on the nearby Cyphers cricket ground blew out the just completed temporary repairs at New Beckenham station as well as those which had been carried out at Clock House a few months before. The very last bomb to affect the Borough and its railways was a V2 which, on 10th March 1945 fell close to the Marian Vian school damaging it and destroying the lineside telegraph between Elmers End and Eden Park but trains continued to run under emergency regulations. Although no one at the time realised it, for the railways of Beckenham and for the Borough itself the hostilities were effectively over.

Towards the end of the war there was a gradual return to normality, the black out ending locally in April 1945 (having been gradually relaxed some months before) and peak train services were generally restored to their pre-war levels by the summer of that year. There were, however, exceptions and neither the Mid Kent trains to Beckenham Junction nor the full Orpington to Holborn Viaduct services were ever reintroduced – the latter being due to both the heavy bombing of the City and to the gradual shift of offices towards the West End. There was, however, no resumption of residential development in Beckenham since

post-war shortages prevented further house-building and all available resources were diverted to repairing the existing housing stock and, where inter-war houses had been totally destroyed, in building replicas so preserve the uniformity of the street and of house values, typical examples being in Greenways and in Broomfield Road. In the case of West Wickham the green belt legislation halted further expansion and has continued to do so and even today lines of houses face the once-threatened farmland. In 1947 the Borough published its plan for the comprehensive development of the war-damaged North Central Beckenham area which had been devastated by a couple of V1 incidents with the loss of many buildings including the Railway Hotel, part of the High Street and Albemarle Road and the complete disappearance of two other residential streets in the neighbourhood. The plan provided for the reconstruction of Beckenham Junction station with new street level buildings on the site of the station approach where it joined the High Street but the whole scheme was a controversial one and the combined effects of local opposition, the restriction on the issue of building permits and the unavailability of sufficient money caused its eventual abandonment.

Change was, however, still in the air and the new post-war Labour government took little time in implementing their promised programme of nationalisation of the national utilities so that on 1st January 1948, exactly 91 years after the first trains ran to Beckenham, the Southern Railway was taken into public ownership and became the Southern Region of British Railways.

Chapter 7

TOTEMS TO THAMESLINK

"Want to Run a Railway?"
Title of BR booklet issued to commuters, 1962.

Recovering from austerity

Although there were few outward signs of change following upon nationalisation with local trains keeping their green livery and local stations retaining their Southern Electric signage and colour scheme for many years to come, the British Railways typeface and totem device began to appear in Beckenham over the next few years[1]. Train services gradually improved and the pre-war three-car electric multiple units had an additional trailer added so as to increase their capacity. In September 1948 the off-peak service on the Mid Kent line was restored with four trains per hour from Charing Cross to Hayes, two trains per hour from Cannon Street to Sanderstead and, on the Addiscombe line where traffic was declining, a shuttle service from Elmers End was provided. Track alterations were carried out at the latter station so that the connection from the Hayes Branch to the up bay was removed and the cross-over reversed so that Hayes trains could run into the down bay, the up bay becoming reserved for the Addiscombe shuttles. On the same day on the Crystal Palace line off-peak through trains to Victoria were restored, virtually to their pre-war levels and a year later, after agitation from local ratepayer's groups, the Mid Kent off-peak service was again revised down to four trains per hour from Charing Cross to Hayes with alternating shuttle connections from Elmers End to Addiscombe and Sanderstead – in the case of these two destinations no further off-peak through service to London was ever provided.

In the immediate post-war years Beckenham's off-peak train services were still well patronised but by the early 1950s there was increasing local road competition and by the end of that decade a change in social life largely attributable to the rise of television began to have an effect on evening travel with the closure of cinemas in West Wickham and Elmers End (in 1957 and 1959 respectively) while at the weekends the attractions of rural woodland walks in places such as Orpington and Hayes became the preserve of the Morris Minor and Austin Cambridge rather than, as previously, the local train. A continuing decline in traffic led to a further reduction in off-peak services and in September 1958 the Mid-Kent service to Hayes was cut back to three trains per hour while the main-line and Catford Loop services were reduced to a 30-minute frequency – the worst service any of these lines had experienced since electrification. The Crystal Palace line service was again reduced to a shuttle, a decision which, allied to its non-connections at Beckenham Junction, would lose even more of its already sparse patronage. In contrast peak hour loadings on the Mid

Kent, main and Catford loop lines remained high and according to the 1951 census return 37% of the employed population of the Borough still travelled to and from their work in central London by train during the peak hours.

In March 1956, as part of the Southern Region "ten-coach scheme" which had been designed to alleviate peak hour overcrowding, Mid Kent platforms were all lengthened to a standard 675 feet and accordingly local stations received ungainly extensions in an unattractive prefabricated concrete style. At Elmers End the lengthening of the down platform resulted in an alteration of the track layout there

The old order gives way to the new as a Southern Railway target sign on a gas lamp is about to be replaced by a BR totem on an SR concrete electric lamp standard in 1961. (John Scrace)

The replacement for the war-damaged West Wickham up station building – a neat 1950s structure as it appeared in 1992. (John Scrace)

The 11.53 Charing Cross to Hayes service calls at West Wickham on 5 July 1991 with the rebuilt 1950s station in view; the buildings to the right occupy part of the former goods yard. (John Scrace)

Elmers End looking north on 14 October 1961 with the new canopy on the down platform under construction and a brake van and coal wagon standing in the goods siding. The original canopies have lost their decorative SER valancing but appear to be in better condition than they were a few years previously. (John Scrace)

and the junction of the Hayes and Addiscombe lines was moved a few yards south; in consequence the signalbox, which had been in the angle of the old junction, now had both lines passing behind it and only the up bay line remained in front. At the same time three-aspect intermediate colour-lights (the first in the Borough) were introduced at Clock House where the box was reduced to the status of a ground frame controlling the yard, its main functions (including control of the Beckenham Council siding) having been supplanted by the Elmers End box to the south and New Beckenham box to the north. At West Wickham the dilapidated wooden station buildings dating back to the opening of the line were swept away in 1958 and replaced by neat brick and steel structures in a contemporary style while at Elmers End the remnant of the blitzed down platform canopy was removed in October 1961 and a new "butterfly-roofed" steel structure put up in its place. Minor improvements were made at other local stations and in a letter to the Council BR stated that Beckenham Junction was scheduled for renovation during 1957-8 "when consideration would be given to the conversion of gas installations to electric lighting and the carrying out of minor improvements but that there was no intention of reconstructing the station in the foreseeable future."[2]

The Kent Coast electrification

More extensive changes now followed on the mainline as a result of the Kent Coast Electrification scheme.

Elmers End looking north, 6 June 1969; by now the lines had been realigned so that Addiscombe and Selsdon trains passed behind the box and only trains bound for the up bay travelled in front of the box. (John Scrace)

Two generations of signalboxes at Beckenham Junction – the Southern box of 1928 is about to be replaced by the power box of thirty years later which can be seen under construction behind it. (Lens of Sutton)

The fifth and last signalbox at Beckenham Junction – the brick and glass power box with its distinctive light blue lower panels - which did service from 1958 until 1983 and whose closure brought an end the era of the signalman of Beckenham. (John Scrace)

This led to extensive track and signalling alterations on the LCDR lines and the junction at Shortlands was revised so as to avoid the bottleneck that had often caused delay. On the approach to the station the embankment and cuttings were considerably widened and realigned so as to raise speed limits there substantially and the lay out of the four tracks at Shortlands station was changed so that the eastern island platform now handled the down and up Catford Loop trains and the western platform handled the up and down Victoria service in contrast to the previous down-down and up-up arrangement; the mammoth task of laying the realigned new tracks was achieved in the single weekend of 6th and 7th September 1958 – a marked contrast to the speed of more recent engineering works in the area. In addition the Shortlands Road bridge was again rebuilt, albeit with some difficulty, and in consequence of the raising of the track level alterations had to be made to the height of the platforms although the 1892 buildings were retained unaltered. Two new signalboxes of modern design with a brick lower storey and projecting upper operating floor clad in light blue panels were built in the summer of 1958 at Beckenham Junction (adjacent to the 1928 SR box) and at Shortlands Junction (in the angle of the main line and Catford loop); these boxes were provided with Westinghouse push-button route setting interlocking panels, illuminated track diagrams and magazine train describers. On 12th April 1959 colour-light signalling was brought into use between Herne Hill and Beckenham Junction, followed on 31st May by the section

Lower quadrant signals mounted on a lattice post; the distant is for the junction at New Beckenham while the home signal is the main up starter at Clock House. (John Scrace)

An Orpington to Victoria service formed of 4 SUB unit No.4364 passes the new signalbox at Shortlands shortly before its completion with the soon to be superseded 1892 box in the background; the new box, closed in 1982, still survives but the track layout is now entirely different with the construction of the new burrowing junction. (R.C.Riley; Transport Treasury)

New Beckenham – a 1968 photograph of the up-side buildings after the fire which gutted them. (John Minnis)

The small replacement booking office at New Beckenham seen in August 1988. (Andrew Hajducki)

between Bellingham, Beckenham Junction and Swanley. The old boxes at Beckenham Junction and Shortlands were then demolished but the box at Penge East was retained to work the sidings and yard there "as required" and Ravensbourne was retained as a 10-lever ground frame to work the sidings there.

Retrenchment and change

In November 1959 the Sanderstead line entered into a slow but ultimately terminal decline with the withdrawal of all weekday off-peak and Saturday afternoon shuttles from Elmers End and, unsurprisingly, these cuts led to even fewer passengers at stations on the line, most of whom had deserted long ago to buses for Croydon and the faster and more frequent main-line trains. At Elmers End the bomb-damaged down side station house was demolished in 1964 and at Lower Sydenham the 1906 buildings had deteriorated to such a state that they were totally replaced in 1972 by new buildings using a new system-built method CLASP-buildings which, it has to be said, left much to be desired on aesthetic grounds. At New Beckenham a modern booking office was built on the up side following upon a fire which destroyed the original booking office in the spring of 1966. On the Crystal Palace line, the bridges over Beckenham Road was replaced in 1960 as part of a road-widening scheme while a similar exercise was undertaken in 1962 on the Elmers End Road bridge at Birkbeck which had developed serious faults.[3] In 1960 the Sunday shuttle service between Crystal Palace and Beckenham Junction was replaced by a London Bridge to Beckenham Junction via Tulse Hill service but this did not last long and in June 1963 a full service to Victoria was reinstated. Further economies on local train services took place in that same month with the withdrawal of some early morning weekday and Saturday peak hour services due to changes in working hours and the cessation of the six-day week for office workers and the complete withdrawal of the "all night" services from Holborn Viaduct to Orpington via both Herne Hill and the Catford Loop and the reduction of the Mid Kent off-peak service to a mere two trains per hour to Hayes with the Addiscombe branch having shuttle connections only. The fortunes of the Southern Electric locally were sinking to a new low with a steady pattern of deterioration and lack of any innovation and it was ironic that on 1 January 1965 the first posters advertising the new and more positive "British Rail" corporate image appeared on local stations.

From 1964 onwards Catford Loop weekend services terminated at Blackfriars rather than Holborn Viaduct and, for a time, were later diverted to Victoria via Peckham Rye while in April 1965 staffing levels at local stations were reduced with the result that at New Beckenham, Clock House, Elmers End and West Wickham only one of the two platform exits remained in use in off-peak hours. From January 1967 the remaining Saturday shuttles from Elmers End to Sanderstead were withdrawn but due to local pressure following upon the BR proposal to close the line in accordance with the Beeching plan (one of only two Southern Electric lines to be included), a sparse peak-hour service of through trains to London was retained even though few of the protesters used the service with daily patronage being in the region of 250 to 300 passengers. On 10th July 1967 a new Southern Region timetable came into use and brought many changes to local services and, following the installation of a new crossover at Kent House, the revival of the pre-grouping practice of starting and terminating some peak-hour services in the loops there. In the following year the main-line was again re-signalled using four-aspect colour lights and the number of block sections being increased by 50% in order to improve the line capacity. In 1968 a proposal was mooted to extend the planned London Transport Fleet Line service over the Mid-Kent from Lewisham to twin termini at Hayes and Addiscombe although the latter terminus was subsequently dropped from the scheme. Local opposition was expressed on the basis that the Mid Kent line had already reached its maximum capacity and that the tube trains would be unable to keep up with the BR units then in use; the whole plan was in any event later abandoned.

The mid 1960s saw many changes in employment patterns with new office accommodation in local centres such as Beckenham, Bromley and, especially, Croydon and this had an impact on travelling patterns. In 1958 the BR Southern Region administration was devolved into three area local boards (roughly corresponding to the operating areas of the pre-1923 companies) and in 1967 the BR South Eastern Area headquarters, having a juristriction over virtually all of the ex-SECR system, was moved from its city offices to newly-built accommodation situated at Albemarle House at 1 Albemarle Road; these offices included staff-training facilities and a signal training school. Since the new area headquarters was adjacent to Beckenham Junction station a special staff service was provided to run non-stop over the Mid Kent to London Bridge and in addition an up and down Kent Coast service made an additional call at the station for BR employees. The new offices were placed above a public house which was named "The Golden Arrow" after the famous train that ran past there and the pub sign consisted of a large Southern semaphore signal which was mounted on the pavement outside. In 1983 further internal reorganisation at British Rail abolished the need for such area headquarters and thereafter the building housed only a number of miscellaneous departments including the area civil engineer before eventually passing out of railway use and being later redeveloped as upmarket apartments.

Signalboxes no more

On 30th October 1966 the Norwood Spur line, which had seen little regular use in the past decade other than the occasional excursion train or enthusiasts special, was officially taken out of use and the ground frame at Spur Junction removed; the line itself was lifted in January 1969 and the trackbed, which was derelict for some time, has now

Norwood Spur Junction looking towards Beckenham with the small signal hut in use, July 1964. (J J Smith; Bluebell Railway Archives)

The impressive Norwood Spur Junction signal, seen from a special train on 15th April 1950. (H C Casserley)

U1 class 2-6-0 No. 31901 approaches the bridge at Sunnybank on the Norwood Spur line with a Sheerness to Brighton excursion train on 5 July 1952. (John Minnis collection)

The view from a special heading along the Norwood Spur with the small junction signal hut visible in the background in 1954; the houses visible on the right are in Cromer Road. (R C Riley; The Transport Treasury)

The main up side booking hall building at Elmers End, dating from 1882, shows clear signs of wear, tear and wartime damage some eighty years later; it burnt out in 1973 and is now replaced with a modern structure. (R C Riley collection)

been partially built over.[4] On 11th May 1969 colour light signalling was introduced over the section of the Crystal Palace line between Bromley Junction and Beckenham Junction and the signalbox at the former location was closed as from 13th July when its functions were taken over by the Norwood Junction box. The final chapter in local semaphore signalling was now to take place. On 4th April 1971 four- aspect colour-light signalling was introduced between Ladywell and New Beckenham, the signalbox at the latter being retained to work the signals to the south while the box at Lower Sydenham was abolished on that date. On 28th September 1975 the colour-light signals were extended to Hayes and the signalboxes at New Beckenham, Elmers End and West Wickham were closed and from then on the whole of the Mid Kent line (with the exception of Addiscombe) was then controlled from a panel in the new London Bridge Signalling Centre; on the same day the down bay platform at Elmers End was relegated to the status of an engineer's siding before being disconnected at a later date. On the main line and Catford Loop the end of local signalling control came with the gradual phasing-in of the Victoria Signalling Centre which was actually situated at Clapham Junction on the site of the former Falcon Lane yard. On the night of 19th/20th June 1982 the Centre took over the functions of Shortlands Junction box[5] leaving, appropriately, the box at Beckenham Junction to be the last remaining signalbox in use in the Beckenham area. Then, on 13th February 1983, the operation of the signals on the remaining section of the main line through the area were transferred to the Victoria Centre and, without ceremony, more than a century and a quarter of service by railway signalmen at Beckenham came to an end.

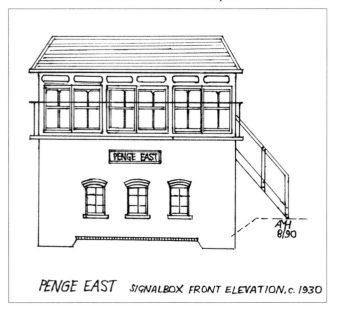

PENGE EAST SIGNALBOX FRONT ELEVATION, c. 1930

The buildings at the east end of the up platform at Kent House await demolition in 1970; in the background is the Plawsfield Road station approach. (Tony Harden collection)

The same buildings reduced to their skeleton - the cheaply built structure is typical of the LCDR frugal attitude towards passenger accommodation. Note the roof and upper storey of the main ticket office and station masters house. (Tony Harden collection)

The striking glass and steel booking hall at Elmers End seen in 1992 – a pleasant replacement for the 1882 building which had reached the end of its life well before it was set alight. (John Scrace)

The 16.30 Elmers End to Selsdon train formed of BR standard 2 EPB unit No. 5725 on the last day of services over the line, Friday 13 May 1983. (John Scrace)

The 12.23 Charing Cross to Hayes service makes a brief call at Eden Park on 5 July 1991 with a Bulleid-design EPB unit approaching the end of its life; to those who used such trains in the post-war years it is strange to think that they last ran some twenty years ago. (John Scrace)

Decline and fall

The 1970s would probably now be seen as representing the true nadir of the railway in Beckenham with a further decline in local train services, cuts in staff levels at stations and an increase in anti-social behaviour with widespread vandalism and graffiti appearing virtually everywhere. It was an era of frequent late-running and cancellation of trains caused by staff shortages, increasingly ageing and unreliable stock and poor labour relations so that a BR local manager was forced to apologise to local travellers with the statement that *"actually getting commuters to London is a daily miracle."* In 1970 the buildings at Kent House on the eastern end of both the up and down platforms were demolished. While on 16th December 1973 the up side buildings at Elmers End, dating from 1882, were gutted by a fire possibly started deliberately; within months they were demolished and replaced by a new glass and steel structure of contemporary design which, although unlike anything else on the Mid Kent line, is of a pleasing and practical design. In the following year the Greater London Council announced a new "park and ride" scheme with a proposed 35,000 designated parking places at London outer suburban stations to be completed by 1977; Elmers End was chosen as the prototype but, like many other proposed schemes of that decade, the plan was later dropped.

Although the off-peak service on the Mid Kent saw an increase from two to three trains per hour from May 1976, the remaining peak-hour through services from London to Addiscombe and London to Sanderstead were withdrawn two months later, both services then being reduced to shuttles from Elmers End to their respective termini. In the case of the Sanderstead line this was to prove to be virtually the last straw and, despite protests from the many who never actually used the service, the thought of having to change trains en route and then enduring a slow and overcrowded journey from Elmers End to London proved so unattractive to the relatively wealthy commuters of the area served by the stations that patronage declined even further to the extent that by 1983 the heavy subsidy paid to maintain the hopelessly uneconomic service could no longer be justified even by the most ardent enthusiast. On, most appropriately, Friday 13th May 1983 the last train carrying an estimated 200 passengers as opposed to the usual twenty or so, ran from Elmers End to Sanderstead accompanied by the traditional railway closure sound of exploding fog detonators and the Woodside and Selsdon line was finally closed to all traffic. Much of the line was subsequently lifted although sections were abandoned and laid derelict under the encroaching vegetation for many years while the short segment between the junction at Selsdon and the nearby Cory oil depot remained in use until March 1993. The cessation of all services over the Woodside and Selsdon line was a fate shared by only a few Southern Electric lines and the stations at Selsdon, Bingham Road and Coombe Road also had the dubious distinction of being the last gas-lit stations in the London area although this and their run-down state which set new records even by the then contemporary standards of British Rail can hardly have been said to have been attractive to the few final passengers. The one encouraging note, however, was that the trackbed was to be preserved from future development pending any further transport innovations and this far-sighted proviso meant that much of the route could again be used in the not-so-distant future.

On the Crystal Palace line the weekend through service to Victoria was again withdrawn as from 12th October 1976, being replaced by a two-coach Saturday and Sundays shuttle from Crystal Palace to Beckenham Junction serving the often almost non-existing passenger load. On the same date Birkbeck station, which had already been closed on winter Sundays from September 1969, was now closed on Sundays throughout the year. In May 1977 the peak-hour service between Orpington and Holborn Viaduct via Penge East was further cut back and two years later the weekend Crystal Palace to Beckenham Junction service was entirely withdrawn although the Saturday service was later reinstated. Then, in February 1983, the line between Bromley Junction and Beckenham Junction was reduced to single track as an economy measure with the up line being lifted

and the former down line being operated on the tokenless block system with two-way signalling. The up platform at Birkbeck was abandoned and before long the inevitable vandals had set light to and damaged the station building on that side; it was later demolished before the site was cleared to make way for the Tramlink line. The last local line singling took place in the summer of 1987 when the up line of the New Beckenham to Beckenham Junction spur line was removed and the former down line re-signalled for two-way traffic while at the same time Eden Park, Kent House and Ravensbourne stations were all closed on Saturday evenings and on winter Sundays, although these latter economies were later reversed.

A railway renaissance

In the 1980s there was something of a renaissance in local passenger services. On 15th May 1985 the ailing Beckenham Junction to Victoria via Crystal Palace service was replaced by a new service to London Bridge via Tulse Hill with properly worked out cross-platform interchanges at Beckenham Junction. The basic service was, however, an hourly one and there were still no weekend trains – a somewhat shortsighted decision in view of the growing popularity of the sports centre at Crystal Palace. From the same date some off-peak trains from Victoria to Ramsgate and Dover Priory began to call again at Beckenham Junction,

By the time this picture was taken the up line had been lifted and the platform and buildings demolished although this derelict area was later utilised by the Tramlink line; 456 unit No. 023 enters the remaining down platform with the 1022 Victoria to Beckenham Junction service on 1 July 1993. (John Scrace)

restoring a direct service to the coast as well as first-class travel to and from London and the opportunity for passengers from Kent to access areas of South London and the South West without having to change stations in London. These improvements, together with a general increase in the number of travellers commuting to London as a result of the economic "big bang", ensured that Beckenham Junction remained the dominant local station and in the year 1985-6 the total value of ticket sales there amounted to some £1.2 million.

In the decade leading up to the privatisation of Britain's railways there were many alterations to railway services in the Beckenham area, perhaps the most welcome of all being the new corporate image introduced under the banner of Network South East, the brainchild of that most successful of BR managers, Chris Green and it is perhaps unfortunate that subsequent politically motivated reorganisation brought about the premature end of NSE and the only occasion on which the railways of the Greater London area were truly operated as a single entity. Other innovations in the same era included, as from 15th May 1988, the diversion of twelve off-peak Catford Loop services to run through the re-opened Snow Hill tunnel between Blackfriars and Farringdon as part of the new "Thameslink" network – this was a radical innovation given that even at the height of the steam operated SECR system there were few cross-London workings from the Beckenham area. This new service proved so popular that in May 1990 a regular hourly service from Sevenoaks to Luton via Ravensbourne was inaugurated, alternating with the more traditional service to Blackfriars, Holborn Viaduct having been closed to all traffic on 29th January of that year. At the same time that the Luton trains began their operation a half-hourly Beckenham Junction to Victoria via Crystal Palace service was re-instated. An important operational change on the Mid Kent line was inaugurated in October 1988, although it was a change that was not necessarily one welcomed by passengers – this was a pilot scheme involving the de-staffing of stations during off-peak hours and the widespread introduction of ticket machines and the redeployment of former booking office clerks as travelling ticket inspectors, despite the complaint of their complaint that, in the absence of corridor connections, they could not pass from carriage to carriage between stations. Nevertheless the pilot scheme was judged a success and became a blue-print for other suburban lines.

In a round-up of other local alterations and innovations, the canopies with their original decorative valances were cut back in length at New Beckenham and Clock House, the down side canopy at the latter station being removed altogether while at Elmers End the up bay at the station was trimmed back to 63 yards in length; two years later the main platforms were extended northwards to pass under the rebuilt road bridge there. At Ravensbourne, following fire damage to the booking office on 6th May 1986, the street level building was demolished and replaced with a new building of modern design with brick walls and a pitched roof the following year. From 1990 to 1992 the former WEL&CPR line enjoyed something of a swansong when works in connection with the upgrading of "Boat Train Route No.1" at Bickley and Brixton meant that many weekend services were diverted from Beckenham Junction to run via Crystal Palace. Then, in May 1993, the whole pattern of train services on the ex-LCDR main line were recast in anticipation of the inception of the through London to Paris and Brussels service and on 14th November 1994 Watkin's dream became a reality when the regular Eurostar services were inaugurated the Channel Tunnel trains were seem trundling through Beckenham Junction en route for the continent.

Trams at Beckenham Junction – 2356 in the original red livery and 2533 in a garish "Nescafe" overall advertising livery on a test run pass Dell Cottage prior to the opening of the Tramlink system in 2000. (Cliff Watkins)

Beckenham Road tramstop, June 2009. This stop lies on the site of the up platform of the long-vanished Penge station of the WEL&CPR, closed some 140 years before and, like the modern tramstop, accessed by a flight of stairs leading up from the road. On the left of the picture is the former down, and now bi-directional, sole line from Crystal Palace while the tall tree opposite the tram signal marks the site of Penge Loop South Junction. (Andrew Hajducki)

Chapter 8
BEYOND THE MILLENIUM

"Will Connex pay my employer for lost working time?"
Hansard, 27 November 2001.

Mid Kent to the Junction

On 28th May 1995, in an unheralded and somewhat surprising move, a full service was reintroduced between Beckenham Junction and New Beckenham as part of an hourly Orpington to Cannon Street via the Mid Kent service alternating with an hourly service starting at Beckenham Junction. The reintroduction of such trains after an absence of 55 years (or, in the case of the trains beyond the Junction, of some 129 years!) was said by BR to be on an "experimental" basis and initially the service was well used even if some of the passengers were merely attracted by its novelty value. It appears that traffic expectations were not, however, realised and although the increase of trains north of New Beckenham was appreciated by some there were few passengers from stations to beyond Beckenham Junction, local travellers using faster trains on other routes and new bus services in the area. In 2003 the service was quietly withdrawn with the exception of a pair of daily trains run to avoid formal statutory closure procedures; once again, the spur line was allowed to lapse into obscurity.

South Eastern Again

On 14th October 1996 the railways of Beckenham entered a new phase when the Conservative government of John Major, in implementation of their privatisation of British Rail, transferred the operation of services on the former South Eastern & Chatham lines to a franchisee, Connex South Eastern and this transfer included in Beckenham the Mid Kent line, the Chatham main line through Beckenham and the Catford Loop line. At the same time the former London, Brighton & South Coast system became the responsibility of a sister company, Connex South Central and locally this included the Crystal Palace to Beckenham Junction service. All of the infrastructure, including all of the stations within the former Borough, were transferred to another private company, Railtrack plc and the electric multiple units serving Beckenham became the property of private leasing companies. Almost immediately the train liveries and station premises were transformed with new colour schemes, although the former Network South East colours have, in places, survived well in to the new century. The wheel had turned and half a century after the Southern Railway had been nationalised, its assets were again in private hands. The reign of the two French-owned Connex companies were short-lived and full of controversy for it was perceived that their style of operation was even worse than that of British Rail in its later years. A typical complaint was

that of Jane Williams, a 28-year old secretary who travelled daily between Beckenham Junction and Victoria and who, when interviewed by the BBC said that "Its been delay after delay and I'm sick of having to turn up to work late and blame it on the train." On 24th October 2000 Connex South Central had the dubious distinction of being the first train operating company to be stripped of its franchise after criticism of its management and performance and this was followed on 1st November 2003 when the South Easern franchise was also removed from Connex for "financial mismanagement". Govia were then awarded the south central franchise and now operate it under the brand-name "Southern" with the trains in a partially green livery. On 9th December 2003 "South Eastern Trains" was formed as a wholly-owned subsidiary of the Strategic Rail Authority and effectively the system was brought back into public ownership. Local travellers noticed an immediate improvement but the Labour government of the time appeared unwilling to continue operating South Eastern Trains in the public sector for political reasons and on 1 April 2006 a new franchise was given to a private company, London & South Eastern Railways Ltd who trade under the name of "Southeastern" and is owned by Govia. The general perception is that things are a lot better than in the days of Connex but that there is no room for complacency. The ownership of the infrastructure and of the local stations are, strangely, back in the hands of the government following the collapse of Railtrack plc and its replacement by the in effect renationalised Network Rail, a government agency.

Trams Return to Croydon

It was now time for trams to return to Croydon and, for the first time ever, to enter Beckenham. The growing traffic problems and commercial expansion of Croydon town centre led, in 1990, to Croydon Council and London Transport jointly promoting a modern system of continental-style trams under the name of "Tramlink". After public consultation, when the vast majority of consultees expressed a favourable response to the proposals, a draft Bill was prepared and three separate routes were identified, namely a line from to Wimbledon, using the trackbed of a former LBSCR West Croydon to Wimbledon line, a line to New Addington which would include a long semi-rural section to serve the isolated estate known as 'Little Siberia' due to its windswept isolation as well as part of the abandoned line from Woodside to Selsdon and finally a line to Beckenham which followed the route of the Selsdon line through Bingham Road and Woodside stations and then serve both Elmers End and Beckenham Junction. This third line was then split into two separate line, with the southern branch terminating at Elmers End station and the northern line running to Beckenham Junction. The Croydon Tramlink Act passed the royal assent on 21st July 1994 and the successful tenderer for the project was Tramtrack Croydon Limited, a consortium who were given a 99-year concession to run the system. TCL was composed of several partners namely Centre West Buses Ltd, part of the Scottish-based First transport group, were to operate the system; Bombardier EuroRail, who designed and built the trams; Royal Bank of Scotland and 3i, who provided the necessary finances and a joint venture between Sir Robert McAlpine and Amey Construction Ltd as contractors for the civil engineering and track works. One consequence of putting into effect the Tramlink scheme was that the by now little-used Elmers End to Addiscombe branch would require to be abandoned so that part of its trackbed could be used by the trams; the total cost of the whole Tramlink venture was estimated at £200 million of which £125 million was to be contributed from central government funds.[1]

Farewell to the Addiscombe branch

Tramlink construction work began in January 1997 and in order to progress matters, closure notices were posted at Elmers End, Woodside and Addiscombe stations. The branch had, by this time, been reduced to single-line working following the malicious destruction by fire of the Addiscombe fringe signalbox in March 1996. Events, however, progressed rapidly and the last service train to run on the branch was the 21.40 Addiscombe to Elmers End on Saturday 31st May 1997 – a Networker unit that carried handwritten commemorative stickers on the cab windows; this was followed by an enthusiasts' special which had already performed the last rites on the West Croydon to Wimbledon line that had closed a short time before. The track on the Addiscombe branch was lifted in early 1998 and the station platforms at Woodside were demolished in June of that year although the roadside building on the bridge was left intact but boarded up. The terminus and carriage sheds at Addiscombe remained in place until 2000, when they were demolished and replaced by a housing scheme for Bellway Homes after an unsuccessful attempt by the South Eastern & Chatham Railway Society to preserve them as a transport museum. The former Selsdon line underwent a radical restructuring north of Sandilands Junction where the Beckenham and Elmers End branch left the New Addington line. The embankment through Bingham Road station and the bridges over both Bingham and Addiscombe roads were removed so that the trams would cross those roads on the level and the soil taken from the site was dumped on the former trackbed of the Addiscombe line east of the former Woodside Junction. The proposed opening date of the

Looking across to the end of the up bay at Beckenham Junction in June 2009 with a Crystal Palace train on the right and a tram in the background. (Andrew Hajducki)

Tram No. 2549 about to depart from the Beckenham Junction tram stop in 2000; the tall building in the background is Albe-marle House the former home of the BR South Eastern Division headquarters; fortunately it has now been refurbished and its stark lines now somewhat modified. (Cliff Watkins)

Tramlink system was to be November 1999 but delays were caused by problems with contractors and certain legal issues and the first tram was not tested on the streets of Croydon until June 1999 and a test tram, hauled by a service vehicle, reached Beckenham Junction on Sunday 15 August. The first part of the system, the New Addington line, was opened to the public on 10th May 2000 while the Becken-ham Junction route was opened a fortnight later on 23rd May and the final part of the system, the Elmers End to Wimbledon line, was opened a week thereafter on 29th May. The trams were deservedly popular from the start and have proved to be a most useful addition to the Beckenham railway scene.

By tram to Beckenham

The Beckenham tram lines physically diverge at Arena Junction, situated on the former Elmers End to Woodside line, some 2m 24ch from East Croydon and within the Borough of Croydon. The Beckenham Junction line then swings to the north, taking a sharp left bend on an upward gradient on a reservation running through the South Norwood Country Park before reaching Harrington Road tramstop (2m 76ch). This, in common with all of the inter-mediate stations, consists of simple low platforms with

glass shelters, ticket machines and nameboards bearing the LT roundel in green. Up to now the line is double track but on crossing over the boundary into Beckenham becomes single as it climbs up via a sharp curve to join the former WEL&CPR line to the north of the Beckenham Cemetery. At Birkbeck (3m 35ch) the tramstop is on the site of the former up platform and separated from Birkbeck railway station by a fence – passengers wishing to change between the two systems at this point must go down and cross under the lines at the Elmers End Road bridge – hardly a great example of easy interchange facilities.

The tram track continues to occupy the former up line up to the next stop, Avenue Road (3m 73ch). This stop, serving the Churchfields and Birkbeck areas of closely-packed terraced houses never previously directly catered for by the railway, has a passing loop with two platforms, the construction of which necessitated the widening of the cut-ting at this point. To the north of the stop and passing under the only remaining footbridge on the Tramlink network which links the Birkbeck estate and the area to the east of it, the line becomes single again and continues as such to Beckenham Road (4m 27ch), a single platform situated on the embankment immediately to the north of the bridge crossing the eponymous highway and, co-incidentally, in exactly the same location as the original but short-lived

Avenue Road tram stop seen shortly before its opening in 2000. In the background a train from Crystal Palace to Beckenham Junction passes by the only tram stop in the Beckenham area not to be sited at a present or past station. (Cliff Watkins)

WEL&CPR Penge station. Approaching the former Penge Junction, the tram line has another passing loop, the only one which is automatically controlled while the trams are on the move. The line now runs to the south and parallel to the former LCDR main line and, after crossing over the Mid Kent, passes Blakeney Road electricity sub-station and the last house on the north side of Rectory Road, Dell Cottage, a small Victorian building which was formerly a stables and whose owners apparently refused to yield any of their small garden for the tramway with the consequence that clearances are extremely tight here. Now parallel to the platforms at Beckenham Junction station, the tram line occupies part of the former up carriage sidings, car park and bus stop. The terminus is reached at 4m 72ch and consists of an island platform with two faces and the usual shelter; from here it is a minute's walk to the station.

The Elmers End line occupies the up line of the former Addiscombe branch and, passing a little-used cripple siding on the north side enters Beckenham a quarter mile south of Elmers End station. At the terminus (2m 70ch) the line occupies Platform 1, the former up bay, and the track is raised up on a bed of ballast in order to avoid an expensive rebuild of that platform. Ticket machines are situated at the front of the station and although passenger interchange is by an easy cross-platform link there is no actual physical connection between the Network Rail and Tramlink lines.

The trams operating the Croydon Tramlink network are of the Bombardier CR4000 design and were constructed in Vienna; they are 30m long and capable of carrying 200 passengers, 70 of whom can be seated. Bearing the fleet numbers 2530 to 2563 (in direct continuation of the pre-1952 London tram numbering scheme), they were originally in a nostalgic red and white livery but in 2008-9 were repainted into a new corporate livery of lime green, blue and white.

Shortlands Junction and the Channel Tunnel Link

Shortlands Junction was always regarded as a strategic point on the lines from the channel ports to London. The traditional main line from Victoria, Boat Train Route 1, (BTR 1) travelled via the LCDR line through Herne Hill, the Penge Tunnel, Beckenham Junction and Shortlands and Sevenoaks while Boat Train Route 2, usually regarded as the diversionary or secondary route, travelled via the Catford Loop and Maidstone East. In the London area the two "pinch points" were at Brixton, where Boat Train Route 1 and Boat Train Route 2 diverged and Shortlands where they rejoined and with the eventual opening of the Channel Tunnel to regular passenger trains in November 1994[2], these routes became of new importance with Eurostar trains from Brussels and Paris to the new terminal at Waterloo Interna-

The sole surviving Mid Kent working from Beckenham Junction, the 1612 to Cannon Street, crosses over into New Beckenham headed by class 456 unit no.008; in the background can be seen the three-way bridge. (Cliff Watkins)

tional using the redesignated Channel Tunnel Routes 1 and 2, the former BTR 1 and BTR 2. The use of these routes, which saw Eurostars regularly passing through Shortlands, Ravensbourne, Beckenham Junction, Kent House and Penge East, was made especially difficult by the high density of existing domestic traffic and the comparatively low speed restrictions on both routes. Although some upgrading of the route had been undertaken, it was not originally envisaged that Shortlands Junction, where trains via the main-line and via the Catford loop, had to cross each other's paths, would need any work carried out on it. Operational experience, however, dictated a different course and in 1999 it was decided that a new grade-separated junction at Shortlands would be required so as to eliminate conflicting movements and increase the capacity of both lines. After public advertisement and consultation, parliamentary approval for the rebuilding of Shortlands Junction was given on 27th January 2001[3] and work on the £60 million project commenced; the main work needed was in connection with the box underpass needed to carry the Catford Loop under the LCDR main-line and this concrete tunnel structure was installed on 11th October 2001. The new underpass finally came into use in May 2003, along with the associated £1.7 million re-signalling scheme and immediately proved to be of considerable benefit in alleviating congestion. Eurostars ceased to use the routes regularly at the end of 2007 when the second

part of the new high-speed link was opened to the new international terminus at St Pancras, thus effectively breaking the cross-channel links which Beckenham had been associated with since 1860. From 2009 certain "high-speed" Kent commuter services were also run over the new line but the remodelled junction continues to be for use to domestic and freight services to and from the SE&CR hinterlands and more than justifies the works carried out at Shortlands.

The present

Present train services in Beckenham are enjoying good patronage, and the Summer 2010 services on the LCDR main-line consist of a basic quarter-hourly off-peak service of stopping trains between Orpington and Victoria on Mondays to Saturdays and a half-hourly Sunday service; the weekday peak-hour service is, surprisingly, less regular but includes a handful of trains which begin their journeys at the down bay platform at Beckenham Junction or the loops at Kent House and run to Victoria or Bedford or St Albans via the Thameslink line. (the terminal platforms at Blackfriars having being closed for redevelopment from 2nd March 2009). The Crystal Palace line has basic half-hourly service to London Bridge via Tulse Hill on weekdays with a few services running to Victoria over the original WEL&CPR; there have been no regular Sunday trains

The fourth and current station at Lower Sydenham seen in November 1992 with Bulleid-pattern 4 SUB No. 5445 on the 1223 Charing Cross to Hayes service. (John Scrace)

over the route since 1979. On the Catford Loop a basic 30-minute service operates to Thameslink destinations and at the weekends trains run to Victoria via Denmark Hill. On the Mid Kent, now shorn of its branches, weekday services from Hayes consist of four trains per hour calling at all stations to Ladywell from where one pair run fast to London Bridge, Waterloo and Charing Cross while the other calls at all stations to Cannon Street.; additional peak hour trains are run but on Sundays the service is reduced to half-hourly. A Monday to Friday oddity is the 0924 from Cannon Street which terminates at Beckenham Junction and a mid-afternoon return service which, uniquely, omits a London Bridge call – these are the sole surviving advertised services on the New Beckenham to Beckenham Junction loop although it is still used by special or diverted trains on occasions. Somewhat strangely, a small number of daily passengers appear to use the service between the two Beckenham stations. The Tramlink service from Beckenham Junction to East Croydon via the central Croydon loop operates at 10-minute intervals during the day, while during the evenings and on Sundays the service is reduced to half-hourly; a similar pattern of services operate between Elmers End and East Croydon.

How local stations fared

In relation to local railway architecture much has survived and indeed with a comprehensive repainting and cleaning up operation begun in 2008 many local stations appear to be clean and well-kept. On the main line Penge East retains its buildings, including the canopies, 1876 footbridge and former crossing-keeper's house and, possibly of all the stations on the line, the spirit of the LCDR is most prevalent here, notwithstanding the loss of the distinctive valancing of the canopies which, like most of the stations on the line, survived until recent times – perhaps a more enlightened railway management of the future will restore this feature to Beckenham's stations. The main station building now bears its name in large blue letters affixed on its front and the former stationmaster's accommodation there is now a children's nursery convenient for commuters. Kent House has had its long canopies shortened and the platform buildings restyled as a result of a fire there in 1990 so that only the boarded-up down side buildings still give a hint of what the station looked like in its heyday, while the former stationmaster's house has been divided into flats and the subway beneath it has been altered. Nevertheless Kent House still retains its quiet air and, if one takes a walk down the adjoining Barnmead Road to observe the remains of the overgrown Penge Loop line, the atmosphere of Beckenham past still survives in the unmade roads and well-kept Victorian houses. Beckenham Junction retains its original booking hall and is largely unchanged from its condition after the 1890 rebuilding, retaining all of its canopies, the two bay platforms (the up bay being yet again extended in length in March 2007), the 1890 footbridge and the wooden down-side buildings with their separate entrance and it still looks, and feels, like the premier station in the Borough. At Shortlands the 1892 station is much the same as it has always been and although the stationmaster's house has gone and the subway is blocked to the east, the decorative ironwork around the stairs and the general atmosphere still give it a period air. Ravensbourne, with its modern booking office, is virtually unchanged at platform level and still manages to retain its air of being a quiet country station while Birkbeck, on the former WEL&CPR line, with its one remaining platform and adjacent Tramlink stop is, although never picturesque, at least quiet and unassuming.

On the Mid Kent the journey begins at Lewisham (now an interchange with the Docklands Light Railway) and Ladywell retains its original and distinctive MKR buildings while Catford Bridge the main building is a Victorian one in a more ornate two-storied Italianate style. Lower Sydenham, damaged by fire in 1989 and rebuilt with more pleasing pitched-roof brick structure in 1992 is, apart from the platforms, entirely new but is nevertheless neat and functional. New Beckenham retains its 1904 brick retaining walls and 1969 booking office, part of the SECR canopies on both platforms and its lamp hut as well as its two parallel subways, one for passengers and the other for pedestrians, the latter using the route of the former crossing. From here

once a day the intrepid passenger can travel over the original Mid-Kent route to the Junction accompanied by squealing wheels and the regular thump of overhanging vegetation on the train windows – surely the other passengers cannot all be railway enthusiasts! On the Addiscombe extension the original station house at New Beckenham has gone, the victim of a redevelopment scheme in 2003 and the nearby now culverted Chaffinch Brook is not easily visible. Clock House at platform level is a sad sight for its South Eastern canopies have been cut back on the up side and removed altogether on the down leaving forlorn high walls and an absence of proper provision (ignoring the bus stop shelter) in the rain and one can only regret that BR did not consult a more sympathetic architect before savaging what was an interesting late Victorian station. The roadside buildings at Clock House are, however, in good repair and a welcome addition is the coffee shop in the former booking office accommodation. The goods yard at the station has given way to housing and the site of the nearby Beckenham UDC siding is lost in the undergrowth. At Elmers End the down side is bare apart from a glass shelter and butterfly canopy. The former down bay was in filled in 2010 to provide access to a new bus stance while the up side sports its glass and steel

The new order for the new century as a Eurostar working heading for the Channel Tunnel passes a 456 unit in the Mid Kent berthing siding in the summer of 2000; note how the tram lines have been squeezed in to a narrow space between Rectory Road and the Crystal Palace line. (Cliff Watkins)

thirty-year old building, its SER canopy and 1882 covered footbridge – a not altogether unpleasing ensemble. In the up bay there often sits a waiting tram but the junction of the Addiscombe and Hayes line is lost in vegetation and it is difficult to imagine that it is not that many years ago that Elmers End was a true railway junction. Round the tight curves the train slowly picks up speed and emerging on to an embankment runs through a stretch of nostalgic pre-war suburbia with panoramic views over the 1920s and 1930s landscape. At Eden Park, with its up side wooden buildings (rebuilt in the early 1920s in the original style) and small down shelter and subway still surrounded by trees, only a little imagination is needed to conjure up a feeling that one has stepped back in time and is standing on a small South Eastern country station. Through another swathe of verdant suburbia we reach West Wickham, again retaining its 1882 footbridge but with its 1950s station buildings largely unaltered and thus providing an interesting contrast to the other stations in the former Borough.

Back to the future

On the Tramlink system various additions and extensions have been proposed over the years but with two exceptions these do not affect Beckenham. The first possible extension was from Beckenham Junction to Shortlands and Bromley town centre suggested by local residents but deemed impractical by Transport for London. The second extension was that suggested by TFL and put out for public consultation, namely a proposed northern extension of Tramlink to Crystal Palace. In 2004 funding was obtained for a feasibility study for a line from Harrington Road to Crystal Palace Parade parallel to the former up line of the WEL&CPR and, possibly, with some on-street running up Anerley Road and Anerley Hill on the former route of the 654 trolleybus. Coupled with a service of trams from Croydon to Crystal Palace and a continuation of the existing Croydon to Beckenham Junction service, the proposal would also include a possible discontinuance of the "heavy rail" service between Beckenham Junction and Crystal Palace via Birkbeck and its replacement by a through tram service between these points, made possible by the total elimination of the Network Rail line and the doubling throughout of the tram line on the former WEL&CPR trackbed, although a turn-back facility for the Southern Trams or a re-instalment of Norwood Junction bay platform would be required. Judging by the favourable public response and by local support by the relevant councils, it had seemed likely that the Croydon to Crystal Palace services will be the first extension of Tramlink since its initial opening in 2000 but, at the time of writing, the present financial recession has resulted in the project being put on hold. Perhaps more fancifully a scheme to rebuild and re-open the Selsdon to Elmers End line was announced in April 2010 as part of the Brighton Main Line 2 proposal to provide a duplicate line from Brighton to London to alleviate congestion on the ex-LBSCR main-line. BML2 would involve a new link from

Brighton to Uckfield and thereafter use of the existing line from there to Selsdon, the rebuilding of the Woodside & Selsdon line with associated Tramlink re-routings and a new viaduct and then the running services over the Mid Kent and East London lines to a terminus at Liverpool Street. A possible quadrupling of the Elmers End to Lewisham section with associated new bridgework and the replacement or repositioning of stations at Clock House, New Beckenham and elsewhere together with the elimination of conflicting train movements of Hayes branch services at Elmers End are all suggested and there are curious echoes of the earlier Beckenham, Lewes and Brighton Railway schemes to say nothing of a virtual resurrection of the Mid Kent's lost branches but whether BML2 is a line too far and will ever see the light of day is, at best, debatable.[4]

Beneath the blue suburban skies

And what of Beckenham and West Wickham in the twenty-first century? Despite the loss of local autonomy with Beckenham Borough being subsumed into the amorphous clutches of the London Borough of Bromley in 1965 along with their unpopular enforced divorce from the county of Kent, both of the local communities have largely retained their character. The High Streets of both towns remain recognisable, although few of the long-established shops that gave the area much of its pre-war atmosphere are still in business and like in so much of suburbia the majority of the trade seems to be in the hands of national multiples and charity shops. In Beckenham the parish church of St George looks more impressive now that the surrounding bombed area has been landscaped as parkland romantically named Beckenham Green but a major loss has been that of the idiosyncratic town hall of 1932, perhaps Beckenham's most memorable, unusual and architecturally distinguished building, needlessly sacrificed for the banality of a car park for Marks & Spencers. Many of the Victorian villas which gave the former Borough much of its distinctive character have, alas, gone beneath the developer's hammer to be replaced by flats and town houses the design of which would even stretch the use of the word architecture – a process that begun at the end of the 1950s and still, unfortunately, persists as a reminder of how the Town & Country Planning Acts do not always produce successful results but at least the wide tree-lined streets themselves remain. But all is not lost for, as John Betjeman commented of Victoria station in his 1972 work, *London's Historic Railway Stations, "The suburbanites from the Continental side go to less fashionable parts than those from the Brighton side. These parts will be coming into fashion again soon, the brick houses round the Crystal Palace and Norwood and Beckenham. High over the chimney pots, carried on its arches these suburban trains of the old London, Chatham and Dover Railway system run."* And the trains still continue to run over that system and serve the now again fashionable and often cherished Victorian villas and terraces, the neat lines of Edwardian and now appreciated pre-war semis, the more

AH 7/90

0   5   10   15   20

Feet

Scale drawing of the Mid Kent booking hall as originally built. Although the porch is now long gone, the building still survives to serve as the main entrance and booking office to Beckenham Junction after 150 years.

substantial residences hidden in the trees and the occasional modern interlopers marking the spot where a bomb fell or the developers struck.

West Wickham, sometimes maligned as being almost a parody of pre-war suburbia, still has its trees laden with blossom in May, its mock Tudor or Dutch-gabled houses and its reluctant morning commuters trudging to Eden Park and West Wickham stations and it is not hard to imagine that one has been mysteriously transported back in the era of the Southern Electrics, Austin Sevens, bridge parties and that cosy prosperity that lasted right up until Germany stopped play in 1939. Whatever one's views of the lost Arcadia and what replaced it, frequent electric trains are still heard to rumble through the quiet evenings and on frosty nights contact with the conductor rails still produce flashes which light up the skies like a firework display to celebrate the genius of Sir Herbert Walker. Despite all the changes since the railways first arrived, it is possible to feel that Beckenham is still very much Beckenham and West Wickham still very much West Wickham.

On the whole the future of the local railway network seems to be more assured than it had been in past years and, one would hope, the future of the remaining railway buildings is also secure. After all Beckenham Junction is now one of the oldest intact buildings in the town and surely it deserves to be listed and have its recent 150th Anniversary suitably commemorated on a plaque while Penge East is an

architectural delight, Kent House, Shortlands, Eden Park and New Beckenham have character and are worthy of recognition as such and West Wickham is now something of a 1950s period piece. Much remains of interest in almost all of the local stations and they deserve more sympathetic care with an enhancement of their historic features and the provision of better amenities to suit conditions in an age that Forbes and Watkin could only have dreamt of. Trains still convey more than one in five local inhabitants to their daily work or education and, at the end of the day, one can confidently predict that, for as long as Beckenham and West Wickham remain places in which people choose to live and bring up their children in, the much derided but secretly often well-regarded local trains will continue to clatter their way through the new millennium.

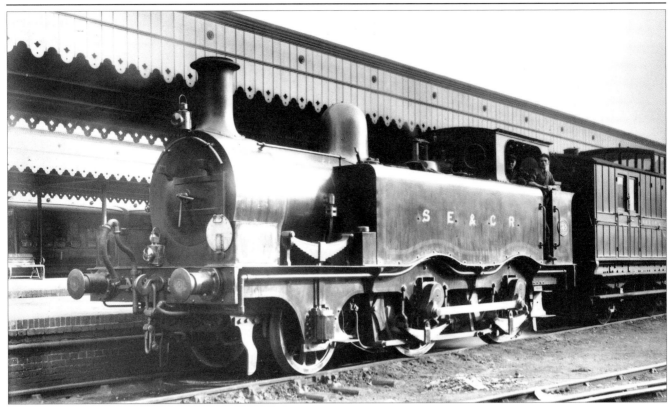

"Sondes" class No.523 (formerly No. 64 "Chatham") in the up bay at Beckenham Junction with a Norwood train in about 1905 – this beautiful study shows a locomotive originally built in 1858 as an 0-6-0ST for the opening of the Chatham to Faversham line and recorded as having broken down five times in its first month in service. Rebuilt as a 2-4-0T at Longhedge Works in 1865 the engine worked the Norwood service for a period in the early twentieth century as well as being a stalwart of the Isle of Sheppey branch until withdrawn in September 1909. (A F Selby; John Minnis collection)

Stationmaster Edward Allen speaks to the crew of Martley 'Sondes' Class 2-4-0T No. 521, rebuilt in 1865, shortly before it was withdrawn in 1909. (A. F. Selby/Lens of Sutton collection)

Chapter 9

FOOT WARMERS AND FLOODS
Passenger Trains in Beckenham

"The dog travelled safely as far as Beckenham station on the LCDR line."
Pleadings in Ashendon v LBSCR, 1882.

High caste and out cast

In the early years purely suburban trains were a rarity and Beckenham passenger services tended to be typical local trains of that period. On virtually all services three classes of accommodation were provided in four and six-wheeled wooden carriages, the first class being relatively comfortable with full upholstery and adequately lit at night, the second class less luxurious but still upholstered while the third class was poorly lit with unyielding spartan seating. The South Eastern had a reputation for parsimony and its carriages were no exception, the third class carriages being subject to much criticism and described as "cheerless rectangular boxes which had wooden seats" while the first

class carriages, although comfortable, were subject to the view that "the first-class fare for any distance above 20 miles was considerably more than the carriages were individually worth."[1] In 1859 the *Bromley Record* pointedly mentioned that on the Brighton line in winter all the third-class carriages were protected from the elements and there is no doubt that original Mid Kent carriages were rudimentary, the three classes of accommodation being described as "high caste, low caste and out cast." These coaches were replaced in June 1864 by thirty composites, ten thirds and ten third brakes specifically constructed for that line by the South Eastern at a cost of £15,900 and similar in style to those supplied for the Greenwich line but the public was still dissatisfied with adverse comments appearing in the

Kirtley D class 0-4-2T No. 554 (formerly "Albion") built to the design of Patrick Stirling of the Great Northern Railway and seen in about 1905 with her crew posing in front of the Beckenham Junction signalbox; the headboard "Catford" is somewhat misleading. In the background are some of the Copers Cope Road houses. (John Minnis collection)

135

A selection of SECR (ex LCDR) four-wheelers of an earlier era in store at Beckenham Junction following their displacement by electrification.(Rev A.V. Mace; R. C. Riley collection)

A London-bound excursion train with passengers in a party mood stands in the up loop at Kent House in about 1910. (J Holdsworth)

An Orpington train passes the signalbox at Beckenham Junction in about 1905 in the charge of Kirtley R class 0-4-4T No. 663; this trim little suburban tank engine dated from 1891 and survived in to nationalisation being finally withdrawn in the month of Elizabeth's coronation. (A F Selby;R J Brasier collection)

press about local railway carriages right up to the present day. LCDR coaches were little better internally in the early years although it was said that they had a neater exterior outline but, like the SER stock, improvements were gradually made even if the need for such had long altered from being desirable to being virtually mandatory.

Carriage lighting was originally provided by oil lamps but whereas first class passengers were treated to one lamp per compartment the third class suffered from having to share a lamp between compartments. Some lamps had a drop feed device fitted and this often required passengers to adjust the flow by means of poking the lamps with their umbrellas and it was remarked sardonically that "as the South Eastern were always well to the fore in regard to mechanical appliances for rolling stock an occasional oil-lamp was apparently constructed on the slight-feed lubricator principle and delivered about one drop of oil per minute on to the heads of the passengers."[2] For a short period oil-gas lighting was used but after the start of the twentieth century electric lighting in carriages became standard and by 1914 all Mid-Kent carriages were electrically lighted even if the low-wattage incandescent bulbs contributed to a dingy environment even in the later electric multiple units running into the 1980s with many a traveller remarking that even the meanest of local landlords would not stoop to using such feeble lighting. Unfortunately misguided passengers would sometimes unscrew the bulbs as trains passed through Penge Tunnel, thus adding to the general melancholic gloom.

Heating in carriages was initially by means of foot warmers which were, in effect, hot water bottles made of tin and although initially confined to first-class carriages only the station staff at Beckenham Junction, where a boiler was available to supply the water needed, were told in 1905 that during the winter months footwarmers "must be supplied to passengers travelling in any class upon application and they must be only filled with boiling water."

Typical Beckenham train formations in Victorian times consisted on the LCDR of one first class, one second and two or three thirds, all 4-wheelers, together with one or more six-wheeled vans while on the Mid Kent, where loadings were generally lighter, a total of four coaches and a van often sufficed. Trains were supposed to be marshalled so that first-class coaches were in the centre, second class flanking them and third class stock at the ends but this could not always observed in practice. Mails and parcels were placed in vans at the front of passenger trains except on the Crystal Palace and Norwood Junction shuttles where they were placed in the guard's compartments. As suburban services became better patronised trains increased in length to ten or twelve coaches and were sometimes composed of such a mixture of different types of four and six wheeled carriages so that the overall external appearance of individual trains was often very untidy. Towards the end of the century both the LCDR and the SER built new 13 or 15 coach close-coupled fixed formation trains of short wheel-base suburban stock and were described by one writer as being "very neat compact little things, beautifully finished outside and very comfortable within."[3] For a period in the 1890s twelve-wheeled carriages were used on the Mid Kent and at a later date some suburban bogie stock was built but, somewhat anachronistically, long trains of four-wheeled stock were the mainstay of virtually all Beckenham suburban services up until 1925. One oddity was the 8.37 am semi-fast from Hayes to Charing Cross which, in 1909, was composed of the stock which then formed the 10 am continental boat express to Folkestone.

Scotchmen and terriers

Initially Mid Kent trains were hauled by a variety of early SER locomotives including Cudworth 2-4-0s, the Company possessing virtually no tank locomotives prior to 1865. Gradually 0-4-2 well tanks appeared on the line and by 1880 were commonplace and were also used on the Liverpool Street to Addiscombe trains between 1880 and 1884. In later years the Mid Kent service was provided by a variety of purpose-built tank locomotives including non-condensing Stirling Q class 0-4-4Ts and these continued to work the line until well into the next century with occasional appearances of other locomotives including Watkin 2-4-0s and Wainwright J class 0-6-4Ts. Mid Kent locomotives were normally shedded at Bricklayers Arms although some engines stationed at the Deptford sub-shed were also used – the Deptford Q1s were invariably allocated to individual trains and became well-known to local commuters. The Hayes branch was served by locomotives shedded at Purley and often specific locomotives spent long periods on the branch – examples included No. 238, which drew the first train, and Cudworth 2-4-0s Nos. 34A and 223A.

LCDR trains were initially hauled by many different examples of the somewhat motley motive power. By the late 1860s those trains serving Shortlands, Beckenham Junction and Penge became increasingly short-distance local trains rather than Canterbury and Dover trains with additional stops and by the following decade were exclusively suburban with dedicated locomotives shedded at Bickley. For many years trains from Beckenham to London were

Pickersgill designed Great North of Scotland Railway 4-4-0 in its guise as SECR No.676 with a train of mixed passenger stock travels through Beckenham Junction in about 1905 with a selection of SER and LCDR goods wagons in the up sidings. This handsome locomotive, one of five bought from the builders, Neilson, Reid & Co, in 1900 when the GNoSR decided they did not wish to take delivery of them, lasted in its new homeland until 1926 and brought a touch of the exotic to the Kent landscape. (A F Selby; John Minnis collection)

SECR H class 0-4-4T No. 548 makes a spirited departure from Beckenham Junction with a Victoria-bound train in about 1905; these useful locomotives had a long life and this particular example became BR No. 30548 until finally displaced with the spread of Kent Coast electrification . (A F Selby; R J Braiser collection)

SER Q class 0-4-4T No. 181 awaiting departure from Beckenham Junction for Norwood in about1905; the carriage is an ex-LCDR second class six wheeler of 1886 – second class survived on the SECR lines until 1923. (A F Selby; John Minnis collection)

A Mid Kent train made up of typical suburban 4-wheeled elliptical roof stock arrives at Beckenham Junction behind a Stirling Q class 0-4-4T No. 406. (A F Selby; John Minnis collection)

R class 0-4-4T No. 709 with a typical suburban train of the period approaches Shortlands Bank on a Victoria to Orpington working in 1910. (H. Gordon Tidey; R C Riley collection)

Sondes class 2-4-0T No. 520 (formerly "Crampton") simmers away in the up bay at Beckenham Junction while employed on a Norwood service in about 1906. (A F Selby; John Minnis collection)

A Norwood train enters Beckenham Junction in the charge of 2-4-0T "Vulcan" at the turn of the century – the locomotive was originally ordered for the Smyrnia & Aidin railway in Turkey but later delivered to the LCDR when that order fell through and, in its rebuilt form, lasted until 1906 while the first carriage of the train was an elderly brake van of an 1862 design. (A F Selby; John Minnis collection)

A Kirtley B2 goods locomotive passes Beckenham Junction in about 1905 – built in 1891 by the Vulcan Foundry at a cost of £2,445 this engine was one of a class upon which the very successful SECR "C" class engines were based. (A. F. Selby; John Minnis collection)

Instructions for detaching Carriage from 5.0 p.m. Down Train at Beckenham without stopping.

Before leaving **Herne Hill** the Guard of the detaching Carriage must see that it is properly coupled with the patent coupling, and that the side chains are **not** coupled, but hung up.

The Carriage **must not be detached** until the Guard has seen that the Distant Signal for **Beckenham** is all right. If at **danger**, the Driver will of course stop the Train, and the Guard must on no account detach his Carriage.

In the event of the Guard finding from any cause he cannot detach the Carriage, he must immediately show a **red flag or light** on the **off side** of the Train. The Two Guards of the Maidstone portion must, on approaching **Beckenham**, always be on the look out on the **off side** for a Signal from the Guard of the Slip Coach, and if a **red flag or light** is shown by him, they must at once pass this Signal on to the Driver, who will then pull up at the Station, but after the Guard of the Slip Coach has once shown the **red flag or light**, he must make **no further attempt to detach the Coach**, but must wait until the Train has stopped at the Station.

Care must be taken that none but Passengers for **Beckenham** are put in the Carriage to be detached.

The Carriage will be worked from Ludgate Hill, and the passengers from Victoria must change into it at Herne Hill.

The Maidstone portion of the Train will carry **one** tail lamp as usual, and the Beckenham Carriage will carry **two** tail lamps.

K class 0-4-2T No. 559 "Scotia" at Beckenham Junction, 9 March 1901; this locomotive was finally withdrawn in 1913 but for a time was used by the Army for re-railing practice and was then converted into a sawdust burning stationary engine at Ashford Carriage Works until being finally scrapped in 1923. (John Minnis collection)

divided at Herne Hill with one portion running on to Victoria and the other to Holborn Viaduct. From the 1870s onwards Martley 0-4-2 well tanks (known as "Scotchmen") operated most Bickley to Holborn Viaduct trains and also the Beckenham Junction to Crystal Palace shuttles, although D class "large Scotchmen" were also used on the former. Other locomotives used included various 0-4-2T and 2-4-0T designs and 0-4-4T examples of the A and R classes. In SECR days Q and H class engines were common in the area and in 1906 Bickley shed was closed, being replaced by a new shed at Orpington. From 1913 onwards P class 0-6-0T locomotives were deployed on the New Beckenham to Beckenham Junction and Elmers End to Hayes shuttle services. A typical local train of the SE&CR period was the 8.11 am Kent House to Holborn Viaduct service; in the turbulent years from 1914 to 1919 the locomotive, an R class 0-4-4T (usually one of Nos. 663, 665 or 672) ran light from Orpington and collected its train of 16 four-wheelers which had been stored overnight on the Penge Loop siding.[4]

The Norwood shuttles

On the Beckenham and Norwood Junction service a variety of motive power was used over the years. In view of the light loadings a number of elderly locomotives served out their declining years on this service – LCDR examples included, between 1898 and 1905, rebuilt "Aeolus" class 4-4-0s Nos. 531 and 532 and from 1905 to 1909 a venerable

"Sondes" class 2-4-0T. In October 1909 "motor-train" experiments using the prototype P class 0-6-0T, No. 753, sandwiched between two LCDR bogie carriages, were carried out and these were so successful that in July 1910 another member of the class, No. 323, was assigned from new to work the service. The small locomotive was popular with train crews and passengers alike due to its attractive appearance in full lined SECR green livery, but a drawback was the limited coal capacity of the bunker and in consequence the inability of the engine to work the full daily service without needing to return to Orpington to refuel; this resulted in the provision of a new coaling stage at Beckenham Junction adjacent to the up platform. New passengers, however, failed to materialise and the Company came to the view that the motor-train accommodation was too lavish for the handful of passengers using it. At the end of 1910 a new locomotive was drafted in to work the service. This was No. 751, an elderly LBSCR 0-6-0T of the famous "Terrier" class which had been purchased from the SE&CR some years previously and was affectionately known as "Litle Tich" after a contemporary music hall artist; coupled with a six-wheeled LCDR carriage No. 2101, the resulting train provided a total of 40 third-class seats in four compartments. Remarkably both P class No. 323 and Terrier No. 751 survive to this day – the former as "Bluebell" on the railway of that name and the Terrier, restored as LBSCR No. 54 "Waddon" by the Canadian Historical Association. Although the SECR railcars were not normally used on the

Martley 'Large Scotchmen' 0-4-2T in the up bay at Beckenham Junction circa 1905, the number unfortunately not quite visible. (A. F. Selby; John Minnis Collection)

Norwood shuttles it may well be that they saw some use on that service between 1914 and 1915.[5]

Billy Beckenham

The Beckenham Junction to Crystal Palace services were, in Victorian times, provided by a locomotive and single carriage, the train being locally known as "Puffing Billy" or "Billy Beckenham". Patronage was never great and in July 1907 Wainwright steam railcars shedded at Orpington, No. 4 and 8, were assigned to the service. The railcars had a diminutive locomotive and saloon carriage combined into a single unit and their operating costs were said to be about one-half of the operating costs of a traditional train. One writer commented that "The steam rail motorcars were handsome little things finished in the standard carriage 'lake' [maroon] and this colour was continued forward to include the cab sides and the tank sides of the locomotives. The domes were polished brass as in the ordinary locomotives."[6]

The railcar did not, however, prove popular with passengers, who complained of the grimy interior and rough riding of the railcar while the crews found them unreliable and difficult to operate along with the fact that derailments

were frequent, particularly on the approaches to Beckenham Junction where the re-railers kept there were frequently required. Despite these shortcomings railcar operation was continued and in 1910 No.7 was allocated to the service and continued to operate it until an accident at Beckenham Junction in April 1913 when a push-pull motor train was then substituted for a few months. By 1914 a railcar (No. 5) was again running the Crystal Palace shuttles – this was, in fact, destined to be the very last SECR steam railcar deployed on a suburban service. When the service was suspended in December 1915 this railcar was stored at Crystal Palace High Level sidings and was never used again on normal passenger services. For a brief period in 1906 railcar No. 4 appeared on the Hayes branch services (including an extended service to and from New Cross shed) but these trains soon reverted to conventional operation.

Pushing and shoving

Although on the whole passenger steam services in the Beckenham area were worked in a conventional manner there were certain features worthy of note. On the Mid Kent from 1866 onwards up portions of trains from Beckenham Junction were propelled to New Beckenham by a tank loco-

Railcar No.7 bound for Beckenham on the stretch of line between Orpington and Bickley on Monday 19 September 1910; this working brought the car from the sheds at Orpington to Beckenham Junction from where it would then shuttle all day to Crystal Palace. (H L Hopwood)

Crystal Palace Low level with a P class motor train awaiting departure for Beckenham Junction in September 1913 – the usual railcar was still under repair following its accident at the latter terminus in April of that year; note the overhead wiring used by the LBSCR "elevated electrics". (John Minnis Collection)

No. 323, the P class loco which formerly worked the Beckenham to Norwood service in Edwardian times and now resides on the Bluebell Railway. (John Minnis collection)

The SECR Terrier No 751 seen at Ashford in 1921; this engine, known as "Little Titch" after a music hall performer of the time, operated the Beckenham to Norwood push-pull shuttles for some time in and after 1910 and, restored in its former guise as LBSCR No. 54 "Waddon", is preserved in Canada. (R C Riley collection)

Beckenham Junction with a P class tank No. 178 about to depart on its short train bound for Crystal Palace in the summer of 1913. (H J Patterson Rutherford; R.C.Riley collection)

Stirling B1 class 4-4-0 No. 454 at Ravensbourne with a train of assorted vans and empty carriage stock in about 1926. This Bricklayers Arms locomotive survived until December 1948 having a year earlier starred in the film "Anna Karenina" where Tattenham Corner doubled as deepest Russia.(John Scrace collection)

Previous Page - M class 4-4-0 (as SECR No. 473) heads a down express past the Westgate Road bridge, Beckenham in about 1910. (John Minnis collection)

A Holborn Viaduct to Orpington working formed of 4 SUB No. 4338 (one of the original three-coach units built new for the Eastern lines electrification in 1925 with a 1945 Bulleid augmentation trailer) emerges from Penge Tunnel and passes the SECR Edwardian signalbox with, to the left, the upper storey of the old LCDR box doing duty as a linesman's hut and in the background one of the large villas of the Lawrie Park estate (John Minnis collection)

A Charing Cross train enters West Wickham in about 1960; somewhat unusually a single 2 EPB unit forms the service. (Tony Harden collection)

motive in the rear before being joined on to the back of the train from Addiscombe portion which was already waiting there. The practice was apparently adopted following the removal of the turntable at Beckenham Junction and there were complaints from local passengers that "they push and shove us about as they like" between the two stations. From about 1870 to 1886 the Beckenham Junction portions formed the front part of trains from London but after this the portions were reversed, causing again complaints to be made from Beckenham Junction passengers. In 1904 operations at New Beckenham were simplified by the provision of a centre run-round road and locomotives could then be detached and attached with greater ease. The practice of dividing and combining trains at New Beckenham finally ceased in 1916 and thereafter Addiscombe and Beckenham Junction trains were run independently, trains to and from the latter being augmented by P-class motor trains on a New Beckenham to Beckenham Junction shuttle service.

At Beckenham Junction between 1863 and 1866 five to eight minutes were allowed for the detaching and attaching of SER coaches to LCDR trains; this appears to have been an optimistic estimate and its non-observance led to habitual late-running on both lines. Normally between four

and six carriages were attached to the rear of the LCDR train while on the up journey these were detached from the front and taken away by the Mid Kent train before the Victoria train could depart. The SER working timetable of 1864 warned that "At Beckenham Junction drivers of the Company's down trains must approach the junctions with extra caution, drivers having trains well under command." From 1873 to 1881 a carriage was slipped at Beckenham Junction from the 5 pm Victoria to Maidstone train – one of the extremely rare examples of slip coaches being used in the suburban area and, given the operational complexities of returning the slip coach to Victoria, it is surprising that such a practice continued for so long.[7]

Drivers of passenger trains often had to observe specific whistle codes in the Beckenham area and these included "on approaching the Norwood Spur Junction, drivers must whistle once when going through to Norwood Junction and twice when going to Crystal Palace" and, at Beckenham Junction, where trains using the through platforms were to give one long whistle while those entering the up or down bays gave three whistles and two when leaving although these codes were later revised and drivers were then required "to sound their whistles at Beckenham Junction

The quintessential Kent Coast electric trains for a period of nearly half a century, the 4 CEP based on the contemporary BR Mark I stock. Refurbished unit No. 1539 heads the 12.23 Victoria to Ramsgate service through Shortlands on 14 September 1982. (John Scrace)

where staff are frequently engaged on siding lines next to running lines", no doubt to the relief of residents of Rectory and Copers Cope Roads. All suburban services on the LCDR carried headboards with painted destinations such as "Bickley Main-Line" or a fairly complex system of small indicators fixed to the lamp irons in patterns to denote the particular routes operated by that train; at night coloured lamps were shown.

The electric age

With electrification the whole system of train operation was altered with many of the displaced steam locomotives scrapped or relegated to secondary duties. For the Southern's South Eastern suburban electrification schemes a number of brand new 3-car multiple units were built but, ever-anxious to trim costs, the company also utilised ex-SER and SECR wooden-bodied coaches (but not, apparently, ex-LCDR coaches as they were not considered suitable for conversion) which were joined together and mounted on new underframes and cabs added so that they resembled the custom-built units. Both first and third class accommodation was provided, second class accommodation having been abolished on the former SECR lines in September 1923 with the exception of certain continental boat trains. Passengers appear to have been willing, at least in the early days of the units, to pay the premium to upgrade from third class and one local resident commented that "Luxuriously appointed in tapestry, first class compartments, identified by a large 1 on the doors, offered a particularly high degree of comfort. One immediately felt warm, secure and cosseted on entering them."[8] In off-peak hours a single 3-car set sufficed to cater for local needs but in peak hours trains were normally run as 8-car set consisting of two 3-car units with two unpowered trailer coaches of pre-grouping origin sandwiched in between; when not in use the extra unit and trailer coaches were stabled at various points locally including Beckenham Junction, New Beckenham, Elmers End and Hayes. The new electric multiple units were maintained in the carriage sheds at Slade Green (near Dartford) and at Addiscombe. For a time following electrification rakes of four-wheeled stock were stored at Beckenham Junction pending conversion and for several months were used on certain steam services such as the 4.50 am Orpington to Holborn Viaduct train and on a number of local peak-hour services, usually as a "fill-in" for unavailable electric units; the steam stock included a 4 carriage set No. 692 and a 3 carriage set No. 639. The "all night" service from Holborn Viaduct continued to be steam-hauled as did weekend through services from local stations to the coast, these being normally hauled by "King Arthur" class 4-6-0s and ex-SECR locomotives often on tight timings – the pre-war National Sunday League services having a 9-minute stop to stop timing on the rising gradient between Herne Hill and Beckenham Junction and 4½ minutes from there to Bromley South. On the Mid Kent there were few scheduled steam-hauled services apart from regular but in-

frequent excursion trains – one example of these were the Lewisham to Brighton via Selsdon and Horsted Keynes summer services run in the late 1920s and throughout 1930s.

The old steam headcodes were replaced by stencils displayed on the front of the electric trains and the letters O,V,H and P became common sights in Beckenham standing, respectively, for Orpington, Victoria, Holborn Viaduct and Crystal Palace. Other route codes included H, I and T on the Mid Kent and O, S and U for, respectively, Hayes, Addiscombe and Selsdon through trains and shuttles from Elmers End. After the war roller blinds and numerical headcodes became common and locally numbers such as 36 (Crystal Palace line), 70 (Orpington to Victoria), 24 (Charing Cross to Hayes) and 83 (Holborn Viaduct to Sevenoaks via the Catford Loop) were well recognised.

In 1941 first class compartments on the electric units were downgraded to third class and in order to make operations easier trailer vehicles were incorporated into the existing 3-car units to make them into 4-car units – these "augmentation trailers" were originally from existing intermediate trailer vehicles but were latterly new coaches built to a standard SR-design were used and, when the original units were withdrawn, these trailers were incorporated into new 4 SUB units of similar design. The Crystal Palace shuttle service was provided by a single 2 NOL unit while in 1941 the new prototype all-steel suburban unit No. 4101 made its debut on the Victoria to Orpington service – this unit, which were designed to maximise passenger numbers s by using every available inch of the loading gauge, was joined in 1944 by No. 4102 and they were dubbed "Shebas" under a Biblical reference to the Queen of Sheba entering Jerusalem "with a very great train" but, continuing the analogy, it has been pointed out that the commuters of Orpington were not known to travel with camels, spices or quantities of gold![9] Why such a forward-looking company as the Southern persisted in a units of such an antiquated design of compartment stock at this time is a matter for conjecture but the company claimed that they were technically more reliable, needed less maintenance and were quicker to load and unload than the sliding door stock fitted in contemporary underground and mainline stock such as the LMS Southport or LNER Shenfield units; whatever the reason the basic design of the "Shebas" was experienced locally for another half-century or so.

The deterioration of the wooden-bodied pre-war stock which by now had seen service for almost half a century, led to the building of large numbers of 4-car all-steel units classified as 4 SUBs of a S.R. pattern originated by the company's chief mechanical engineer, Oliver Bulleid. The general design of these units was continued in the form of stock known as the 4 EPB units (the code standing for their electro-pneumatic brakes which rendered them incompatible with the SUB units). These were supplemented by mechanically identical units of similar designation with bodies of the standard BR Mark 1 suburban pattern. Two-car units of both patterns were also built and these were to be found

The sleek lines of Britannia 70004 "William Shakespeare" are evident as she storms Shortlands Bank with the down "Golden Arrow" in the summer of 1957 – in her train is an SR utility van, three BR Mark I third class coaches and, at the rear, a string of Pullmans. (R C Riley; The Transport Treasury)

running either singly on the Addiscombe to Elmers End shuttle services or in rush hours attached to two 4-car units on Mid Kent services with the introduction of the "ten-car" scheme.

In 1956 third class was re-branded as second class which, in a later and more egalitarian age, was then dubbed standard class. By 1957 the old wooden-bodied units had been banished from the Mid Kent and by 1960 from the main line and Catford Loop services, and all of these lines became the sole preserve of the EPB units. The Crystal Palace line soldiered on with pre-war 4 SUB units and pairs of 2 NOL (no lavatory!) units until, in the late 1950s, post-war 4 SUB units replaced them and these units then operated the service until the mid 1980s. Latterly there were joined by 2 HAP units of SR design, providing the unusual variation of side-corridor accessed compartment stock on the weekend shuttles. Occasional variations were seen locally including on the main-line local services the use of 4 CEP Kent Coast stock and more frequently, trains composed of BR pattern 2 HAP semi-fast stock. In the era before sliding doors on trains local passengers often boarded up fast trains when they were held at signals at stations (to the disapproval of station staff who informed the travelling

public somewhat erroneously that "they should not board as this train does not stop here"). On occasions confused passengers also boarded down fast trains which had come to a halt at stations in the fond belief that they were on an Orpington all-stations service – a school friend of the author was involuntarily carried non-stop from West Dulwich to Dover on this basis. Gradually the all-compartment trailer vehicles on the SUB and EPB units were replaced by saloon vehicles to combat vandalism and fears for the safety of passengers. On the Crystal Palace services, the old practice of "For Ladies Only" stickers affixed to the outward compartments of motor coaches of 4 SUB units was discontinued thus heralding the end of an era. From 1962 onwards the amount of non-smoking accommodation was greatly increased in local trains and, in concert with changing public tastes, smoking was eventually completely banned from both trains and stations.

Steam and diesel

Passenger steam trains on the Mid Kent were rare after the war with the exception of a few excursion trains bound for the Oxted line via Woodside and Selsdon. On the

A class 70 tackles Shortlands Bank with the down "Golden Arrow" in the snow covered winter of 1962-3 (John Scrace)

The up "Night Ferry" in the capable hands of H class 4-4-0 No.31545 and Battle of Britain class 4-6-2 No. 34073 "249 Squadron" with SNCF luggage vans and distinctive dark blue Wagon-Lits coaches glides through West Dulwich on the last stage of its journey to Victoria on 6 June 1959, having passed through Beckenham minutes before . In the background, the bulk of Sydenham Hill with the newly-built Crystal Palace television mast. (J J Smith; Bluebell Railway Archives)

Merchant Navy 35015 "Rotterdam Lloyd" enters Penge East with the down "Golden Arrow" – the down LBSCR Sydenham to Crystal Palace branch is carried on the high arch with the ex-London and Croydon line carried over the lower bridge. (R C Riley collection)

E5004 with the down "Golden Arrow" at Ravensbourne after having been diverted via the Catford Loop due to engineering works on the main line, 7 April 1963. (John Scrace)

main-line steam continued through Beckenham and a variety of mainly Southern Railway steam locomotives were seen while Bulleid Pacifics replaced the Lord Nelsons on boat trains and supplemented King Arthurs on the Thanet coast trains. 1957 saw the transfer of Stewart Lane's two Britannia Pacifics (70004 "William Shakespeare" being the author's particular favourite) to the London Midland Region, in return for two B.R. Standard Class 5s, which supplemented the ten already allocated to Kent coast services, while the "Golden Arrow" reverted to Bullied Pacific haulage.

Apart from boat trains, most steam workings through Beckenham disappeared in 1959 with the inauguration of Phase I of the Kent Coast Electrification scheme; the rest followed in 1961 with the inauguration of Phase II. From then onwards there were few locomotive-hauled passenger trains seen on the main-line with the exception of diesel-hauled cross country services and the two remaining prestigious Continental services, the Wagon-Lits "Night Ferry" service whose distinctive dark blue sleeper carriages were shunted on to the deck and carried by the Dover to Dunkirk overnight sailing thus providing a through service from Victoria to Paris and Brussels[10] and the "Golden Arrow" Pullman train which ran from Victoria to Dover before its passengers crossed the channel on the "Invicta" and were met

at Calais by the Arrow's French counterpart "Le Fleche D'Or". With increasing air competition the "Golden Arrow" ceased operating in 1972 and the "Night Ferry" was withdrawn in 1980 when its coaches were life-expired but not replaced because it was becoming increasingly likely that the Channel Tunnel would be built.

The regular flooding of the Mid Kent when the Chaffinch Brook burst its banks close to Clock House continued to cause problems when the electric conductor rails were covered by water, despite the works to raise the level of the line carried out by the SR in 1928 and by BR thirty years later. A rake of loco-hauled stock was for many years kept in a siding parallel to the up line immediately south of the original New Beckenham station and, when the waters rose to the level that an alarm was sounded in the signalbox at Beckenham Junction, a steam shuttle was provided between New Beckenham and Elmers End, often with a locomotive at either end to avoid the need for propelling trains in the up direction – an example of this was on 2nd June 1958 when SECR C class goods locomotives Nos. 31037 and 31102 were seen on this duty attached at either end of a rake of eight corridor coaches. On other occasions electric units were steam hauled or replacement buses were hired and special arrangements due to flooding at Clock House had to be made on ten separate occasions in 1960 alone. From

Penge East with unit 375629 on down working in 1992 – these units had just begun to replace the 4 CEP stalwarts of the Kent Coast. (Terry McCarthy)

1961 onwards flooding provided the only example of diesel-hauled local passenger services when BRCW Type 3 (Class 33) locomotives, their undersides protected by a special plastic casing, were used to haul electric units; these trains were subject to a 5 m.p.h. speed limit through the flood water. Otherwise diesel-hauled passenger trains in Beckenham were not common although excursion trains and cross-country services bound for Dover were regularly seen.

New trains for old

In 1985 sliding-door stock of a new generation appeared on the Crystal Palace services in the form of Class 455 units replacing the EPB units which themselves had replaced the older SUBs a few years previously. Later these units were supplemented by two-coach Class 456 units, but today it is not unusual for express units of Class 377 to be found operating the services, especially off-peak. On the Catford Loop Class 319 dual-voltage trains appeared on the Thameslink through services, while in 2010 First Capital Connect also began to use them on trains from Beckenham Junction to destinations north of the Thames. Remaining local services continued to be operated by traditional EPB units, some of them face-lifted. The semi-fast services introduced to call at Beckenham Junction were made up of 4 CEP and 4 VEP units of classes 411 and 423, the former being rebuilt from their original state by BR in 1979-80. From 1993 onwards Class 465 "Networker" 4-car units, and their 2-car variant, the Class 466s, appeared on local services. Compared with the units previously used, they were technically a great advance on the EPB units, which were finally displaced in the spring of 1995. As a result, the South Eastern fleet now operating on all local services is, in railway terms, comparatively young.

After 1965 a plethora of train liveries was seen – the ubiquitous Southern green giving way to plain blue on the suburban units with the corporate BR blue and white livery for semi-fast and express units and later extended to the face-lifted suburban units as well. In the 1980s the newly designated sector Network South East introduced a curious brown and orange livery, referred to affectionately as "Jaffa Cake" although this was later replaced by the NSE red, white and blue livery which was ultimately extended to all units. On privatisation the NSE livery was gradually replaced by the yellow, grey, blue and red col-ours of Connex. By 2003 the last of the BR Mark 1 stock (the CEP and VEP units) had been phased out on the Kent Coast services after a life of almost 45 years and replaced by Class 375 and modified Class 465s; thus the South Eastern corporate colours became universal with the exception of the Crystal Palace line where trains now operated by "Southern" reappeared in a green and white livery vaguely reminiscent of the SR and BR colours of an earlier age.

Miscellaneous traffic

Passenger trains also conveyed numerous items of a miscellaneous nature in the guard's van and the Mid Kent charges for such traffic from London to Beckenham included 5s 0d for coffins (leaded, empty), 3s 6d for coffins (wooden, empty), 10s for pianos (at owner's risk), 1s for harps (accompanied, at owner's risk), 1s for perambulators (childs, at own risk), 1s for accompanied barrel organs and 2s for monkeys, goats, sheep, small pigs and lean calf while more prosaically a newspaper was 1d and a bundle of newspapers 3d. This traffic continued well into the post-war period by which time there was little call for coffins, harps, goats or barrel organs and the principal traffic handled was now mail and newspapers; the sight of mail bags and bundles of the *Evening Standard and News* being flung out of the vans onto the platforms were commonly experienced at many local stations including Penge East, Beckenham Junction and Clock House. Small parcels and boxes were also handled and these included machine parts and hand tools, bicycles and lawn mowers, food (mostly boxes of tinned food, butter, cheese and breakfast cereals destined for local grocers including Woolworths), small livestock (mostly day-old chicks) and pharmaceutical supplies for the Wellcome research laboratories and a whole variety of other goods were frequently unloaded. In 1958 West Wickham despatched 1,261 parcels and received 552 while Elmers End and Lower Sydenham, both serving local factories, handled 1,838 and 3,348 and 5,339 and 3,655 parcels respectively. Parcels and mail traffic dwindled towards the beginning of the 1960s but was temporarily revived when Beckenham Junction and certain other local stations became "Red Star" depots before the traffic was finally abandoned in 1992.

On occasions items were mislaid and an unusual example of this was provided by the case of Ashendon v LBSCR when, on 2nd March 1880, it was alleged that when an unaccompanied Italian greyhound was sent from Brighton to Rochester via Norwood Junction and Beckenham Junction

"the dog travelled safely as far as Beckenham station on the LCDR line where one of the servants of the company lifted it into the van and it slipped its collar, ran down the line, escaped and was lost."

One can only hope that, through the negligence of the railway staff, Beckenham added yet another pet dog to its population.

Chapter 10

CORN AND COAL
Goods Trains serving Beckenham

"If the LCDR's train is late and has cattle for the SE line, this train will wait at Beckenham
for 30 minutes for its arrival, if telegraphed to do so."
SER Working Timetable, 1883.

Prize cattle and sand

Although passenger traffic always dominated local railway operations, several Beckenham stations also handled goods. Beckenham Junction was always the most important of these and for many years was an extremely busy centre for the handling of a wide range of both inward and outward freight. Early facilities provided here were modest, consisting of little more than a goods office on the down platform and two sidings but following upon the rebuilding of the station in 1890, more lavish siding accommodation was provided on both the up and down sides; in 1910 the station was listed in the Railway Clearing House handbook as having a 10-ton crane, a 20-ton weighbridge and facilities to handle furniture vans, highway carriages, motor cars, portable engines, machines on wheels, live stock, horse boxes, prize-cattle vans and coal staithes. Three principal classes of goods were handled here – coal, building materials and agricultural goods. The coal, which was mainly for domestic purposes, was supplied from pits in South Yorkshire, Nottinghamshire and the North East and came via the Great Northern, Midland and Great Central systems while coal from Lanacashire came via the London & North Western and anthracite for central heating boilers was transported via the Great Western from south Wales. In 1864 W T Kelsey was advertising "double-screened Wallsend coal and gas coke at the lowest market prices" delivered directly from the yard. A few years later Walter Matthew and Frank Moore were in partnership as coal merchants and advertised that they could supply "thoroughly screened, all the best qualities of coal obtainable at the lowest prices for cash" while their "Moore & Mathews" private owner wagons were a common sight in Beckenham[1]; in addition between 1880 and about 1900 the firm also acted as agents for Fremlin's Maidstone Ales and Stout. In 1914 the coal merchants based at Beckenham Junction included, as well as Moore & Matthews, depots of Carr Brothers, The Tyne Main Coal Co. and Rickett, Smith & Co (a subsidiary of William Cory & Sons Ltd.).

Having regard to the rapid development of Beckenham from 1870 onwards it is not surprising that building materials should have formed an important part of traffic at the yard and consisted mainly of wagonload traffic of sand, cement, timber, lime, slates, tiles and, notwithstanding the presence of local brickworks, London stock bricks. A number of builders merchants had offices and showrooms in the

yard at different times including that of the Otford Lime & Cement Co., the Sevenoaks Sand Co. and R & G Dimmock and it would be fair to say that the majority of the borough's older houses contain materials that arrived by train via Beckenham Junction.

Agricultural traffic was two-way in nature and it is easy to overlook the fact that when the railway arrived in Beckenham it was a largely rural farming community, remaining so until the turn of the century. In 1885 there were still some 400 head of cattle in the parish and by 1925 about half that number, while in 1866 Beckenham had 1,600 resident sheep and still by 1914 some 200. In late Victorian times there was a considerable acreage of arable and permanent pasture land in Beckenham and it was only in the 1930s that the last vestiges of this land gave way to the richest cash crop of them all – the suburban semi while a similar position was found in West Wickham parish. Goods handled at Beckenham Junction yard in 1864 included potatoes, hay, straw, malt and hops for W.T.Kelsey and in 1885 included, for the local and long-lived firm of Henry & William Carr, oats, maize, flour, pollard straw, beans, buckwheat, poultry mixture, oatmeal, barley meal, clover, tares, linseed, middlings, oilcake and manure; in addition farm machinery was also handled – it is, perhaps, interesting to see that by 1929 the emphasis of the same firm's advertisements had shifted to them being removal contractors and builders' merchants and they claimed that "crazy paving, burrs, lime and all garden requisites can be promptly delivered" and they no longer advertised that they were "agents for Benskin & Co's celebrated Watford Ales.". A good source of revenue were horticultural goods for the newly established gardens of Beckenham houses and this traffic included manure and compost as well as plants, seeds, bushes and trees and it is no coincidence that such businesses were often carried on in the vicinity of local stations, an example being T. Horman, florists and nurserymen, who had premises at Clock House and Beckenham Junction, the latter establishment being referred to as the "Station Conservatory", a somewhat grandiose name for what was, in reality, a large wooden greenhouse. Livestock was well catered for and until 1928 pens and watering facilities were provided at the up sidings and until 1914 these were well-used with a considerable amount of stock handled en-route to local farms or the slaughter-house situated behind the village butcher in the High Street. In 1896 the aptly named Richard Sheepwash, a farmer from New Brompton

The 5.36 p.m. Victoria to Margate express, hauled by M2 class No. 664, passes through Beckenham Junction on 19 August 1903 with an eleven-coach load travelling at an estimated speed of 50 m.p.h.; of particular interest is the Moore & Mathew private owner coal wagon visible on the right. The load and speed of the train was written on the back of the print by the photographer himself. (H. Dixon Hewitt; R.C.Riley collection)

SECR C class No. 584 which entered service in June 1903 and when still quite new, passes the second generation signalbox at Penge East with a down goods. (John Minnis collection)

[Gillingham], was summonsed to appear before the Bromley magistrates on a charge of ill-treating and torturing a cow in transit at Beckenham Junction but this appears to have been an unusual if not unique event at the station. Horse boxes were common and catered both for farm horses and the more patrician horses kept by the owners of the larger villas and, on occasions, hunters and hounds were conveyed by rail to the station – a late example being the meet of the West Kent Hunt in 1905 where the hunters assembled in front of the Railway Hotel in Beckenham High Street, notwithstanding the gradual suburbanisation of the area.

Beer and rubbish

Apart from Beckenham Junction the only other LCDR stations in the area to handle goods were Penge East and Ravensbourne. At Penge the yard was a busy one and included wagon turntables and a large goods shed situated on the up side next to the passenger station buildings; coal and building materials were the two biggest sources of traffic here and coal merchants operating from here included in the nineteenth century Carlton, Mead & Company, Booth Brothers and A.D. Clifton & Co and n the twentieth Charringtons, the Mid Kent Coal Company and the Tyne Main Collieries In the 1870s S.T. Prior & Sons supplied coal, cement, plaster, gravel and drain pipes and in later years M Bailey, sand and lime merchants, provided materials for house building. From a fairly early date Shepherd Neame &

Co, the Faversham brewers, established a depot at the station and the sidings became the railhead from which barrels of beer were transported onwards by horse and dray with daily deliveries advertised to the Penge and Beckenham districts. The Crystal Palace was probably the most important local customer and the distribution of beer from here seems to have reached its zenith about 1910; the traffic was subsequently lost to the motor lorry. Another feature at Penge was the tunnel maintenance siding parallel to the up main line and this still survives. Ravensbourne sidings catered solely for coal although for a period from 1893 building materials for the Cator estate were also handled. A twice weekly pick-up goods served the station and latterly this was hauled by a SE&CR C class 0-6-0 arriving at 9.50 pm; much of the traffic was, apparently, destined for R Robinson & Co, civil engineering contractors whose work had included the construction of the SR Allhallows-on-sea branch.

On the Mid Kent yards were provided at Clock House, Elmers End and West Wickham. Clock House sidings were busy with large quantities of coal handled both for domestic purposes and for the Beckenham UDC electricity works; in 1910 there were three coal merchants with depots there – H & W Carr, J A Bennett and F Button. Elmers End Coal Sidings (there was never a general yard here) handled both domestic coal and fuel for the nearby factory premises and for many years Gill & Co and the aptly-named Collier & Co had offices here. West Wickham primarily handled coal, building materials and agricultural requisites and for many years there was a coal depot here run by J W Laurence of Shortlands Road, R.E.Ray (later Mary Ann Ray) and the Lightwood Coal & Coke Company; the station also boasted a dock on the up line which was used for horse boxes and private carriages. Elmers End, Clock House and West Wickham were sufficiently busy to justify the running of at least one daily Mid Kent goods train until 1963 – indeed as late as 1958 Elmers End was handling over 4,000 tons of coal annually – equivalent to eight full wagon loads per week. – and West Wickham 11,000 tons. There was only one private siding, that of the Beckenham UDC at their electricity works and depot between Clock House and Elmers End (a single trailing siding on the up side) and this principally handled coal and general refuse. There were no other goods yards or sidings in the Beckenham area although in 1889 there was local agitation for a coal yard at New Beckenham while eight years earlier a plan had been put forward for a new yard at Shortlands to relieve overcrowding at both Beckenham Junction and Bromley South yards.

Goods by steam

The principal starting point for Beckenham-bound goods trains was the depot at Bricklayers Arms, on the Old Kent Road about half a mile south of London Bridge; opened in 1844 and closed to passengers in 1852 when supplanted by London Bridge, the former terminus remained in operation as a goods station until 1981. Early freight services included, in March 1864, a daily pick-up goods under the control of Guard Murphy which left Bricklayers Arms depot at 9.45 pm and an via the Mid Kent to Beckenham calling en-route at Catford Bridge and arriving at 10.45. The return service, conveying empty wagons, left Beckenham at 11.45 pm and after its passage the Mid Kent was closed for the night. In 1883 the service included a 6 am light engine from New Cross to Addiscombe, a 6 a.m. general goods from Bricklayers Arms to Beckenham Junction "which call at Elmers End when required and shunts at Lower Sydenham for the 6.3 am passenger train to pass" and a 10.20 pm Mid Kent goods calling at all sidings and returning from Beckenham Junction immediately "although if the LC&DR's train is late and has cattle for the SE line, this train will wait at Beckenham for 30 minutes for its arrival if telegraphed to do so."

By 1947 the Mid Kent services consisted of 11.40 pm, 12.20, 12.50 and 1.35 am coal trains from Bricklayers Arms to the Lower Sydenham gas works, followed by a 3 am pick-up goods which included wagons for Catford Bridge, Clock House, Woodside and Addiscombe and a front portion for Lower Sydenham and Beckenham Junction yards; this portion was detached at Catford Bridge and conveyed independently from there at 4.35 am. At 4.47 am another service from Bricklayers Arms set out for Hayes and included wagons for Catford Bridge, Elmers End, West Wickham and Hayes, with a separate portion for Addis-

combe going forward from Elmers End at 11.45 am.

Goods services over the main-line varied greatly over the years and in 1877 consisted of a 4.40 am Stewarts Lane to Swanley calling at Penge and Beckenham Junction. In 1916 there were seven goods trains booked to call at ex-LCDR Beckenham yards, three Mid Kent services and a solitary Norwood Junction service. After the second war the main-line yard's service consisted of a single night-time pick-up while the Norwood Spur was used only by trains from the Kent coal fields bound for the Croydon B power station at Waddon Marsh.

Guards and number takers

Operating instructions for goods traffic contained in the 1905 and 1918 supplements to the SE&CR working timetables include a prohibition on goods traffic between Herne Hill and Beckenham Junction between 7 and 10.30 am and 4 and 7.15 pm and noon and 7.15 pm on Saturdays. On the Mid Kent line large goods engines were permitted a maximum of 45 wagons, ordinary goods engines 40 and passenger engines 35 with any goods trains for Beckenham Junction being given a clear run through New Beckenham. Between there and Norwood Junction the load of goods trains "must not exceed 15 wagons when hauled by a P class 0-6-0" and, rather oddly, under the heading of "Coal traffic ex-Great Eastern Railway via Norwood Junction" the following appears: "The guards working the Norwood and

Stirling Q class 0-4-4T No. 360 with a down Mid Kent goods passes through New Beckenham on 22 February 1926; this Purley-based locomotive was withdrawn in November of the same year. (H C Casserley)

Oposite Page - The Mid Kent goods timetable for 1916. Q trains ran "as required" and note the amount of early morning activity. This basic pattern of services survived into the diesel age.

MID KENT LINE.

Down Trains—WEEK DAYS.

	Brake Van Working No.										Coal		GN Q	GN Q	Coal	Coal	Q	GN Q	GN
Dist.		a.m. arr. dep.	a.m. M O	a.m. arr. dep.	a.m. dep.	a.m. arr. dep.	a.m.	a.m.	a.m.	no'n	p.m.	p.m.	Coal p.m.	Q p.m.	Q p.m.	
M. C.			SO	NS					SO	NS	NS	NS	NS	SO	
.	**Bricklayers' Arms**	12.0 midt. ex Hither Green Sidings.			4 0	6 12	10 30					1 0	4 45	
2 45	Surrey Canal Junction			4 8		6 22	10/40				12/28	1/10	4/57	9/35
3 18	New Cross	12 7 12 20	12 52 12 57	4 10		6 27	10/45					1/13	5/ 0	
3 62	St. John's	12 23	12 59	4 12										
	Park's Bridge Junction													
3 52	Lewisham Junction						10/48				12/34	1/15	5/ 2	9/42
4 31	Lady Well	12 26	1 1											
5 16	Catford Bridge	12 30 2 0	1 4	4 15 4 30				11 15 12 0	12/40				9/47
6 50	Lower Sydenham	2 5			6 37 7 10 7 30 10 58	11 20 12 5	12 45	1 10	1 25	5 12	9 52 10 30
7 34	New Beckenham				Stop	Stop Stop		Stop	Stop		
8 11	Clock House			4 38 4 48	7 15 7 25						
8 60	Elmer's End			4 54 5 5 6 5							
10 74	West Wickham			CS							
12 9	Hayes			6 20							
9 63	Woodside and South Norwood			5 10 5 20 Stop							
12 11½	Selsdon Road			5 32							
10 52	**Croydon** (Addiscombe Road)			Stop	7 35						
7 69	**Beckenham Junction**	2 10			7 38 Stop			1 17			

Up Trains—WEEK DAYS.

	Brake Van Working No.		Q			Eng		noon.		Q						
Dist.		a.m. NM arr. dep.	a.m. NM arr. dep.	a.m.	a.m. NS arr. dep	p.m. NS	p.m. NS arr. dep.	p.m. NS arr. dep.	p.m. SO	p.m. SO arr. dep.	p.m. SO
M. C.			5 35		12 0						6 20
.	**Beckenham Jnc.**										
.	**Croydon** (Addis. Rd.)										
.	Selsdon Road .. arr./dep			5 47							
0 69	Woodside & S. Norwood			5/52							
	Hayes / West Wickham					1 20 1 15			5 25 5 20	
1 72	Elmer's End			5 55		1 45 1 30			5 50 5 35	6 25
2 41	Clock House					2 0			Stop	Stop
3 18	New Beckenham									
4 2	Lower Sydenham	12 40		12 6 12 16	1 55	2 8	3 10	3 55	
	S. Suburban Gas Sidings			12 10		2 10 2 20			
5 36	Catford Bridge	12 45		12 26	2 0	2 25	3 15	4 0	
6 21	Lady Well								
7 0	Lewisham Junction	12 50 5 50			12/31			4/8
6 70	Park's Bridge Junction			12 29		2/5		
7 34	St. John's	12 52 5 55		12 23	2 8 2 30	3 25 3 25	4 10
8 7	New Cross	12 55 5 58		12 33	2 35		
	Surrey Canal Junction						
10 52	**Bricklayers' Arms**	1 5 *1 25 6 10	12 42	2 45		

Up Trains—WEEK DAYS—contd. | SUNDAYS.

	Brake Van Working No.	Q Coal p.m. SO	p.m. SO arr. dep.	p.m. NS	p.m. SO arr. dep.							Q a.m. arr. dep.
			8 48								
	Beckenham Jnc.										
	Croydon (Addis. Rd.)			7 35							
	Selsdon Road .. arr./dep										
	Woodside & S. Norwood										
	Hayes / West Wickham										
	Elmer's End			8 10							
	Clock House										
	New Beckenham										12 40
	Lower Sydenham	8 54 9 15								
	S. Suburban Gas Sidings	6 12	CS							
	Catford Bridge	9 27	8*58 8 21 9 0							12 45
	Lady Well									
	Lewisham Junction	6/22								12 50
	Park's Bridge Junction	9 30	9/3 9 6							
	St. John's	6 24	9 6							12 52
	New Cross	9 36	Stop 9 10							12 55
	Surrey Canal Junction									
	Bricklayers' Arms	9 50	9 20							1 5 *1 25

* Arrives Catford Bridge 7.50 p.m.

Beckenham goods trip must not accept the above traffic at any time one or more trucks be tendered to them."

Number takers (checkers) at Beckenham Junction sidings were required to remove all special labels before the despatch of empty trucks and ensure that all 'foreign' (i.e. non-SE&CR) vehicles were expeditiously returned home. At the same station a lay-by siding was provided on the down side adjacent to Blakeney Avenue was provided "solely to enable trains to shunt or for trains to pass and must not be used to put off trucks" and the siding had the capacity to hold an engine and up to 37 wagons and 2 vans. The 1946 SR working timetable lists Austerity, N1, Q1, C and O1 locomotives permitted to run on the Mid Kent to Lower Sydenham but beyond that point only C and O1 classes were allowed.

Goods by diesel

From the 1950s onwards there was a sharp drop in revenues from local goods yards caused by a combination of lorries, a decline in building operations and most significantly of all a decline in domestic coal consumption with the advent of newer forms of gas and electric home central heating. The first facility to go was the Beckenham Council siding, which had been out of use by 1960 and was officially closed on 16 July 1961 when the siding and the ground frame controlling it were disconnected. Ravensbourne sidings lost their regular goods service in 1959 and were closed to all traffic on 4th September 1961 when the ground frame was taken out of use; the signalbox was later demolished.

In June 1961 BRCW Type 3 diesel locomotives had taken over all local freight workings. On the main line Penge East sidings were served only in the up direction by an 11.27 am Mondays, Wednesdays and Fridays only service from Herne Hill Sidings which arrived at Bromley South at 11.50, returning from there at 12.26 pm and calling at Penge East to set down wagons, shunt and pick up wagons from 12.35 until 1.30. On the Mid Kent line the goods service was still quite traditional in nature. Beckenham Junction was served by a daily 11.40 pm from Bricklayers Arms that served Catford Bridge and Lower Sydenham yards en-route before arriving at Beckenham Junction at 1.44 am; the engine then worked forward "as required" any traffic for Bromley South at 2.15, returning from there to Beckenham Junction and setting out at 3 am for Lower Sydenham Gas Works Sidings, Catford Bridge and Bricklayers Arms, arriving back there at 4.32. This was followed by a 3 am Bricklayers Arms to Addiscombe service which took traffic for Beckenham Junction, Clock House, Woodside and Addiscombe, arriving at that terminus at 4.25. The third down goods on the line was the 4.7 a.m. from Bricklayers Arms to Hayes, arriving there at 5.18 am, with two additional Hayes workings leaving Elmers End at 10.58 am and 8.55 pm. At 10.50 pm the latter train left Hayes and travelled to Addiscombe via Elmers End, returning from Addiscombe at 12.48 am and arriving back at Bricklayers Arms at

2.32 am.

The retrenchment, however, continued and all remaining goods facilities went as part of the strategy adopted by Dr Beeching to concentrate freight in a smaller number of large, well-equipped yards. Elmers End coal sidings closed on 6th May 1963 and at neighbouring Clock House goods facilities were discontinued from 19th May 1965 and the signalbox there closed. At Penge East general goods facilities were withdrawn on 30th November 1964 although the coal depot remained in use until 7th November 1966; latterly this was served by a special Mondays, Wednesdays and Fridays only trip working which left Bromley South at 12.26 and arrived at Penge at 12.35, being the return working of the 11.27 from Herne Hill, the reason for Penge yard being served by the up working only being so as to avoid cross-line shunting operations at the station. The sidings at Penge East remained in situ but out of use until 25th February 1968 when the signalbox there was closed and the site, with the exception of a single siding for tunnel maintenance vehicles, was cleared for housing.

The general goods yard at Beckenham Junction, which had remained moderately busy with coal traffic and occasional traffic for Harrison Bailey, the last local builder's merchants to use the railway, was closed to all traffic on 18th April 1964. This was, however, not quite the end of the story for on 1st November 1966 a rail-served House Coal Concentration Depot was opened on the site of the goods yard. Operated originally by Ricketts, the depot

The small Fowler diesel locomotive which was used to shunt wagons in the Coal Concentration Depot at Beckenham Junction in the late 1960s – a good example of a subject, taken in 1968, which others deemed to be of little interest at the time but which forms a valuable record of a short-lived method of working in the yard. (John Minnis)

A 1968 view of the mechanised hoppers and conveyor belts of the coal concentration depot at Beckenham Junction which replaced the general goods yard in 1966 and which survived until 1982 as the last remaining railway goods facility in the area. (John Minnis)

Beckenham Junction goods yard as seen from the window of a departing Victoria service in 1962. The headcode displayed by the unit in the down bay proclaims it to be Holborn Viaduct to Hayes via the Mid Kent line working. (John Minnis collection)

contained two sidings and three tall hoppers with a conveyor system to load them from the wagons. At first a small yellow Fowler 0-4-0 of considerable vintage was used to shunt the wagons but at a later date mechanical shunting devices and a road tractor were used in its place. The wagons arrived on a 10.28 am working from Bricklayers Arms and after they had been dropped off and the empties collected the train set off again on its return journey at 12.30 pm; the motive power used was a class 33 and, latterly, a class 73. By 1981 the service had become a twice-weekly working from Acton Yard which arrived at Beckenham

Junction at 13.50; a 10.26 return working on the following day took the empty wagons back to Acton. The depot at Beckenham Junction, latterly operated by Charringtons, finally closed on 1st February 1982 and alternative uses were sought including that of a rail-served aggregates distribution depot. Local opposition led to the abandoning of the aggregates plan and in 1985 the site was cleared and subsequently used for a Sunday market (a prohibition against which even the Cators had not thought of) before, in 1988, a Waitrose supermarket was built in its place, thus effectively completing the rise of the middle-class in Beckenham.

73142 "Broadlands" on an experimental aggregates working to assess the suitability of the former coal concentration depot at Beckenham Junction, 25 March 1982. (R C Riley)

Chapter 11

LINE BLOCKED
A chapter of accidents and incidents

*"It was fortunate that the train destroyed was not a passenger train for if it had been the case
a fearful loss of life would have been inevitable."*
Kent County Coroner, January 1864.

A singular accident

Despite the fact that Beckenham's railways have had a long and busy history accidents have, fortunately, been rare – a fact which is hard to explain having regard to the somewhat haphazard working practices adopted by local railwaymen, particularly in the earlier years. The earliest reference to a mishap is reported in the *Bromley Record* of May 1860 when it was reported that a spark emitted from an engine working on the WEL&CPR line close to Beckenham had caused a serious fire in the haystacks of a farm belonging to a Mr Watkins. This was not a one-off incident and there were many subsequent reports of the fire-beaters being called out to deal with outbreaks of fire particularly on embankments and cuttings in the Shortlands area.

Under the heading of "A Singular Accident", the same paper reported in December 1861 that:

"At about 8.20 this morning (30th November) as Mr Gripper of West Wickham, with another gentleman and a groom, were near the Beckenham railway station, his horse took fright, and dashed through the palings beyond the station, upsetting the three persons who were in the cart, but fortunately without serious injury to either. The horse was stopped near the tank a little distance from the station towards Pimlico by some men holding up their hands, but instantly turned and started back through the station between the platforms and down the line at full speed till it was ultimately stopped between Shortlands and Bromley stations. No further injury appears to have been sustained other than a few fractures to the cart. Danger signals were immediately passed from Beckenham through Shortlands to Bromley and Bickley to stop the 8.35 up train."

It would be difficult to imagine a similar occurrence in the middle of the rush hour today!

Snowdrop unsprung

During the early years of the LCDR there were a number of local accidents starting with the that of 26th September 1864 when "Snowdrop", a Sharp Stewart 2-4-0 dating only from May of the previous year, was heading the 7.30 a.m. Victoria to Dover express with a train consisting of one second, two firsts and a large van, was derailed near to the site of the present Kent House station. Due to it being a foggy morning the train was travelling at a reduced speed estimated as being as between 25 and 30 m.p.h. After pass-

ing through Penge station the driver "suddenly perceived a racketing" on the right side of Snowdrop's driving wheel splashers and the fireman observed that the ballast was flying against the engine and carriages. The fireman applied the brake for the distant signal at Penge Junction which was at danger whereupon the engine left the rails and plunged about 8 ft down the embankment, taking the leading coach with it.

"There were twelve passengers, (seven men, two women and three children in the second class carriage, which was much damaged and it is wonderful that they were not all killed".[1] The crew were, however, less fortunate than the passengers in that the driver sustained two broken legs, the senior guard lost three fingers and the unfortunate fireman died the following day from severe burns incurred when the locomotive turned on its side.[2] "It is plain that some system of strict examination is much needed to prevent an engine from being sent out, as in this instance, to run an express train with five of its springs, out of eight, in a defective condition."[3] The accident was said to have occurred because of a broken leading spring on the locomotive and an unequal distribution of weight and served to underline the necessity for thorough examinations of locomotives prior to their use and regular servicing – matters which, at that period, sometimes received scant attention. As a result the LCDR Board instructed their locomotive engineer to keep proper records of engine weights and to have engines properly inspected before they commenced their duties.

Tacita takes a plunge.

On 10th January 1866 another accident occurred barely half a mile from where Snowdrop left the rails. About 400 yards west of Beckenham Junction the LCDR line crossed a small stream, the Beck or Rusher Brook, a tributary of the Pool River which flowed through the centre of the village. The bridge involved, a flat iron girder supported by brick piers set 18 inches into the bed of the stream, was bounded on one side by osier beds and on the other by a ploughed field. On Saturday 9th melting snow caused the Beck to raise its level to its highest seen within living memory and the flood waters began to scour the piers of the bridge which dated from the days of the West End of London & Crystal Palace Railway but when a routine inspection of the line was carried out at 4 p.m. nothing unto-

The Beckenham disaster, Sunday 14th January 1866. "Tacita" and the remains of her train can be seen lying in the stream. This engraving ensured the accident a contemporary notoriety, being published in the "Illustrated London News" the following week. (Author's collection)

ward was noted. However on the following morning at 3.57 a.m the early morning Blackfriars to Ramsgate goods, comprising of 40 wagons hauled by Stephenson 0-6-0 "Tacita", was approaching Beckenham and, as it crossed over the stream the bridge collapsed under its weight and "Tacita", her crew and the first 13 wagons of the train were thrown down the embankment. The driver was thrown clear and the guard, although severely bruised, managed to clamber out of a window in his van but the stoker (fireman), 19-year old John Maxted of Whitstable, was buried beneath the locomotive and died instantly. The accident was witnessed by W. Baxter, the Beckenham Junction signalman who had been keeping a special lookout for the train, the telegraph wires having been brought down in the storm and he, and another signalman, Amos Grinsted of Penge Junction, who had also heard the crash, took immediate steps to protect the line.

Daylight revealed a scene of much destruction with the wagons which had left the rails being completely smashed while the remainder were damaged. The train's cargo was scattered across the site and items such as firewood and biscuits "of which there was a great quantity" had been carried away by the flood waters while heavier merchandise lay in and was spoiled by the waters. William Mills, the LCDR engineer, was present at the scene at 7 a.m. and directed the operations so that by the following day

the line had been partially restored, in the interval trains being terminated on either side of the locus and passengers having to walk over the girder of the damaged bridge. It was not until Wednesday 17th that Maxted's body could be extricated from the debris and, at the inquest held two days later at the Railway Hotel in Beckenham, it was established that the swollen stream had caused the piers to give way, the saturated ground beneath having contributed to this. The jury returned a verdict of accidental death with a rider that it was for Mr Mills to consider the evidence taken as to "the state of these streams and bridges and such matters"; Mr Carrtar, the Kent County Coroner commenting that "it was fortunate that the train destroyed was not a passenger train, for if that had been the case, a fearful loss of life would have been inevitable."

Gorgon to the rescue

The third and last of these three early accidents occurred on 6th February 1868 when "Gorgon", a Hawthorn 2-4-0, was hauling one first, a second brake, four thirds and four vans on a stopping train from Chatham to Victoria. After calling at Shortlands, Beckenham and Penge the train entered the Penge Tunnel at about 9.25 a.m. when, after travelling for 600 yards, the driver felt a sudden jolt and thought that he had run over some object. He stopped the train but not before the leading carriages became derailed and ended up fouling the down line. Realising that a down train was due, he had the presence of mind to uncouple Gorgon from the coaches and proceed to Sydenham Hill signal box where he alerted the signalman to the danger. The signalman at Herne Hill, having heard of the occurrence, immediately attempted to communicate with Penge box but the signalman there was too busy with the crossing gates to hear the warning. Happily the down train was halted in time and no ill effects were felt. The Board of Trade Inspector, Captain Tyler, found that the cause of the derailment was a broken rail but he had comments to make on the tardiness of preceding train drivers to notify the signalmen of an apparent problem with the rails in question and on the method of communicating between boxes and in particular with Penge box. The passengers were, understandably, distressed by being marooned in the tunnel and many Victorians who had a horror of railway tunnels in general and accidents in them in particular would have hardly have had their faith restored when, seven months later, one of the Penge Tunnel shafts suffered a partial collapse.

A rarity of accidents

On 5th September 1881 the 6 a.m. Bricklayers Arms to Beckenham Mid Kent goods, consisting of 13 wagons hauled by Cudworth 0-6-0 No.6, collided with a South Eastern passenger train just outside Beckenham Junction. The passenger train was, however, less crowded than normal and those on it suffered only a shaking. As the *Bromley Record* commented: "had the accident taken place earlier in the morning it might have been serious. Considering the small size of Beckenham Junction for goods purposes and the quantity of traffic through the station it confers great credit to the officials that the accident of the smallest moment is a rarity."

Another collision took place on the Mid Kent line on January 1st 1887 when, following the block signalling system being put out of use by storm damage, the driver of a train from Addiscombe passed two signals at danger owing to the limited view caused by the severe curvature of the line to the south of New Beckenham. He then proceeded to run into the back of the preceding train from Addiscombe which was patiently waiting for carriages from Beckenham Junction to be propelled in to the station and then attached to the front. Three carriages of the waiting train were wrecked but, despite the alarming nature of the crash, injuries were slight. Three years later a light engine ran away and smashed through the level crossing gates at the same crossing, much to the alarm of the signalman.

On 25th October 1913 the 7.52 a.m. Elmers End to Charing Cross workmen's train, hauled by F class No.9, crashed into the rear of the 7.35 a.m. train from Blackheath at Waterloo Junction; both trains were full and three passengers were killed and 22 injured, including three residents of Beckenham. Penge station was the scene of an accident on

19th June 1918 when evening shunting operations were in progress at the sidings. Owing to a misunderstanding between the signalman, guard and driver, wagons being attached to a goods train standing on the up main line were derailed fouling both the running lines. Before any warning could be given the 10 p.m. Holborn Viaduct to Orpington service emerged from the gloom of the tunnel and collided with the derailed wagons, overturning the locomotive and telescoping the front three passenger coaches. Remarkably there were no deaths or serious injuries although one passenger, Alfred Johnson of Westfield Road, Beckenham, had both of his legs broken; he later sued the Company after they refused to adequately compensate him and the court awarded him the not inconsiderable sum of £1,000 in damages.

Unfortunately Beckenham residents were not necessarily safer on other companies' lines as was illustrated on 4th May 1890 when William Ford of Yew Tree Cottages, Croydon Road was killed in a railway accident far from home – it occurred when he was travelling as a passenger to Scotland and his train collided with a light engine outside of Carlisle station.

Railcars off the line

On the Crystal Palace line the steam railcars had a rather unfortunate history during the relatively brief period that they operated that service. The first mishap occurred on Thursday 19th August 1909 when the *Beckenham Journal* reported that

"A railway accident at Shortlands on Thursday caused a good deal of inconvenience and delay on the S.E.&C.Railway. Just before 8 o'clock the steam railcar known locally as "Puffing Billy" and which travels between Beckenham and the Crystal Palace, with one journey during the day to Bromley, jumped the points and ran off the line. The accident occurred at a time when the traffic from the city is particularly heavy, and through the train running off the metals considerable delay was caused; in fact it was over two hours before the line was cleared."

The second accident occurred at Beckenham Junction on Tuesday 3rd May 1910 when the same paper carried another report in the following terms.

"On Tuesday morning the steam car which has for a year or so has acted as the train to and fro the Crystal Palace ran off the metals just where the up-main line joins the shunting branches on to the side platform. The result was that the up-main line was blocked for several hours but traffic was maintained with fair punctuality by the use of the down line for a distance of a few hundred yards. A large crowd were attracted to Rectory Road by the occurrence, and the work of the break-down gang from Battersea, coupled with the accident, occasioned a mild excitement for several hours, while the passengers of passing trains maintained a keen interest in the cause of late trains and the busy scene of railway workers. The derailed train was got back on the metals by being jacked-up, and then additional

sleepers and lines being put into position to guide the wheels back to the proper line. With the long coach and engine attached it proved a heavy job and a long one, and just towards the end as the car was being pulled back into position, more trouble seemed imminent as one of the metals snapped clean in two. However patience and care won, and before 2 o'clock the engine and attached coach were on the line again."

The most serious, and in many ways the most interesting, incident took place on 22nd April 1913 when, according to the *Journal*

"The steam railcar which connects Beckenham Junction with the Crystal Palace Low Level came to grief on Tuesday evening through a collision with a light engine and though the accident was fortunately not attended with such serious consequences as might have occurred had the car been travelling at a higher rate of speed the injuries to the guard were sufficiently serious to render his immediate removal to the hospital necessary.

The accident occurred at 9.21 p.m. just after the car had left the Junction station, and as it was passing the signal box a light engine, which was engaged on shunting operations, dashed in to the rear section of the car wrecking the guard's compartment, shattering the glass in most of the windows and damaging the steering gear, whilst the engine had one buffer completely carried away and the front portion considerably bruised. The guard, William Moss, aged 60, of Paddock Cottages, Orpington, was found to have sustained serious injuries, and after first-aid had been rendered by a ticket collector he was seen by Dr Williams who ordered his removal to the Beckenham Cottage Hospital. Here he was attended to by Dr Curtis who found that he was suffering from scalp wounds, a broken nose, shock and loss of blood. The driver of the car was also thrown forward by the concussion, sustaining a nasty cut and being considerably shaken. Fortunately there were only two passengers in the car at the time and they were lucky to escape with nothing more than a severe shaking and they were able to proceed to their destinations. They were Mrs Lovell of 5 Playden Road, Upper Norwood and Mr James Emmery of 8 Corby Road, Gipsy Hill.

The cause of the accident is said to be due to the fact that the driver of the light engine mistook the dropping of a signal for another train to be his signal to proceed and he started the engine and it ran too far before he realised his mistake. It was a very good thing that the speed was not great in either case for had there been a main-line express passing at the time – as might easily have occurred – the loss of life must have been considerable. The back part of the steam railcar which is largely the guard's portion was so badly damaged that it is not expected that the car will be available for public service again. Extreme care had to be exercised in order to take the car to the siding on the Rectory Road side of the station where after such "first aid" was rendered as was necessary to keep it in position, a tarpaulin was placed over the whole of the damages It has been rather wondered that the force of the collision did not

throw the car off the metals but it was saved by the fact that at this point there is a check rail on the bend of the lines thus holding the wheels on one side and effectually preventing the coach being pushed off the rails. It was due to this also that no damage was done to the permanent way. An enquiry was subsequently held into the matter by Railway Officials from London. It has been suggested that there should be catch points at this position as there is a perfect maze of cross lines and perhaps now that an accident has occurred something will be done in this direction."

Fortunately the injured guard made a good recovery. In an unusual coda to the accident the police sergeant despatched to Beckenham Hospital to make arrangements for the treatment of the injured guard himself required treatment after coming to grief when his bicycle collided with a dog on Church Hill.

Railwaymen at risk

Being a local railwayman seems to have been a hazardous occupation. On 5th June 1875 William Chitty, LCDR signalman at Beckenham Junction, left the box after signalling the 10.16 p.m. up express and was crossing the lines when the connecting rod of a passing engine "struck him with fearful violence on the right side, causing his death." The life of the Kent House signalmen seems to have been somewhat precarious one. On 15th May1900 the 8.10 p.m. Bickley to Victoria and Holborn Viaduct service was waiting in the up loop at Kent House for an express from Dover to overtake it. The driver of the local train, Thomas Leonard, then misread the signals and started his train up just as the express was due and, failing to stop at the end of the platform proceeded northwards. Fortunately the points were set against him and rather than reaching the main line the engine was diverted into a siding terminating at Kent House A signalbox which it then rammed and in the process smashed up the lower storey. The signalman, seeing the accident about to happen, promptly escaped from his box but fortunately for all concerned the wrecked box halted the engine in its tracks and thus prevented it from dragging the train in to the road below. There were no serious injuries and the Board of Trade inspector commented that "When I inspected Kent House fourteen (sic) years ago, I had doubts as to the expediency of the arrangement, the use of facing points on passenger lines not being allowed. Now I am glad that I did because [otherwise] the train would have run in to the up fast train."

Three years later James Evenden, a signalman at the B box, was not so lucky and he was "cut to pieces" by a train while leaving the box; his widow sued the SECR and was awarded compensation of £238 14s 8d.

Other grades of railwaymen were also at risk in an era before risk assessments and large compensation payments. In March 1870 the *Bromley Record* reported that Frank Marsh, a Beckenham porter, slipped as he tried to board a slowly moving engine "and his foot was run over by a wheel and smashed". He died two months later in Guy's

Hospital from a pulmonary embolism and his grave in St George's churchyard bore the inscription "He was much beloved and his death was very much regretted by all who knew him." In June 1880 the *Beckenham Journal* recounted that "the unfortunate porter, Howard, who met with such an untimely end by accident at the Beckenham Station, on Derby Day, left a widow and three little children totally unprovided for. We are glad, however, to record that a few energetic friends set to work and collected about £50, which has been handed over to the widow, who desires through our pages to return her sincere thanks to all who have assisted her in her hour of affliction and bereavement."

At Penge on 7th October 1881 the fireman of an engine shunting in the yard there fell off his steed and was run over by the wheel; he died the following day of his injuries. On 14th September 1892 John Shorter, a new recruit who was working as a porter at the station, was walking backwards checking the doors of a departing train when he caught his foot on a box of butter that he had previously unloaded and fell between the train and platform with fatal results. Platelayers and other track staff sometimes found themselves imperilled and they included Baranbas Aspinell, killed in 1886 by the 8.20 am Dover to Victoria express 140 yards west of Beckenham Junction, David Hayter of Shortlands who was also killed by the up Dover express near to Beckenham Junction in 1908 and Robert Herbert run down by a train at New Beckenham in 1928, while porter Albert Wakely was killed by an express train passing through the station there in 1903, and William Aldridge, a porter at Clock House died there after being struck by a train in March 1921. In addition there were numerous reports in the local papers of "near misses" involving railwaymen, particularly at New Beckenham and Beckenham Junction and a number of suicides over all of the local lines, particularly in the Penge Tunnel when passengers jumped from trains or, as in the case of a German governess in 1913, placed their head on the line. The tunnel was also hazardous to railwaymen working in it as they were forced to lie down in the space between the up and down lines when trains were approaching due to the absence of adequate side refuges to shelter in until, in 1915, the SECR agreed to install additional refuges at a cost of £4,700, no doubt as a result of rising workman's compensation awards. A permanent reminder of the need for vigilance on the part of the public is provided for the footbridges which cross the main-line between Shortlands and Bromley South on the edge of the parish. These date from a decision of the LCDR Board in October 1887 to replace the footpath crossings formerly in use here following upon a series of fatal encounters between pedestrians and locomotives on this busy stretch of line over which an estimated 170 trains passed daily – in one incident alone that summer there were three deaths.

Electrification brought its own hazards. In April 1926 a ten-year old boy from Camberwell who had apparently been exploring in Beckenham Place Park was electrocuted while crossing the line close to Ravensbourne station. Later in that same year a platelayer, William Mathieson,

inadvertently touched the conductor rail with his pick and the shock threw him straight into the path of a passing express train with fatal results. In January 1930 George Scotney slipped and fell across the live rail while working in the Penge Tunnel and in the same month Charles Knapp, a signalman at West Wickham, was crossing the line outside his box in order to catch a train home that was waiting at the station when he slipped and caught his foot between the live rail and the collecting shoe of the train; it took half an hour to extricate him and he died later in Beckenham Hospital from terrible injuries.

Recent times

Kent House seems to have been a favourite place for derailments and on 29 January 1931 a most unusual incident occurred when No. 853, "Sir Richard Grenville", a Lord Nelson class 4-6-0, was passing through the station with the up "Golden Arrow" Pullman express. As the train crossed over the points that gave access to the up loop to the east of the station the leading wheels of the locomotive became derailed and although extensive damage was done to the trackwork the engine's wheels re-railed themselves at the west end points and the train arrived at Victoria on time the driver being unaware that anything untoward had happened; the report held that the accident was caused by a combination of factors including excessive speed on the curve leading into the station.[4] On 2nd July 1968 an Ashford to Victoria train, composed of four 2 HAP units, was derailed at the west end of the station due to the rails having buckled during a heat wave; there were no casualties although the line was blocked for three days and the parapet of the bridge over Kent House Lane damaged. Almost exactly twenty years later, on 20th July 1988, a down Hoverspeed boat train comprised of a single 4 CEP unit was derailed at virtually the same spot – the train was isolated in the down loop and only minimal disruption was caused; the passengers, reported to being mainly French and German tourists, suffered no injuries and were taken back to Victoria.

The most serious accident to have involved a Beckenham train occurred on 4th December 1957 when the 5.16 p.m. Charing Cross to Hayes service, a 10-coach train made up of virtually brand new EPB stock and carrying an estimated 1,500 passengers, was struck in the rear by the steam-hauled 4.56 p.m. Cannon Street to Ramsgate in the charge of 34066 "Spitfire". Both trains were running late due to thick fog and the Hayes train was stationary when "Spitfire" ran through a red signal and collided with it close to St Johns. The eighth and ninth coaches of the Hayes train were destroyed and the heavy girder bridge carrying the Nunhead to Lewisham line over the scene of the accident collapsed on to part of the wreckage. Casualties were high with 90 dead and 177 injured (the Hayes train figures alone being 38 and 107 respectively), making this the third worse accident in British railway history. A temporary shuttle service between Hayes and Catford Bridge was put into operation for a couple of days. Inevitably many of those killed or injured

Battle of Britain class 34066 "Spitfire"passing through Beckenham Junction in 1958. This locomotive hauled the 4.56 p.m. Cannon Street to Ramsgate train that ran into the back of the 5.16 p.m.Charing Cross to Hayes train in the fog near to Lewisham on 4 December 1957 with great loss of life ensuing. A great irony here was that the photographer who took this view was a regular traveller in the last coach of the 5.16 and, but for the fact that on the fateful day the trains were running late, would have probably been killed or badly inured in the crash. (John Penfold; Terry McCarthy collection)

were from the Beckenham area and of the dead 6 were from Eden Park, 4 were from West Wickham and a substantial number of others from the Clock House, New Beckenham and Elmers End areas; a number of funerals and commemorative services were held in local churches with the Mayor of Beckenham and Philip Goodhart, the constituency M.P. both attending a memorial service held at St Mary's Parish Church in Lewisham on 15th December. The driver of the 4.56 was later charged with manslaughter but was found unfit to stand trial. A plaque in memory of the victims was placed on Lewisham station in 2003.[5]

In the last two decades of the twentieth century there were a spate of minor accidents on the Crystal Palace line. On 23rd December 1981 six passengers were injured when 4 EPB unit 5007 on the 08.22 West Croydon to London Bridge service collided with 4 SUB No. 4725 the 08.23 Beckenham Junction to Victoria at Bromley Junction. Both trains were damaged and the accident was attributed to error on the part of the 08.22 driver. More spectacularly at 6.30 am on Friday 1st November 1985 an empty train, made up of one of the new Class 455 units, entered the up bay at Beckenham Junction when the brakes failed and it ploughed

through the buffer stops demolishing staff accommodation and public toilets. The incident was graphically described in the *Beckenham Journal* under the headline "Runaway Train Crash – Engine wrecks station as driver flees for life"; new building work marks the site of the crash. On 22nd January 1990 4 EPB unit 5408 on the 07.45 incoming service from London Bridge collided with the replacement buffer stops at the same location, damaging he train but causing no serious injuries; a similar incident occurred in February 2002. At Shortlands on 12th February 1976, hours after a lorry had collided with the bridge there, the 15.50 Victoria to Gillingham service consisting of a single 4 VEP unit was derailed close to the signal box after the driver had inadvertently passed a signal at danger; one female passenger was slightly injured but the lines were blocked for several hours.

Natural causes

Natural phenomena have often disrupted trains in the Beckenham area including numerous flooding incidents at Clock House as well as the widespread Kent floods and consequent landslides of September 1958 and September

1968, both of the latter blocking the main line for several days. In May 1922 giant hailstones ("some of them 3½ inches in diameter") fell on the lines at Clock House station and for a time visibility in the vicinity was down to a few yards while, in the words of the *Times* "frozen clouds swept along the streets of Beckenham." In July 1934 a spectacular storm flooded the subway at New Beckenham and caused the embankment between Hayes and West Wickham to collapse – according to the *Times* "at that time 500-600 day-trippers were stranded and the railway authorities arranged for a service of single-deck omnibuses to convey passengers to Elmers End."

The regular flooding of the Chaffinch Brook at Clock House station had long been a problem and despite work carried out in 1927 and 1957 to raise the line at the point where it crossed the river, the flooding became even more frequent especially from 1965 onwards when remedial works being undertaken by the local authority caused the

problem to become progressively worse. Special arrangements for passengers continued to be necessary and "much-handled and very dog-eared posters would be brought out of store to warn passengers of delays inherent in these emergency procedures."[6] The BR South Eastern Divisional manager to issue the following letter to passengers on 17 August 1967:

FLOODING AT CLOCK HOUSE

I want to apologise personally to all passengers who suffered delay and inconvenience because of the flooding which occurred at Clock House yesterday evening and on previous occasions.

This is a problem of long standing and I believe that you would appreciate a resume of its history, future prospects and our arrangements for emergency services when flooding occurs.

CLOCK HOUSE.

FLOODING OF LINES.—1. The person in charge of the platform at Clock House must keep a careful watch on the permanent way in the vicinity of bridge No. 685 at the London end of the station when flooding is likely, especially after prolonged or heavy rain.

2. Should flooding occur, the person in charge of the platform at Clock House must immediately inform the station master and the Train Supervision Office at Orpington. The latter must advise the electrical control operator at Lewisham Control Room, the District Engineer and the District Motive Power Superintendent (electrical inspector's office, London Bridge, telephone Waterloo, extension 2256). Arrangements will be made by those departments to send representatives to the site. Trains may continue to run until

    (a) the electrical control operator at Lewisham Control Room requests the Train Supervision Office at Orpington to suspend traffic owing to leakage of current.

          or

    (b) the water level reaches the danger mark referred to below.

3. Whilst trains are continuing to run, speed when passing through the flood water must not exceed 3 m.p.h. in order to avoid damage to the electrical equipment. The station master must arrange for all trains to be stopped at New Beckenham or Elmers End, as the case may be, for the motormen and guards to be advised of the flooding.

4. A board is fixed to the down side abutment of bridge No. 685, near the platform ramp and the danger mark is indicated thereon by an arrow. When flooding has occurred, the station master must keep this board under observation and immediately the water level reaches the danger mark, he must arrange for all services between New Beckenham and Clock House to be suspended and for the Train Supervision Office at Orpington to be advised. Traffic must not be resumed until the water level has subsided below the danger mark. If, on the resumption of traffic, it is still necessary for trains to pass through the flood water, the provisions of the third paragraph of these instructions must continue to be observed.

5. The Line Traffic Manager will issue separate instructions concerning the emergency train service arrangements, etc. to be introduced when normal working is interrupted.

COUNCIL SIDING.—This siding is on the up side between Elmers End and Clock House with access by a trailing connection in the up line. The points are operated from a ground frame controlled from Elmers End signal box and the working is in accordance with electrical release lever control arrangements.

Extract from B.R.(S) sectional appendix, 1960.

Summer flooding at Clock House with a BRCW Type 3 diesel locomotive hauling a dead electric unit on a New Beckenham to Elmers End shuttle service on 1 June 1964; the underside of the locomotive was fitted with a special plastic casing in an effort to avoid damage to what was then a comparatively new machine. (P F Sumner; Railway Magazine)

Bottom Left - Floods in Beckenham affected other form of transport but fail to halt the progress of an RF bus on Green Line service 725 in September 1968 at the junction of Manor Road and the High Street – one business still there is Furley & Baker whose sports shop was a good source of model railways to the schoolboys of the 1960s. (Nancy Tonkin collection)

Bottom Right - A red RF on the 227 ploughs through the floodwaters at the same location. (Nancy Tonkin collection)

The Chaffinch Brook adjoining Clock House station has flooded with increasing frequency and speed over recent years. To alleviate the effects on our services, we raised the track level by 5 inches at a cost of £9,000 in 1958. To do more would have cost over £50,000. In October last year the Greater London Council announced a £3m flood prevention scheme on the River Ravensbourne and its tributaries including the Chaffinch Brook, to be completed by March 1968. The G.L.C. hope that this will nearly eradicate flooding. Unfortunately in the mean time it seems that the effect of the works now in progress is to constrict the flow of water more than normally with the result that flooding is likely to occur more frequently and more suddenly until the work is finished.

Now let me explain the emergency arrangements we operate, in conjunction with the buses of the London Transport Board. When the level of water reaches a certain height, an alarm bell operates in Beckenham Junction signal box. All concerned are then warned, and the L.T.B. are advised that buses may be required. If the water seems likely to reach danger level, arrangements are then made for the special train and special buses. The train is hauled by two diesel locomotives as electric traction obviously cannot be used when water reaches the conductor rail. To obtain and prepare special locomotives and coaches takes about two hours, so you will gather that flooding at short notice presents difficulties in providing the emergency rail service. You may ask why we do not have a special train always standing by, but the train is a very costly item which we cannot afford to have lying idle for most of its time. Furthermore, last Thursday the flood waters were so high that even the special train could not be operated.

You will gather, therefore, that the increased tendency of then Chaffinch Brook to flood more quickly adds to the problems we face, in that now we frequently have less time to provide the special train, finding special buses and warn bus crews that they can accept rail tickets.

Details of the standard emergency train and our bus arrangements are exhibited at this station for your information. Despite the increasing difficulties, you have my assurance that everything possible will continue to be done to minimise the difficulties of travel in flood conditions until next March when, as we all hope, the trouble will virtually cease to occur.

The frequent flooding did cease in 1968 although over the years there have been a few reoccurrences.

January 1881 brought exceptionally heavy snow which caused the Mid Kent to be blocked between Lower Sydenham and New Beckenham for almost a week while in both January 1987, February 2009 and January 2010 brought blizzards which isolated the Beckenham area for a period. Fallen trees have been a problem in Beckenham, the last major incidents being in 1987 when the great October storm caused a complete suspension of local rail services when the electricity supply was breached and for a considerable time the main-line, Catford Loop and Hayes branch were all blocked by trees blown over. Other weather phenomena included the great winter freezes of 1947 and 1962 and the recurring problems of fog which bedevilled local train service timekeeping for many years. On a more esoteric level, on 20 November 1966 a trainload of passengers at West Wickham saw mysterious lights in the sky and one passenger told the *Times* that "there seemed to be 50 or 100 of them going from north to south, travelling at various speeds." The lights were seen across Britain and were attributed by experts to a shower of meteorites breaking up when re-entering the atmosphere or, perhaps, to the return of a Russian satellite into the earth's atmosphere.

The darker side

The darker side of local rail travel was represented by the last journey of that luckless Victorian heiress Harriet Staunton on the 8.26 am from Bromley to Penge on Thursday 12th April 1877[7] and the finding on 10th September 1903 of the bodies of a young couple from Plumstead in a train at New Beckenham; subsequent verdicts at the coroner's court were of the wilful murder of Ada Cook by Charles Speller followed by his own suicide under mental derangement. A more recent and unsolved local train murder was that on 23rd March 1988 of Deborah Linsley between Brixton and Victoria in one of the single compartments of the 14.16 stopping service from Orpington, heralding an end to the use of such stock in off-peak hours.

The suffragette campaign of 1913 resulted in the Times reporting on 16th June of that year that "A bomb has been found inside one of the leather-covered seats in the ladies' waiting room at Eden Park railway station near Beckenham. It was examined by the police who ascertained that it had been set to go off at a stated time, but that the clockwork had stopped. The station is not much used, and it is thought that the intent was to set it on fire." Presumably it was not a coincidence that this incident occurred on the same day as the funeral was to be held in Northumberland of Emily Davidson, who had thrown herself in front of the King's horse at the Derby.

Eighty years later the IRA were engaged on a bombing campaign in London and on Wednesday 3 February 1993 a warning was given by them that two bombs had been placed aboard the 0905 Victoria to Ramsgate service and that these bombs were due to explode in thirty minutes time. The train had by the time the warning was given already left the terminus and was progressing upon its southward journey but it was stopped in the down loop at Kent House station and the seventy passengers were promptly evacuated. The immediate area, including the nearby Royston Primary School and its 285 pupils, was cleared by the police and local helpers and at 9.39 a device exploded in the seventh coach of the train, blowing windows out and scorching the interior of the carriage. A second bomb was not found and the line was reopened to all traffic on the evening of the following day.[8]

A selection of the Beckenham Junction staff in Edwardian times are anxious to have their picture taken on the up platform. Although clearly posing this was not an official postcard but would have sold well to members of their proud families. (Lens of Sutton)

Chapter 12
RAILWAYMEN & PASSENGERS
Some Noteworthy Characters

"We now have a railway to Beckenham."
Letter from Charles Darwin to W.D.Fox, 8 Feb 1857.

Stationmasters and others

In the nineteenth and early twentieth centuries railways were heavily labour intensive and it is not therefore surprising that about 200 men were employed by the SECR in the Beckenham area. Many of these men worked at local stations, where six or more staff were commonplace at a busy suburban station, while others worked in the goods yards and signalboxes but there were few employed as train crews due to the lack of engine sheds or indeed affordable housing in the locality. In the railway hierarchy the station master occupied an exalted position for not only was he in charge of the staff and railway property entrusted to his care but was also the local representative of the Company responsible for public relations and the attraction of local trade and, as such, having a position of some authority in the local community. His social status can be seen from the fact that even as late as 1914 the *Beckenham Directory* listed local stationmasters in the "professional" rather than "trade" section.

Each station initially had a station master, his duties and salary according to the importance of that station although Kent House, Clock House, New Beckenham, Eden Park and Ravensbourne later came under the care of neighbouring stations. At what was always regarded as the premier station in the area, the Beckenham Joint Committee seem to have made a fortuitous choice in appointing Michael Moore (1818-1894) as the Junction's first stationmaster. Occupying the post for seventeen years, his office was at times made virtually impossible by the continual disagreements and lack of co-operation between the two companies. However he was diplomatic and hard-working and over the years was presented with several testimonials to his efforts – these included the not inconsiderable sum of £75 in 1866 "in testimony of the obliging manner in which he performs the arduous duties allotted to him; and for the unwearied attention to and uniform anxiety for the safety, comfort and interest to all the classes of passenger in the numerous trains coming into his station." When he retired from his work he became a churchwarden at St George's and when he died at the age of 76 it was said by Borrowman that he was "deservedly popular with all classes of the community … being singularly simple and retiring in manner. One had to know him well to know how keen and punctual he was in all that related to the business part of his office, while his deep personal piety was hidden in the same way." He was later commemorated by a window at St Georges which was destroyed in the war. His son Frank went into partnership with Walter Mathew as coal merchants at the station.

Another Beckenham Junction stationmaster was Robert Blackborrow, who occupied the office from 1879 to 1898 and oversaw the rebuilding of the station. In a bizarre incident he sued a local cheesemonger, Walter Packham, for defamation following upon the publication of a humorous rhyme (described as "a squib") in which Mr Blackborrow's habit of recommending "pitch pills" to all and sundry was lampooned. New Beckenham's first stationmaster was George Hannan and an account of his earlier railway activities stated that in 1858 a Volunteer Review was held in Bickley Park and that this "taxed the resources of the railway", particularly as the Beckenham to Bickley section was still single-track. Hannan was appointed the Pilotman for the day and he "wore a red coat and no train was allowed to go without him personally giving permission. Many trains were worked by the Great Western from Kensington etc and the Brighton Company from Pimlico, and all was successfully carried out." Hannan was also an early member of the Congregational Churc in Beckenham and due to his influence services were held in "an iron room" at the station from 1877 onwards. He died in October 1899, "a very large number of persons attending his funeral." The first stationmaster at West Wickham was John Rudge, who occupied that position between the opening of the station in 1882 and 1901 and was said to "have been conscientious and kindly to all".

Most stationmasters lived in Company houses or close to their place of work and the station masters at Penge East, Kent House and Elmers End all resided in the accommodation provided at the stations, the first stationmaster at Kent House, Edward Huish, being literally able to survey the platforms from his bedroom windows. At New Beckenham the old station of 1864 was used as accommodation for the station masters of the replacement station until the abolition of that post after the First War and in later years it was rented out to private tenants. At Beckenham Junction the stationmaster occupied Rutland Lodge, set back from Southend Road and situated on the down side approach road next to the entrance to the yard; the house was demolished in 1985. The Shortlands stationmasters from 1892 onwards lived at Ivynook, a detached house on Shortlands Road adjacent to up side of the station and now demolished while at Clock House the first stationmaster there, Traiton Matthew Reynolds, lived in a house with the exotic name of Himalaya close to the junction of Beckenham and Sidney roads.

The post of stationmaster was abolished by British Rail in the 1960s but at Beckenham a station manager responsible for the whole area was appointed.

The short-lived Penge WEL&CPR station was apparently inhabited by James Denyer, a platelayer, and his wife who lived there and tended a small garden and orchard alongside although it is not clear whether or not he ever acted as stationmaster there. Mr Denyer seems to have worked as a foreman on the LCDR for many years and gave evidence to the coroner in the enquiry after the 1866 accident to the effect that he had inspected the bridge in question the previous day. The couple continuing to live in the former station building until moving to Penge; Mrs Denyer appears to have survived well into her nineties.[1]

On the eve of the first war the local stationmasters were Edwin Harmer – Beckenham Junction, Traiton Reynolds – Clock House, Thomas Wright – Eden Park, James Davies – Elmers End, H. Harris – Kent House, Thomas Henry Bingham – New Beckenham, Harry John Porter – Penge, Ravensbourne – William Henry Hardy, F. Bowles – Shortlands and J. Jeffries – West Wickham

Lamps, ladies and base coins

The duties of the staff serving under the station master were many and varied and, according to the 1905 appendix to the SECR working timetable, they were forbidden to consume alcohol or smoke while in uniform. The platform staff were responsible for placing footwarmers and rugs in carriages, for filling and trimming carriage and platform lamps and they were offered rewards such as one guinea for the capture of thieves of incandescent gas mantles from stations and 2s. 6d for reporting broken rails while a warning was given to booking staff to look out for "base coins". At Beckenham Junction and Elmers End the inspector in charge was to receive from train guards a record of the arrival and departure of all trains, showing accurately the actual times involved and the reason for any delay. The guards of all trains were "strictly forbidden to read for amusement on journeys". With the exception of a solitary female employed as the ladies' Room Attendant at Beckenham Junction, all staff until nationalisation were male although female porters, guards and booking clerks were temporarily employed at local stations during both Wars and in 1944 it was estimated by the Southern that in that year 16% of its employees were female. One notable First War employee at Shortlands was Woman Porter Gregory who, in 1917, received a citation for lowering the lights at the station during an air raid.

Passenger needs to be catered for included the looking after of amenities such as the waiting rooms and lavatories but these were never lavish, given the fact that neither

"Erin", one of the Kirtley D or "Large Scotchmen" class of suburban 0-4-4 tank locomotives seen at Beckenham Junction with a number of keen onlookers in about 1902 – a nice study of both engine and staff. (Lens of Sutton)

Permanent way workers attending to the line at Penge East after damage caused by a minor derailment on 5 December 1956 with, in the background, the houses in Linden Grove complete with what appears to be post-war replacements for bomb dam- aged houses. (Bromley Libraries)

the SER or the LCDR could ever have been accused of squandering their shareholders' money on stations. A typical complaint was that of a passenger in 1885 who after reporting that during severe weather there were no fires lit in the waiting room at Beckenham Junction was met with the comment that this was due to the fact that "the station had already burnt its ration of coal for the year". Other local station facilities included bookstalls at Elmers End, Beckenham Junction, New Beckenham, Shortlands and Penge East, telegraph and telephone offices at all stations, and parcels and left luggage facilities. Horse cabs and, later on, motor taxis met trains at Penge East and Beckenham Junction and at the latter a wooden cabmen's shelter, holding an office and messroom, was provided on the down side approach road – this seems to have been a den of iniquity for in 1898 a police raid resulted in cabman George Davey being fined the then enormous sum of £60 for illegal betting. Other infamies included railway staff fired for minor thefts and drunkenness and the dismissal in 1916 of a driver and fireman at Shortlands for stealing "a sieve of Kentish cherries" from a wagon on their train.

Signals and kindness

In late Victorian times there were a total of sixteen signalboxes in the area employing a total of 40 men including porter signalmen and signal lads. At the first of these, the Saxby & Farmer wooden box on stilts at Beckenham, the original signalmen included William Baxter, William Chitty and a Mr Cook – the last two named came to unfortunate ends with Chitty, described as "bearing a most excellent character" being killed by a passing train and Cook, of a less than excellent character, being dismissed by the LCDR in June 1861 after falling asleep at his post while intoxicated. By 1900 commencing respectively at 6 am, 2 pm and 10 pm, while all other boxes in the area were worked in two ten-hour shifts commencing at 4.30 or 5 am (6.30 on Sundays and one particular duty of the New Beckenham signalman was to check that the level crossing gates were closed across the railway when leaving the box at night. In 1910 Penge Junction and Shortlands boxes had been added to the list of those operating eight-hour shifts. All lines were opened on Sundays with the exception of the

Norwood spur and Crystal Palace line.

On 2nd February 1897 Thomas Lewis, a porter at Shortlands, was awarded a bronze medal by the Order of St John for having saved the life of a passenger who had fallen off the platform edge there as a train was entering the station and his deed was duly reported in the *Times*. Local newspapers also recorded public appreciation of other railwaymen – an example is of George Pankhurst, the Beckenham Junction goods foreman who was given a presentation and an award for his service in 1904. On a larger scale teas with evangelical overtones were organised for local railwaymen from an early date and these appear to have been popular with a local stationmaster commenting that "Men of that class did need a kind word and could appreciate it far more than was generally supposed" although it is possible that their appreciation was more directed towards the "handsome and substantial repast." In December 1879 a dinner was held in aid of local train drivers at the Bell Hotel, Bromley and "through the kindness of the superintendent of the line, all of the Bickley drivers were relieved from duty in order to be present, and enjoyed a good repast and a convivial evening afterwards, several good songs being sung." Other local activities involving railwaymen included charitable events in aid of the Railway and Old Beckenham Missions, the latter dating back to the days of the railway navvies and Miss Marsh at the rectory, the Signalmens and Switchers Benevolent Society, concerts given by railway employees in the Beckenham Public hall and the establishment of a Beckenham Junction Cricket Team while the present-day activities of the Beckenham and West Wickham Model Railway Club speaks to a continuing local interest in railways.

Passengers (extraordinary)

A number of important railway personalities have, over the years, lived in Beckenham at different times. William Vian (1827-1890) the secretary and one of the founders of the Railway Passengers Assurance Company lived in The Knoll; his daughter Marian served on the Borough Education Committee and had a local school named in her honour. Sir John Fowler (1817-1898), chief engineer of both the SER and Mid Kent and consulting engineer to the WEL&CPR owned the Eden Park estate in the 1860s while John Morgan, secretary of the LCDR from 1876 and afterwards the first joint secretary of the SECR, lived at 21 Rectory Road and was a daily commuter from Beckenham Junction – when he died in October 1900 his funeral was attended by members of the SECR Board and it was said that he was "a man of very retiring disposition and was little known in Beckenham." Another local resident was Sir Josiah Stamp (1880-1941), afterwards Lord Stamp of Shortlands, who was the first Charter Mayor of the Borough and the Chairman of the London, Midland & Scottish Railway; he lived at Tantallon, Park Hill Road and was killed along with his family and three servant girls when his home received a direct hit by a high explosive bomb. James Staats

Forbes (1823-1904) was the General Manager of the LCDR and between 1864 and 1899 lived at Wickham Hall; according to his obituary in the *Beckenham Journal* his loyalty to the company was noted as "when the railway reached West Wickham he continued to travel from Beckenham Junction, presumably to avoid travelling on the South Eastern."

The Royal train passes Shortlands Bank box in about 1905. This small intermediate box had been closed in 1892 but was not removed until about eighteen years later. (SECR Society)

Many notable persons who have travelled through Beckenham stations including Sir John Lubbock, a noted scientist, astronomer and mathematician who became the first Vice-Chancellor of the University of London as well as being the Chairman of the Mid Kent Railway and Charles Darwin, whose achievements need not be repeated here, but who was also a major debenture holder in the company. Both travelled regularly from Beckenham Junction and mention the Mid Kent in their correspondence both as passengers and as shareholders although Darwin, after the opening of Orpington station in 1868, transferred his custom to that station, it being considerable closer to Downe.[2] Other regular travellers included Walter De La Mare, who commuted for 18 years between Elmers End and London Bridge, and the painter Mary Potter, who made daily journeys from Beckenham to the Slade School of Art from 1918 to 1921 while passengers who used local stations included Princess Henry of Battenburg, Enid Blyton,[3] David Bowie and Oscar Wilde – of the latter it was said that when he arrived at Beckenham Junction on Thursday 4th November 1886 in order to give a public lecture on "Art in Dress" he disappointed those who were expecting an exotically arrayed figure by appearing in ordinary evening clothes. On March 31 of that year Penge station witnessed the arrival of the composer Franz Liszt when the LCDR up boat express made a special call to set him down. Although little publicity of this had been given, a little group of his admirers were waiting for him and a lady with a basket of flowers "strewed the floor of the waiting room as the musician entered". Here he was welcomed by a representative of the London Hungarian Association of Benevolence and Liszt, after making a little speech in thanks and shaking hands with the bystanders then "proceeded to Westwood House,

Sydenham, the residence of Mr Littlejohn, whose guest he was." During his stay at Westwood House Liszt attended two concerts at the Crystal Palace devoted to his own works and he is reputed to have said after attending one of them that "I did not know until today that I had written such beautiful music."

Passengers (ordinary)

In contrast probably virtually every inhabitant of Beckenham has, in the last century and a half, used the local railway network at some point or another. The most important source of revenue for the railway was, and will no doubt continue to be, the season-ticket holder and, with the exception of the Crystal Palace line, peak-hour traffic has always been heavy. Initially the city termini of London Bridge, Cannon Street and Holborn Viaduct were the most popular destinations for commuters while leisure traffic was concentrated on Charing Cross and Victoria, a trend so marked that in 1863 Forbes, in giving evidence to the Select Committee on the Beckenham and Brighton Railway Bill, could confidently state that "gentlemen travel to the city and ladies to the West End." Weekend traffic was always directed away from the city and concentrated in Charing Cross and Victoria after the second war travellers to the city (and trains) were much fewer in number. Business peak-hour traffic was and to a certain extent still is, attracted mainly to the city stations of London Bridge, Blackfriars and Cannon Street, and even as late as the 1960s there was an obvious difference in the attire of passengers at Beckenham Junction who were bound for Holborn Viaduct as opposed to Victoria with the former still clad in bowler hats and carrying the regulation furled umbrella and broadsheet newspaper. Female commuters were in evidence from the 1870s onward, and by 1910 clerkesses and "typewriters" were a frequent sight while by the 1930s they had been joined by female shopworkers, civil servants and managers. Workman's tickets tended to attract "the better class" of manual workers and artisans who could not aspire to third class travel.

Their clothing may have changed with the decades

but the daily commuter is still very much with us, now armed with free newspapers, mobile phones and laptops. Travellers to the city, West End and new destinations such as the Docklands via Lewisham and the DLR, Croydon via the trams and the increasingly important and urbanised Bromley, are still seen leaving Beckenham stations in the morning and returning at night. Recent figures (shown in Appendix 6 below) show that Beckenham Junction is still the most used local station, followed by Penge East and Shortlands while Birkbeck and Ravensbourne are the quietest and West Wickham figures have fallen somewhat from their peak in the 1930s. Taken as a whole the figures suggest that one in five of all the inhabitants of the area formerly covered by the Borough of Beckenham still use the railway on a daily basis.

Not all commuters, however, believed in paying their way and the local press over the years contains many examples of fare-dodgers being caught out. Two examples were that of a young woman from Forster Road who was fined £8 in March 1932 for altering a first-class season ticket and thus attempting to get a free month's travel and, in the previous year, a West Wickham inhabitant who instead of paying the 3s 0d fare from that station attempted to buy a London Bridge to Charing Cross ticket "for a few pence". The *Times* commented that "an explanation was given to the court by the Southern Railway that they had withdrawn ticket checks at West Wickham for reasons of economy, thus making it easy for dishonest persons to defraud the Company."

Other regular but hopefully more honest travellers have included school children and their value to the railway was illustrated when the Beckenham UDC successfully asked the LCDR in 1897 to "run the 3.37 down train a little later from St Paul's so as to accommodate pupils returning to Penge, Kent House and Beckenham Junction from Dulwich College." The school was later honoured in having a Southern Railway locomotive named after it – Schools class No.307 "Dulwich". Other schools which attracted local pupils to travel by rail at differing periods included the Beckenham & Penge County Grammar School for Boys at Kent House, the County Grammar School for Girls in Lennard

"Off to work" and "Home again" - The life of a Kent House commuter as seen through a pair of post cards issued by J. Holdsworth at the Kent House Post Office at the turn of the last century. (Nancy Tonkin collection)

No.34089 "602 Squadron" near to Ravensbourne on the 10.46 Canterbury East to Wembley Women's Hockey International special working on 11 March 1961 – some of the sporty girls aboard can be seen at the windows! (John Scrace)

Road which was served by Kent House and New Beckenham stations, the Abbey School near to Beckenham Junction, James Allen's Girls School in Dulwich, the Langley Park schools at Eden Park, the Beckenham Technical institute and School of Art served by Clock House and the City of London School at Blackfriars.

In the case of younger children The *Bromley Record* of June 1871 helpfully advised their parents to "keep their fingers away from train doors as scarcely a day passes without their little fingers getting smashed" while in the not so distant days of compartment coaches the Penge Tunnel was sometimes the scene of much youthful exuberance and mischief-making. The considerable number of sports grounds and clubs particularly in the vicinity of New Beckenham and Eden Park attracted inward traffic and in particular cricket, rugby, tennis and hockey players and at the same Council meeting where the school train resolution had been passed a previous request having been made for a fast train during the summer months "for the convenience of various cricket and other clubs in the district" was noted as having been granted in the form of the 2.25 pm Charing Cross to Beckenham Junction service calling only at London Bridge and New Beckenham.

Special excursion trains were run to Penge East for special events at the Crystal Palace and a good example of this was on Whit Sunday 1885 when the *Times* reported that "a large number of passengers from all parts of Kent alighted at Penge station en route to the Crystal Palace"; these trains were sometimes stabled in the loops at Kent House as were outward bound excursions for local residents. Special stops

A BR Standard Class 2 tender locomotive enters Birkbeck Station in July 1964 with a LCGB special rail tour working. (J J Smith; Bluebell Railway Museum Archives)

by main-line trains were made so that the inhabitants of Beckenham could enjoy reduced fare half-holiday and other excursion fares and when statutory paid holidays became widespread in the late 1930s additional holiday seasonal services were run to the coast and country. Among other local special trains were those providing day trips to "places of interest and resort" and in the July 1875 *Bromley Record* Mr Rogers, a Penge businessman, announced that once again he was running his annual excursion to Margate, Broadstairs and Ramsgate at a fare of 4s 0d (children under 15, half-price). Another typical excursion was that of the Bible Class of the Old Beckenham Mission who, in August 1888, hired a special train from Beckenham Junction to Ramsgate and according to a somewhat dry report in the *Bromley Record* "At 7.30 the return journey was made, Beckenham being reached at about half-past twelve. A pleasant day was spent. The cause of their late arrival was because the train with their own special carriages was empty and left without them."

Inbound special traffic included excursions for poor children from the East End who were invited to picnics in local landowner's fields and a special train from Elephant & Castle to celebrate the crowning of the Newington Rose Queen at Kelsey Manor was run on 19th August 1881. Whether the Cator Agreements were effective in preventing day trippers on Sundays is a matter of conjecture and the

fact that trains would not call at Beckenham stations during many of the daylight hours would not have helped. An example of how rural Beckenham still was occurred in March 1897 when the Colindale Draghounds arrived by special train at Beckenham Junction with their hounds – the day seems to have been a success despite one of the hounds being run over by a train at Clock House. Excursion traffic bound for Beckenham in the twentieth century was rare but local events such as the Beckenham Tennis Week still attracted passengers by rail even though the car was becoming commonplace among the leisured classes.

Hop pickers, train spotters and others

In the twentieth century special trains were less common although Mid Kent stations saw Sussex excursions via the Woodside & Selsdon line at a time when it was closed to normal traffic while Kent Coast trains made additional calls at Penge East and Beckenham Junction right up until summer electrification in 1959. Other Mid Kent specials included services for hop-pickers who would stay for a week to gather in their harvest. These trains were normally run on Saturday mornings in September and travelled from London Bridge to Goudhurst, Marden, Hawkhurst, Headcorn, Staplehurst and Robertsbridge; on a typical day, 8th September 1935, five of these trains were provided with

The Centenarian special leaves Beckenham Junction with its train of six coaches ("part modern and part old-fashioned") in the care of South Eastern Railway O1 class locomotive No. 31048 on a roundabout journey back to Beckenham via the Mid Kent, London Bridge, New Wandsworth and Crystal Palace at an all-inclusive fare of seven shillings (children half-price). Although the signalman is presumably keeping a good look-out in this more innocent age health and safety seem to be a less urgent consideration as illustrated by the schoolboy standing inches away from the conductor rail and the photographer standing on the sleepers. (R C Riley; The Transport Treasury)

another seven running on the following Saturday. The hop-pickers specials resumed after the war but ceased to use the Mid Kent after 1956 by which time the traffic was in a sharp decline. At Ravensbourne one of the sidings was used to house a rake of old SECR stock including a birdcage brake until 1959, being kept for hop pickers and other special services.

Private trains could be hired from the various railway companies (and were not prohibited under the Cator Agreements) but the cost was high – as an example in SECR days 7s 0d per mile was charged, with a minimum total cost of £3. An interesting example of a local private train was the steam-hauled special which was run from Beckenham Junction on 26th September 1938 and organised by a master at the Abbey School in Beckenham. Carrying 500 passengers, 350 of whom were children, this train travelled by a roundabout route to Euston where the children and their teachers were then welcomed by Sir Josiah Stamp Beckenham resident and chairman of the company to the London Midland

& Scottish Railway's Centennial Exhibition. In more recent times there have been a number of railway enthusiasts' specials including the Mid Kent & WEL&CPR Centennial Special run on Sunday 30th December 1956 which was organised by a Crystal Palace man at a fare of five shillings. This train set off from the down bay at Beckenham Junction and travelled via the Mid Kent to London Bridge returning via Crystal Palace. Cheered by local crowds the train was well loaded "in the best traditions of the rush-hour traffic on the Mid Kent" and was hauled by SECR O1 class 0-6-0 No. 31048 on the outward run and by LBSCR 0-6-2T No. 32472 on the homeward run, arriving back to be greeted by the Mayor and Mayoress of Beckenham and, a comparative rarity at that time, being featured on the television evening news.[4] On 5th July 1964 the LCGB "Surrey Rambler" was hauled by a BR Standard 2-6-0 No. 78038 and reached Beckenham Junction via the Norwood Spur and was probably the last passenger train to use that line. Another unusual sight was provided by two Bournemouth-bound excursions

The Centenarian arriving back at Beckenham with 31048 running tender first while at the same time 2 NOL unit No. 1864 arrives with a Crystal Palace service – the locomotive dates from 1893 and its leading coach from 1911 while the electric unit, converted from LSWR steam stock, could also properly be described as having "old-fashioned" carriages. (R C Riley; The Transport Treasury)

The Beckenham, Catford & West End & Crystal Palace Railway Centenaries

SUNDAY, DECEMBER 30th, 1956

To commemorate the opening on New Year's Day, 1857, of the Mid-Kent Railway from Lewisham to Beckenham (the first railway to serve Catford and Beckenham) and the opening in December, 1856, of the West End and Crystal Palace Railway (the genesis of all later rail access to Victoria Station) from Crystal Palace to New Wandsworth (the original temporary terminus), A SPECIAL CENTENARY STEAM TRAIN, hauled by old South Eastern Railway and L.B.S.C. Railway engines, and comprising part modern and part old-fashioned carriages, formerly in use in the Crystal Palace-Beckenham area, will run as follows :—

	Return Fare (round trip)
Beckenham Junction .. .. 2.05 p.m. dep. }	7/-
Catford Bridge (see Note A).. .. .. .. * 2.16 p.m. dep. }	
Crystal Palace.. .. .. * 3.04 p.m. dep.	5/-
New Wandsworth (goods) .. .. 3.26 p.m. arr.	
New Wandsworth (goods) .. .. 3.44 p.m. dep.	
Crystal Palace.. .. .. 4.14 p.m. arr.	
Crystal Palace.. .. .. 4.24 p.m. dep.	
Beckenham Junction .. .. 4.34 p.m. arr.	

Passengers from Beckenham Junction and Catford Bridge, not wishing to make the complete tour, may alight at Crystal Palace on the outward journey and return to Beckenham Junction (see Note A) by 3.15 p.m. ordinary train at a reduced fare of 5/-.

Accompanied juveniles, 3 and under 14 years, half price.

* * * *

Note A.—Passengers wishing to return to Catford Bridge should make their own way from Beckenham Junction to New Beckenham, from where they may use the ordinary 15 minute interval service to Catford Bridge, for which the special Centenary train tickets will be valid. These tickets may be retained as Souvenirs of the tour.

* * * *

The special train on the outward journey will reverse at London Bridge (Low Level) from 2.32 to 2.41 p.m. On the return journey, it will travel from New Wandsworth to Crystal Palace via Selhurst and Norwood Junction, thence back to Beckenham Junction via Birkbeck to include in the tour further extensions of the W.E. & C.P. Railway, opened in 1857 and 1858 respectively.

* * * *

Tickets obtainable from G. R. Lockie, 36 Harold Road, Upper Norwood, S.E.19, by postal application with remittance and addressed envelope, also a limited number from Beckenham Junction, Catford Bridge and Crystal Palace Stations. Enquire at booking offices.

* * * *

BOOK EARLY. ACCOMMODATION IS STRICTLY LIMITED AND WILL BE RESTRICTED TO SEATING CAPACITY OF SPECIAL TRAIN OF SIX COACHES.

CROWN PRINTING WORKS. S.E.19

organised by a Hayes travel agent at Easter and Whitsun 1988 and which consisted of Orient Express Pullman coaches pulled by a Class 47 diesel locomotive and, on another occasion, double-heading by two Class 33s - a first in

An unidentified Class 73 electro-diesel on a down "Venice-Simplon Orient Express" working in 1990 emerges from the Penge Tunnel into the sunlight. (Andrew Hajducki)

Maunsell N class 2-6-0 No. 31411 passes through Beckenham Junction with an up van train from Folkestone in 1956. (John Penfold; Terry McCarthy collection)

several respects for the Mid Kent. On 26th January 1990 the very last train to depart from Holborn Viaduct Station, a special composed of two 4-CEP units used the New Beckenham spur and reversed at Beckenham Junction on its way to call at every one of the ex-SECR London termini. Other regular excursion trains seen in Beckenham have been the Pullman "Venice – Simplon Orient Express" services to Dover and, in the present century, the return of steam-hauled special services which have become regular events on the LCDR main-line through Beckenham using a variety of locomotives - in December 2009 Britain's newest steam engine, the A1 pacific "Tornado" travelled on the line between Penge and Shortlands.

Golden Days at Beckenham Junction

Terry McCarthy, then a pupil at Worsley Bridge County Primary and latterly of Beckenham and Penge Grammar School, was a keen enthusiast and one of the two boys depicted in the painting on the front cover of this book (the other being his near neighbour Keith Gower) and Terry contributed the following reminiscences of golden days

spent in the company of Beckenham's railways:

"En route to my primary school I stopped on the footpath leading to the overbridge on the down side of Beckenham Junction in the morning to see the up "Night Ferry" come through, quickly followed by a down Ramsgate hauled by a vociferous BR standard Class 5. If the "Night Ferry" was late, so too were we and many was the morning that we had to run to school (initially in the old Abbey School building) for registration at 09.30. On weekends and during the school holidays longer visits were made, on a few occasions with the photographer John Penfold. It was not often that we train spotted from the platform – that depended on the ticket collector. One, nicknamed "Taffy", was particularly understanding and let us on, providing that we stayed away from the platform edge and other passengers.

Most of the trains seen were electric multiple units on Orpington and Gillingham/Maidstone West services, the latter being operated by pre-war 2 HAL units. There were, however, many steam passenger workings both to Ramsgate via Faversham and boat trains to Dover and Folkestone. Regular Thanet workings were hauled by a variety of mo-

184

N15 class 4-6-0 No. 30805 passes the substation at Shortlands with an up express from the Kent Coast in 1957. (R C Riley; The Transport Treasury)

West Country 4-6-2 No, 43092 "City of Wells" with the down "Golden Arrow" passing through Beckenham Junction in 1958 – this photograph forms a basis for the cover illustration painting; the locomotive is now preserved on the Keighley & Worth Valley Railway in Yorkshire. (John Penfold; Terry McCarthy collection)

tive power; king Arthurs, Schools, BR Class 5s and Bulleid Pacifics with, after 1957, the air-smoothing removed. Most boat trains were Bulleid Pacifics hauled, aided by the two 73A Britannias. In summer weekends additional trains were run o the coast, bringing older or more unusual locomotives. Coastal excursions appeared with with N and U class moguls, and occasionally with one of the delightful SECR 4-4-0s of the D1 and E1 classes. One Saturday morning I was amazed to note an up train hauled, bunker first, by a Brighton-built Fairburn 2-6-4T (?42095). On another occasion, a down train announced itself with an unusual hooter sound, and was revealed as an LMS "Black 5", No. 45388 of Willesden Junction depot. I saw few freight workings through Beckenham Junction. 33038 wheezed through one weekday morning on a down freight and Sundays often brought an up van train from Dover, which could yield a range of motive power, including N and D1 classes. One abiding memory was on a sunny weekday afternoon when I saw a Battle of Britain/West Country heading in the down direction. Watching it head off towards Shortlands I could see that it had been stopped by the signal between Westgate Road and Downsbridge Road. The restart a short while later could only be described as "volcanic" as a towering plume of smoke and steam rose above the locomotive, which I imagine was slipping in only the way that a Bullied pacific could, from the sound of the distant roar which came back to the station. I recall that it took ages to disappear out of sight. And that was on dry rails!

Often our train watching took place from Rectory Road, by the railings overlooking the Crystal Palace branch trains. Visits to Beckenham Junction, however, became less frequent after 1959, when the Kent coast services were electrified. Complete electrification in 1961 took away almost all the interest, apart from the sight of a diesel-hauled train. I recall that one Sunday I saw the unusual sight of an up working – a train hauled by double-headed class 24 diesels, then allocated to the Southern Region. Latterly, variety appeared with the Class 47s on cross country trains to Dover and, later still, the Eurostar trains.

I was particularly pleased, in 1958, to travel to Beckenham Junction on a steam hauled service train. This was a summer Saturdays only Kent Coast train that that called at about 10.45 a.m.; one week I saw it with a Schools class locomotive at the head but when I purchased a ticket for Bromley South the following week, I had a Maunsell mogul. On two occasions I passed through Beckenham Junction on special trains. In early 1971 I passed through on a Swansea – Folkestone Class 47 working organised by Glamorgan County Council for their annual ski-trip to Austria. The last time I went through the station (in both directions – contrary to the published schedule) was behind 35005 "Canadian Pacific" on a Victoria – Canterbury – Dover – Victoria working in 2002."

School Belles

Terry completes his recollections with some train-spotting when at the Grammar school where an earlier generation of pupils had seen the passing of the Dunkirk specials in 1940.

"I attended this establishment for seven very happy years from 1958-65 and observed many workings on the main-line in the vicinity of Kent House, often in lesson times – music was a particular victim. In my first few weeks there the "Kentish Belle" passed by during music, hauled by a variety of motive power including, I seem to recall, an L1 on one occasion. Later that school year I had the joy of seeing all four lines occupied – three with steam! In the down loop was a goods train with a C at the head, in the other loop a 4 SUB while on the through lines two expresses passed each other. One favourite working was at morning break time – a C class loco returning to Stewarts Lane as a light engine. It was usually held in the loop for a while but we never found out from whence it came, or why.

Special workings caused great excitement. At the end of one lunchtime a 5 BEL Pullman set went down, decorated with roof boards marked "European Free Trade Area Special". Where it went to, again, we never found out, but it was the only occasion that I saw a "Brighton Belle" set on our line. In early 1959 I returned to school from one of my very few absences to hear that a strange new locomotive had run by the day before at morning break, bearing the number E5000. My railway friends and I waited patiently for a reappearance and this time it was E5001. Not long afterwards D5000 went by on a lunchtime training run, anticipating their operation on S.R. routes pending the delayed arrival of the BRCW Type 3s (class 33s).

The Mid Kent line, being all electric, merited little attention. Yes, we saw Clock House station in flood but no trains – well, it was wet! On a couple of occasions when returning home from a friend's house in Brackley Road via Bridge Road and Blakeney Road at about 18.45 I saw a steam locomotive running light in the down direction towards Clock House and on one of those occasions it was a Bulleid pacific. Why, I do not know."

Trouble at The Myrtles

No account of the railway in Beckenham would be complete without a mention of the most famous traveller of all to visit the town. In the adventure of "The Greek Interpreter", Dr Watson records their attempt to reach the unfortunate Mr Melas who had been imprisoned in a house with that most Beckenham of house-names, "The Myrtles",[5]

"It was a quarter to ten when we reached London Bridge and half-past before the four of us alighted at the Beckenham platform. A drive of half a mile brought us to The Myrtles – a large, dark house, standing back from the road in its own grounds. Here we dismissed our cab and made our way up the drive together.
'The windows are all dark' remarked the Inspector. 'The house seems deserted.'
'Our birds have flown and the nest is empty' said Holmes.

The Railways of Beckenham

APPENDICES

Appendix 1

DEVELOPMENT OF THE BECKENHAM RAIL NETWORK 1858 – 2010

Beckenham Junction Station 1861

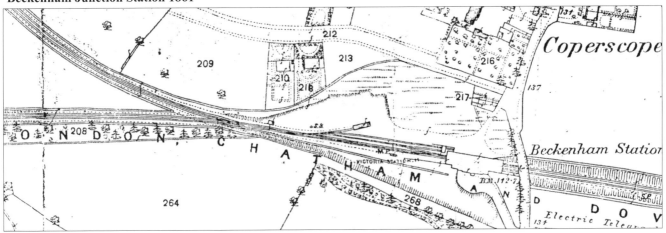

Beckenham Junction Station 1894

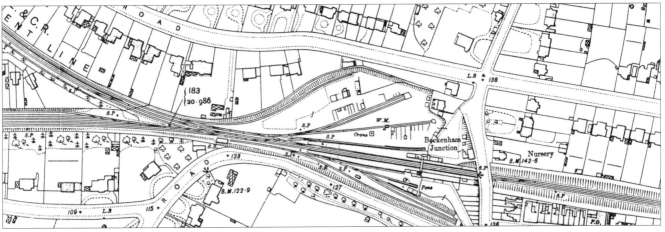

The 1861 map of Beckenham Junction shows the original signal box, goods shed and overall station roof. The later 1894 map shows the recently rebuilt station, the goods sidings on both sides of the running lines and the replacement 1881 signal box. Note how the Cator estate's Copers Cope Road has been developed and now rural Beckenham is no more. The small building to the immediate left of the new signal box is Dell Cottage.

Penge East Station 1894

Map of Penge East circa 1894. The level crossing has been replaced by the foot bridge. Note the goods yard and the second signal box. Penge tunnel would be entered on the immeadiate left hand side of the map.

Elmers End Station 1894

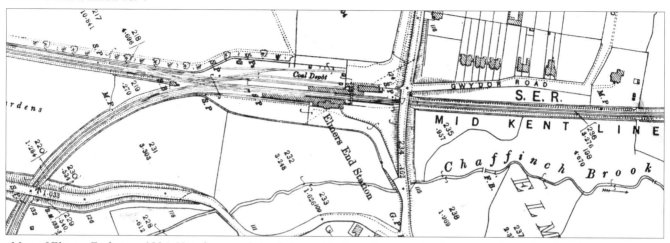

Map of Elmers End circa 1894. Note how much land along side the railway station has not yet been developed.

New Beckenham Station 1894

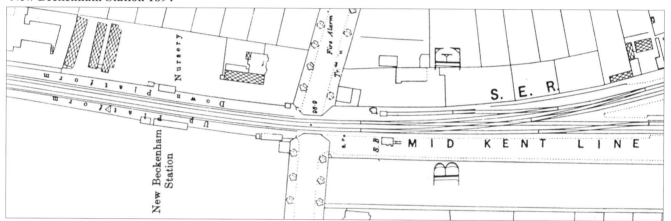

New Beckenham Station 1912

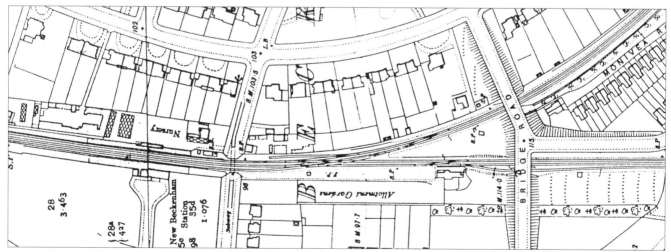

Map of New Beckenham in two stages of development. The 1894 map shows the level crossing and the adjacent signal box on the up line. Heading down the line to the left (upwards) is the spur to Beckenham Junction, and the line to the right (downwards) is for the Addiscombe extension. The scene by 1912 shows the building of the three way Bridge Road, the subway and a new signal box. The new station now has a centre run round line. The first station closed in 1866, and is visable on the map just north of Bridge Road.

Kent House Station 1912

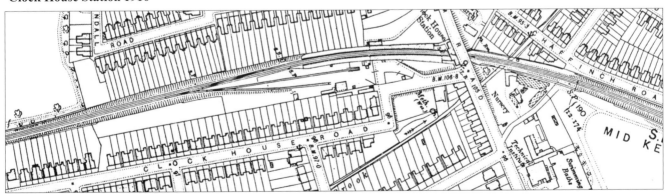

Map of Kent House circa 1912. The main entrance was to the south and the signal box shown is the 'B' box. Although the Penge Loop has been closed a siding has been laid on its formation. The station (disused) is none other than the 1858 Penge Station of the WEL & CPR.

Clock House Station 1910

Map of Clock House circa 1910. The building by that name had been replaced by the Technical Institute and Swimming Baths seen on the right. Note the site of the crossing next to Chaffinch road. Enid Blyton's childhood home in Clock House Road backed on to the station goods yard.

Shortlands Station 1932

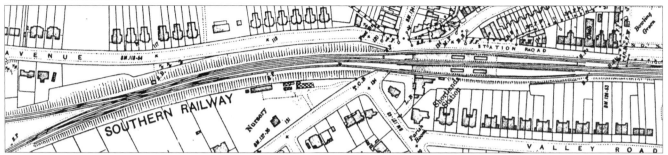

Map of Shortlands in Southern Railway days showing the main line to Beckenham Junction on the left (downwards) and the Catford Loop on the right (upwards). The Station Masters house, (in front of the booking hall), has now gone and the layout of the track work has been entirely altered with the Kent Coast Electrification and the Channel Tunnel improvement works.

Eden Park Station 1894

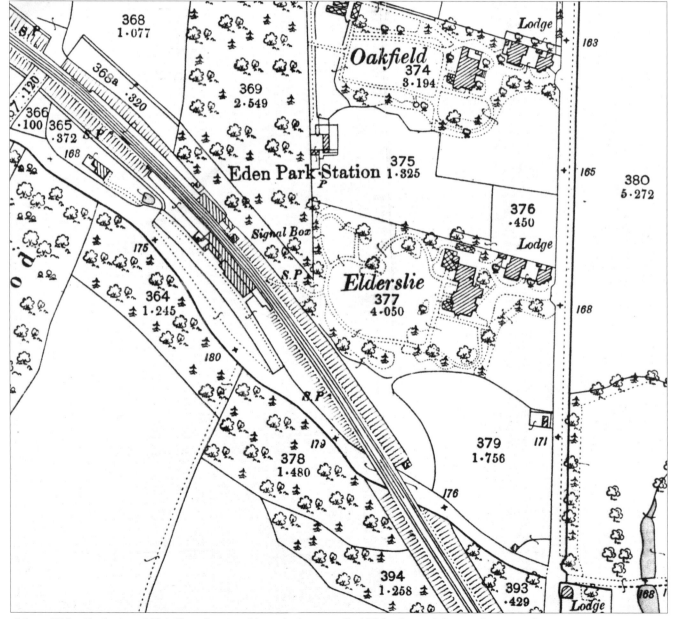

Map of Eden Park circa 1894. Note the signal box, the house called Elderslie and the rural surroundings.

Ravensbourne Station 1894

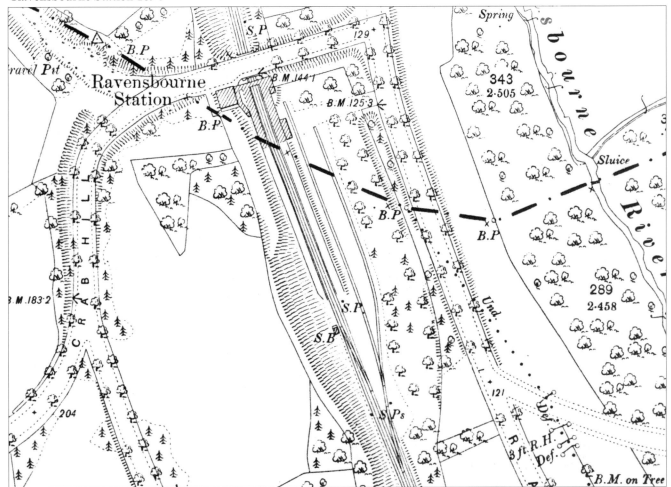

Map of Ravensbourne circa 1894. The County boundary runs right through the station. At this time there was no development at all, and consequently very few passengers.

Lower Sydenham Station 1912

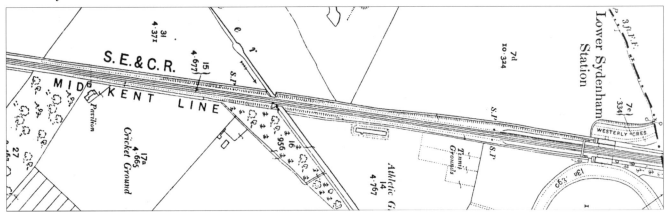

Map of Lower Sydenham circa 1912, after the rebuilding of the railway station in 1906. The county boundary cuts straight across the station. Note how the line to the south and New Beckenham traverses the playing fields and open ground.

THE RAILWAYS OF BECKENHAM

Beckenham Rail Network 1858

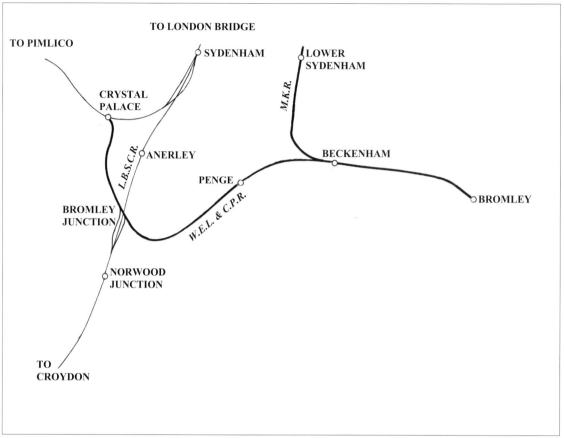

Beckenham Rail Network 1865

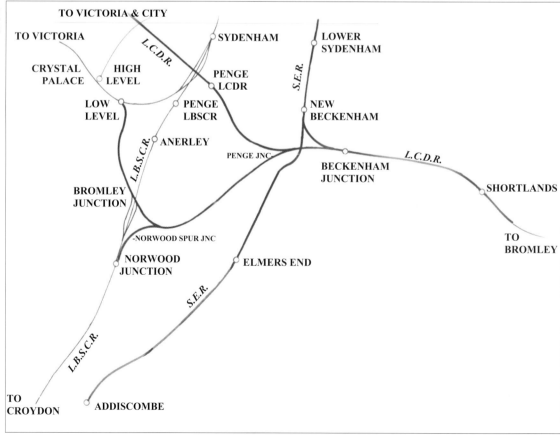

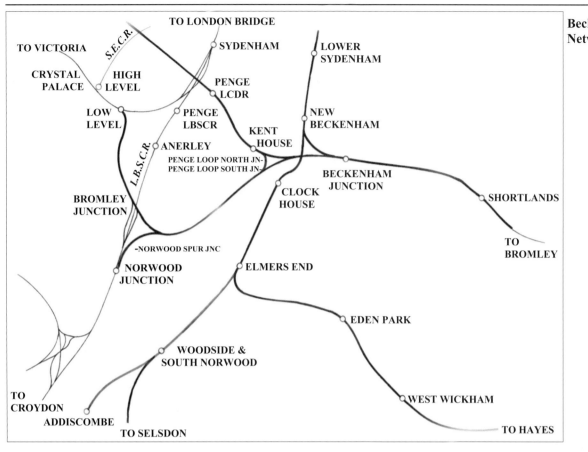

Beckenham Rail Network 1890

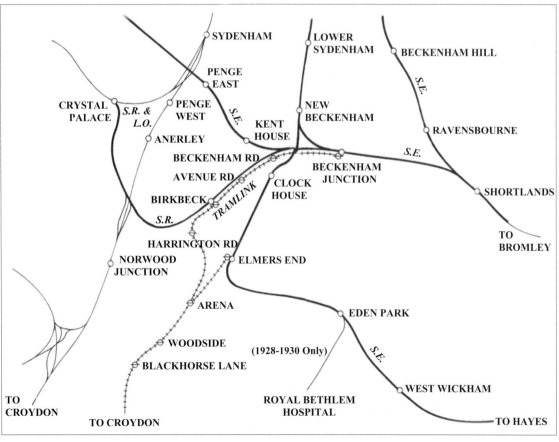

Beckenham Rail Network 2010

Appendix 2
THE CATOR AGREEMENT 1854

Memorandum of Agreement made this 15th day of July, in the year of Our Lord 1854 Between JOHN CATOR, of Beckenham Place in the County of Kent, Esq., of the First Part and the WEST END OF LONDON & CRYSTAL PALACE RAILWAY COMPANY, of the other part.

Whereas a Bill promoting the Company is now pending in Parliament for extending the said railway to Farnborough, with stations and other works and conveniences, AND WHEREAS it is to be proposed that the line of Railway shall be made through the lands of the said John Cator, AND WHEREAS the said John Cator having reason to apprehend that the Line of Works of the proposed Railway, and unlimited Sunday traffic thereon, might be injurious to his Estate, has petitioned the House of Lords against the Bill, AND WHEREAS it is of importance to the Company that the opposition thereto of the said John Cator should be withdrawn, and, at their request, he has consented to withdraw it on the faith of the Agreement hereinafter expressed being on the part of the Company specifically performed. NOW THEREFORE it is mutually agreed by and between the parties hereto as follows:

1. That in case the Bill now depending in Parliament shall be passed into law, authorising the construction of the said extended Railway, the said John Cator will sell, and the Company shall purchase for the purpose of the said extended Railway, and the Works connected therewith, such of his lands shewn on the plans, deposited for the purposes of the Bill, comprising in the whole 25 acres, more or less, and the fee-simple thereof on the terms hereinafter expressed.

2. The compensation for the 25 acres, shall be specific performance by the Company of their part of this Agreement and two perpetual yearly Rent-charges, the one a fixed Rent-charge of £2,000, subject to reduction, as provided in the 18th Article, and the other a Rent-charge of £375, subject, if the quantity of land taken by the Company be more or less than 25 acres, to such proportionate increase or reduction thereof.

3. The Rent-charge of £375 shall cover compensation for all damage to the owner by severance or otherwise (except as expressed in the 4th Article) in the exercise of the powers of the Company's Acts.

4. The Rent-charge of £375 shall not include compensation to the owner for the timber and timber-like trees (down to one shilling a stick) on the land, or compensation to the Lessees or Occupiers of land for their respective rights or interests thereon, or compensation for the damage done at any times of floods to the other property of the said John Cator, by reason of any of the Company's operations, for all of which matters the Company shall from time to time, be liable to make compensation in the same manner as if the present Agreement had not been made.

5. The Company shall, to the satisfaction of the said John Cator or his Agent, as such time or times as he shall require, make all such works and conveniences for the Accommodation of his Estate as are expressed in Section 68 of the Railway Clauses Consolidation Act 1845, and in respect to which, compensation is not hereby agreed to be made, or as not otherwise provided for, in and by these presents, as he shall at any time or times require, provided, that if any difference upon this clause shall arise, it shall be determined by two Arbitrators or their Umpire, in the usual manner.

6. The Company shall forthwith make good all damage occasioned by them, to any of the roads, and approaches, belonging to the said John Cator, or over which he is entitled to any right of way, except where provision or compensation in respect thereof is otherwise hereby made.

7. If any of the part of the land shall, according to the provisions of the Land Clauses Consolidation Act 1845, after having been taken by the Company, being superfluous land, the Company shall reconvey the same to the said John Cator, gratis.

8. The Company shall make and maintain one sufficient and convenient goods and passenger Station, adjoining the high road from Beckenham to Southend, to be called "the Beckenham Station".

9. The Railway shall not cross either of the said roads or the road from Beckenham to Bromley, at a level.

10. The traffic on Sundays, from Midnight to Midnight at that station, and in the direction of Bromley to any other station which may be established nearer to the Beckenham Station, that at or near to the Bromley Bridge and also in the direction of Penge to any other station which might be established to the Beckenham Station than at or about the point where the present proposed extended line crosses the road from Beckenham to Penge, shall, as to every station, be limited as expressed in the following Articles.

11. There shall not be received or delivered at the Station or Stations, as the cause may be, referred to in the Tenth Article, on Sunday, any goods traffic whatsoever, whether heavy goods or parcels, except such as are carried by a Passenger Train.

12. The only Trains which shall stop at the Station referred to, in the Tenth Article, on Sunday, shall be the following ordinary Passenger Trains, to wit, three from and three to London before 10 a.m.; one from and one to London between 1.30 and 2.30 p.m., and three from and three to London after 6 p.m., and such trains as are specified in the 14th Article.

13. The fare for every passenger taken up and set down at the Station referred to in the 10th Article, shall be the full fare as on weekdays.

14. Between 10 a.m. and 6 p.m., on Sunday the only Trains which shall stop at the Station referred to in the 10th Article shall be the one from and the one to London, between 1.30 and 2.30 p.m., and special Trains expressly required by the persons engaging the same to stop there, such special Trains having throughout the whole of the journey, in addition to the Engine and Tender, only one carriage and one brake, and any other van, if considered desirable for greater safety.

15. Provided always, that as the object of the said John Cator, in placing such a limit on Sunday traffic at those stations is to prevent annoyance to his Estate, and other evil consequences to himself and others, which might result from the Sunday Traffic and Excursion Trains, but not to interfere with privileges of Special Trains at any time of the day, in all cases of real emergency, the preceding Articles are not to limit the traffic over the Line, not stopping at such Station or Stations referred to in the 10th Article, and are not to prevent any Goods or Passenger Traffic at any of those stations which the exigencies of the public service (such as the service of the Post Office, the Army, the Ordnance, or Navy, or any other department of Government) which may from time to time absolutely require.

16. The Rent-charge of £375, if more or less than 25 acres be taken from the Company, the reduced or increased Rent-charge to be paid in lieu thereof shall be reserved or paid by equal quarterly portions at Lady-day, Midsummer, Michaelmas or Christmas, the first quarterly payment therof to be made on such one of those days as happens next after the Company take possession of any part of the land.

17. The Rent-charge of £2,000 shall subject to the 18th Article, be reserved and paid yearly on Christmas day next after the Railway is opened to the public.

18. The Rent-charge of £2,000 shall be reserved, subject to a proviso that whenever the whole of the year ending on Christmas day, the terms of the 10th to 15th Articles, both inclusive, are in every respect complied with, unavoidable accidents or delays excepted, then such compliance shall be accepted in lieu of the payment for that year of that Rent-charge.

19. The conveyance of the Company shall contain all such covenants and provisions for carrying this Agreement into full effect, as may be advised by counsel of the said John Cator to be proper.

20. On the faith of this Agreement being specifically performed on behalf of the Company, the said John Cator will not directly or indirectly offer or sanction any further opposition to the passing of the Bill, but on the contrary will, at their expense, use his utmost reasonable endeavours to promote the same.

21. But if anything shall be inserted in the Bill tending to interfere with such specific performance, then the said John Cator may renew his opposition, and the stipulations contained in the 20th Article shall thereupon cease and be void.

22. The Company shall, within six calendar months after the end of the present Session, pay to the same John Cator all his costs, charges and expenses – legal, engineering, parliamentary and otherwise – of and incident to his opposition to the Bill; and the preparation of the same; and the Company shall also from time to time bear and pay all the costs, charges and expenses of both sides, of and incident to the preparing and executing of these presents, and the carrying of this Agreement into full effect, all such legal and parliamentary costs to be as between attorney and client.

23. Provided always, that if the Bill for authorising the said extended Railway does not pass into law in the present year, 1854, this Agreement, except for the 22nd Article, shall be void.

In Witness Whereof,

JOHN CATOR

By His Agent, Peter Cator

Witness, JOHN RANDALL, Solicitor, Temple

Appendix 3

BECKENHAM RAILWAYS – A Brief Chronology

Lines:

LEWISHAM JCT – NEW BECKENHAM: opened as double line 1.1.1857, electrified 28.2.1926

NEW BECKENHAM – BECKENHAM JCT: opened as double line 1.1.1857, electrified 28.2.1926, singled 1.6.1987

BROMLEY JCT – BECKENHAM JCT: opened as double line 3.5.1858, closed to passengers 1.7. 1863, re-opened 1.7.1864, closed 1.12.1915, electrified and re-opened 3.2.1929, singled 13.2.1983

BECKENHAM JCT – SHORTLANDS: opened as single line 3.5.1858, doubled 5.1859, electrified 12.7.1925

SHORTLANDS – BICKLEY: opened as single line 5.7.1858, doubled 5.1859, electrified 12.7.1925

NORWOOD JCT – NORWOOD SPUR JCT: opened as double line 18.6.1862, closed to passengers 1.1.1917, singled 3.2.1929, closed 30.10. 1966, lifted 1.1969

HERNE HILL – PENGE JCT: opened as double line 1.7.1863, loops added at Kent House 2.5.1886, electrified 12.7.1925

NEW BECKENHAM – ELMERS END: opened as double line 1.4.1864, electrified 28.2.1926

ELMERS END – ADDISCOMBE: opened as double line 1.4.1864, electrified 28.2.1926, closed 31.5.1997

PENGE LOOP NORTH JCT – PENGE LOOP SOUTH JCT: opened as double line 12.7.1879 (no regular use), closed by 1884, lifted 1886, re-laid as single siding from North Jct 1.1899, closed 11.9. 1927

ELMERS END – HAYES: opened as double line 29.5.1882, electrified 21.9.1925

NUNHEAD – SHORTLANDS: opened as double line 1.7.1892, electrified 8.6.1925

BECKENHAM JCT – CROYDON [Tramlink]: opened 23.5.2000

ELMERS END – WIMBLEDON: opened 29.5.2000

Passenger stations and tramstops:

AVENUE ROAD [Tramlink] : opened 23.5.2000

BECKENHAM ROAD [Tramlink] : opened 23.5.2000

BECKENHAM JUNCTION: [MKR & WEL&CPR] joint] opened 1.1.1857 as BECKENHAM, re-named 1.4.1864

BECKENHAM JUNCTION [Tramlink] : opened 23.5.2000

BIRKBECK: [SR] opened 2.3.1930

BIRKBECK [Tramlink] : opened 23.5.2000

CLOCK HOUSE: [SER] opened 1.6.1894

EDEN PARK: [SER] opened 29.5.1882

ELMERS END: [SER] opened 1.4.1864

ELMERS END: [Tramlink] : opened 29.5.2000

KENT HOUSE: [LCDR] opened 1.10.1884 as KENT HOUSE (BECKENHAM), suffix later dropped.

LOWER SYDENHAM: [SER] opened 1.1.1857, re-sited 1906

NEW BECKENHAM: [SER] opened 1.4.1864, re-sited 10.1866, re-sited 12.1904

PENGE: [WEL&CPR] opened 3.5.1858, closed 3.12.1860

PENGE EAST: [LCDR] opened 1.7.1863 as PENGE, re-named 9.7.1923

RAVENSBOURNE: [LCDR] opened 1.7.1892

SHORTLANDS: [WEL&CPR] opened as BROMLEY 3.5.1858, re-named 5.7.1858

WEST WICKHAM: [SER] opened 29.2.1882

Goods Depots, Yards and Sidings:

BECKENHAM JUNCTION: opened 1.1.1857, closed 18.4.1964, coal concentration depot opened 11.1966, closed 1.2.1982

BECKENHAM UDC SIDING: (also BECKENHAM COUNCIL SIDING) : opened 11,1900, closed 16.7.1961

CLOCK HOUSE: opened 1.6.1894, closed 19.5.1965

ELMERS END: opened 29.5.1882, closed 6.5.1963

PENGE EAST: opened 1.7.1863, closed (except coal) 30.11.1964, closed (coal) 7.11.1966

RAVENSBOURNE: opened 1.7.1892, closed 31.5.1959

Signalboxes:

BECKENHAM JCT: (1) [MKR/WEL&CPR] opened as BECKENHAM 3.5.1858 and closed c11.1860 [but see Chapter 2]; (2) [SER] opened 11.1860, re-named 1.1.1864, closed c. 11.1881, (3) [SER] opened c. 11.1881, closed 15.9.1928, (4) [SR] opened 18.9.1928, closed 11.4.1959, (5) [BR] opened 12.4.1959, closed 13.2.1983

BROMLEY JUNCTION: (1) [LBSCR] opened 3.5.1858 as CRYSTAL PALACE BRANCH JCT, closed c.1881; (2) [LBSCR] opened c.1881, closed 10.10.1920; (3) [LBSCR] opened 10.10.1920, closed 13.7.1969

CLOCK HOUSE: [SER] opened 1.6.1890, reduced to ground frame 3.1956, closed 19.5.1965

EDEN PARK: [SER] opened 29.5.1882, closed 8.1899

ELMERS END: (1) [SER] opened c.1870, closed 27.5.1882; (2) [SER] opened 27.5.1882, closed 27.9.1975

KENT HOUSE "A": [LCDR[opened 10.5.1886, renamed KENT HOUSE 2.12.1928, closed 28.6.1931

KENT HOUSE "B": [LCDR] opened 10.7 1879 as PENGE LOOP NORTH JCT but commissioned 1884, re-named 10.5.1886, closed 2.12.1928

KENT HOUSE "C": [LCDR] opened c. 1880 as PENGE JUNCTION, re-named 10.5.1886, closed 16.10. 1927

NEW BECKENHAM; [SER] (1) opened c.1864, closed c.1881; (2) [SER] opened c.1881, closed 12.1904; (3) [SECR] opened 12.1904, closed 27.9.1975

NORWOOD SPUR JUNCTION: (1) [LBSCR] opened 18.6.1862, closed 14.4.1929; (2) [SR] opened as hut box 14.4.1929, closed 30.10.1966

PENGE: (1) [LCDR] opened as PENGE STATION 1.7. 1863, closed c. 11.1879; (2) [LCDR] opened c.11.1879, closed 9.02; (3) [SECR] opened 9.02 renamed PENGE EAST 1.7.1923, closed 25.2.1968

PENGE JUNCTION: (1) [LCDR] opened 1.7.1863, closed c.1880, (2) [LCDR] opened c.1880, re-named KENT HOUSE C

PENGE LOOP NORTH JCT - see KENT HOUSE "B".

PENGE LOOP SOUTH JCT: [LCDR] opened 10.7.1879 but never commissioned, removed c.1884

RAVENSBOURNE: [LCDR] opened 1.7. 1892, reduced to ground frame 31.5.1959, closed 4.9.1961

SHORTLANDS BANK: [LCDR] opened c 1880, out of use 1.6.1892, closed 3.1898

SHORTLANDS JUNCTION: (1) [LCDR] opened 1.7.1892, extended 20.12.1925, renamed SHORTLANDS c.1947, closed 31.5.1959; (2) [BR] opened 31.5.1959, closed 20.6.1982

SHORTLANDS STATION: [LCDR] opened 2.6.1892, closed 20.12.1925

WEST WICKHAM: [SER] opened 27.5.1882, closed 27.9.1975

Appendix 4
BECKENHAM JUNCTION STATIONMASTERS 1857 – 1983

Beckenham Joint Station Board (SECR/LCDR)
1857 – 1874 Michael Moore
1874 – 1879 Philip Knee
1879 – 1898 Robert Blackborrow [a]
1898 – 1899 Edward T. B. Allen
SE&CR Joint Management Committee
1899 – 1909 Edward T. B.Allen
1909 – 1911 Edward E.Morgan
1911 – 1914 F. Hopper
1914 – 1922 E. Harmer [b]
1922 – 1923 J. Tickner

Southern Railway
1923 – 1926 J. Tickner
1926 – 1929 Cecil Churchward
1929 – 1933 Henry Fay
1934 – 1942 William Dixon
1942 – 1946 George E. Tucker
1946 – 1947 Sidney J. Wildish
British Railways
1947 – 1954 Sidney J. Wildish
1954 – 1966 Edwin Stringer
1966 – 1976 Edward C. Pays [c]
1976 – 1980 T. Ward Penny
1980 – 1983 Leslie Felton [d]

NOTES: [a] – alternatively Blackborough or Blackboro'; [b] – from July 1921 stationmaster also responsible for Clock House, Kent House and New Beckenham; [c] – from 1966 the post was renamed Station Manager based at Beckenham Junction; [d] – Post abolished in 1983.

Appendix 5
STAFF PARTICULARS AT BECKENHAM STATIONS 1926

BECKENHAM JUNCTION (42) : station master (Grade 1, also controls Clock House, Kent House, New Beckenham), 1 chargehand carriage cleaner, 2 carriage cleaners, 1 checker, 1 goods porter, 1 parcel porter, 8 passenger guards, 5 porters (Grade 5), 3 signalmen (grade 3), 2 station foremen (grade 2), 4 ticket collectors (grade 4), 2 porters, 1 female ladies' room attendant, 1 ganger, 1 sub-ganger, 5 undermen, 1 track lineman, 2 track lineman's assistants.

CLOCK HOUSE (7) : 2 leading porters, 2 porters (grade 2), 2 signalmen (grade 2), 1 ticket collector (grade 1)

EDEN PARK (2) : 2 porters (grade 2)

ELMERS END (22) : station master, (grade 1, also controls Eden park, West Wickham, Hayes), 3 passenger guards, 2 leading porters, 2 porters (grade 2), 2 porter signalmen (grade 2), 2 signalmen (grade 2), 2 gangers, 2 sub-gangerrs, 7 undermen.

LOWER SYDENHAM (14) : station master (grade 3), 1 goods porter, 2 goods shunters (grade 4), 2 porters (grade 2), 3 signalmen (grade 3), 1 porter, 1 ganger, 1 sub-ganger, 2 undermen.

NEW BECKENHAM (11) : 2 porters (grade 2), 3 signalmen (grade 3), 2 station foremen (grade 2), 1 porter, 1 ganger, 1 sub-ganger, 1 track linesman, 1 track linesman's assistant, 3 undermen.

KENT HOUSE (15) : 4 porters (grade 4), 3 signalmen (grade 3, "A" box), 3 signalmen (grade 3, "C" box), 2 station foremen (grade 2), 1 ticket collector (grade 1), 2 porters (grade 2)

PENGE EAST (36) : station master (grade 1, also controls Penge West), 1 goods porter, 6 porters (grade 6), 3 signalmen (grade 3), 2 ticket collectors (grade 2), 2 porters, 2 gangers, 2 sub-gangers, 10 undermen, 1 assistant (gas mantles), 2 gas fitter's assistants, 1 plumber (grade 1), 1 plumber's mate, 1 tinsmith (grade 3), 1 tinsmith's mate.

RAVENSBOURNE (9) : 3 porters (2 grade 1, 1 grade 3), 1 ganger, 1 sub-ganger, 4 undermen.

SHORTLANDS (15) : station master (grade 1), 2 ticket collectors (grade 2), 2 leading porters, 3 porter signalmen (grade 3, Ravensbourne box), 3 signalmen (grade 3, Shortlands Junction box), 2 porters, 2 signal lads.

WEST WICKHAM (8) : 2 porter signalmen (grade 2), 1 porter, 1 ganger, 1 sub-ganger, 3 undermen.

Source: SR staff census, 1 November 1926

Appendix 6

BECKENHAM AND WEST WICKHAM POPULATION AND HOUSING STATISTICS

Beckenham

Year	Population	Inhabited Dwellings	Uninhabited Dwellings	Houses under Construction
1801	955	159	-	-
1811	1,093	164	-	-
1821	1,180	196	-	-
1831	1,228	238	-	-
1841	1,608	285	-	-
1851	1,688	307	13	2
1861	2,124	362	10	7
1871	6,090	976	123	66
1881	13,045	1,995	175	79
1891	20,707	3,451	283	55
1901	26,331	4,701	308	166
1911	31,692	6,227	612	53
1921	33,345	6,925	267	158
1931	43,832	10,308	311	-
1941	51,000*	16,431	518#	-
1951	54,116	19,250	348#	-
1961	56,139	20,000	-	-

NOTES: From 1801 to 1931 refers to Beckenham Parish, Local Board area and UDC areas; from 1941 to 1961 refers to the Borough of Beckenham excluding West Wickham. *-estimate (no census due to war). # - figures include West Wickham.

West Wickham

Year	Population	Inhabited Houses
1801	436	75
1811	494	79
1821	555	86
1831	614	101
1841	651	114
1851	732	136
1861	737	140
1871	884	173
1881	963	176
1891	1,262	249
1901	1,328	259
1911	1,302	294
1921	1,301	281
1931	6,229	1,805
1934	10,080*	3,360
1951	20,720	5,503#
1961	21,051	6,915

NOTES : Census returns except * which is a Beckenham UDC survey figure; # - Beckenham Borough estimate.

Appendix 7

TICKETS ISSUED AT BECKENHAM JUNCTION 1985 – 1986

In 1985 – 6 (the last year in which the traditional fare structure applied prior to the introduction of travel cards) a total of 325,346 tickets were issued at Beckenham Junction in the following categories:

Standard singles and returns	177,441
Cheap Day returns	116,392
Season tickets	25,272
Savers (mainly non SR destinations)	1,010
Ancillary tickets	43
Others	5,020

Source: Letter from BR to author, 1986.

Appendix 8

ANNUAL PASSENGER STATION USAGE 2008-9

	Total no. of Passengers [a]	Season ticket Passengers [b]	Interchange Passengers [c]
BECKENHAM JUNCTION	1,334,067	893,759	46,395
BIRKBECK	19,150	12,929	-
CLOCK HOUSE	566,645	383,349	4,891
EDEN PARK	242,988	152,797	-
ELMERS END	485,341	343,714	-
KENT HOUSE	390,348	258,784	48
LOWER SYDENHAM	270,772	135,070	-
NEW BECKENHAM	429,826	293,000	1,937
PENGE EAST	639,110	392,069	182
RAVENSBOURNE	80,331	55,954	-
SHORTLANDS	681,234	474,234	1,239
WEST WICKHAM	458,200	316,252	-

NOTES: [a] – recorded as station entries
[b] – season ticket holders entries, included in total passenger figures
[c] – interchange with other national services and excluding TFL

SOURCE : O.R.R..

Chapter 1

1. For an explanation of "Beckenham" in this book see p.5.

2. The words are from an anonymous contributor to the *Bromley Record* of April 1894. An earlier description of the 19th century village by Hone is cited by Borrowman, *Beckenham Past and Present*, p.55.

3. From the Tithe Commutation List of 1838, cited in Knowlden and Walker, *West Wickham: Past into Present*, p.155.

4. Edward Walford, *Greater London*, Vol. 2.

5. The Cator Estates Act 1825 (6 Geo. V, cap. xxxvii) has a schedule of all the lands affected. The description of John Barwell Cator (1781-1858) is by Borrowman. Peter Cator was formerly the Registrar of the Supreme Courts of Madras and then practised as a London solicitor.

6. William Hone, *Everyday Book*, (London, 1839).

7. The narrow projection of the parish boundaries up to what was later known as Crystal Palace Park Road was said by Borrowman to have resulted from the Beckenham parish authorities removing an unclaimed body and then claiming the land back from there to the existing boundary. Whether true or not it accounts for the inclusion of Penge East station in the present work. Beckenham Hill station is situated in the Parish of Lewisham and thus, dispite its name, is excluded from this book

8. Cited in Alan Warwick, *The Phoenix Suburb*, (London, 1972). Penge Forest is an authentic but somewhat fanciful name for the woodlands adjoining the common.

9. According to Borrowman for the short section of the line lying within Beckenham parish, the vestry received annual rates of £9 from the railway company.

10. Howard Turner, *London Brighton & South Coast Railway*, Vol. 1, chapter 3 and Vol. 2, chapter 2.

11. The activities of the crossing keeper here were commented on in a letter published in the *Times* of 23 December 1840; the L&CR report of their half-yearly general meeting of 7 September 1841 stated that "The bridge at Penge common is in a forward state and will be very shortly completed" and this would tend to suggest that the crossing was closed shortly thereafter.

12. Quoted by Borrowman at p.251 from a letter which he received from an unspecified source. In Catherine Marsh, *English Hearts and English Hands*, (1858), there are numerous references to Sydenham as being the railhead for Beckenham prior to 1857.

13. Borowman, p.242.

14. Rev Chalmers in the introduction to *English Hearts and English Hands*.

15. LBSCR Half-yearly meeting, April 1854

16. Evidence of James Younghusband and Charles Geach to House of Commons Select Committee on Railway Bills, 23rd and 24th May 1853; note the apparent ten-fold increase in traffic between the "ordinary" and "fete-day" traffic.

17. The terminus and through platforms are the present Crystal Palace (Low Level) station, the later suffix being needed to differentiate it from the High Level station of the LCDR on the branch from Nunhead.

18. Originally known as Crystal Palace Branch Junction, Bromley Junction was actually in Norwood and several miles distant from the town of that name; the nameboard on its signalbox was a cause of confusion to the unfamiliar traveller right up until its closure in 1969.

19. Railway distances are traditionally measured in miles and chains, the latter literally being derived from the length of a surveyor's chain and equalling 22 yards or one-eightieth of a mile; the metric equivalents of a mile and chain are 1.609km and 20.11m.

20. The present Elmers End Road and not to be confused with Clay Hill, a settlement in the eastern part of the parish

21. The Avenue Road footbridge marks the site of the path while the private road is on the site of the later nos. 21 and 23 Mackenzie Road and was the subject of litigation – *reported in Whitehouse v Hugh*, [1906] 1 Ch. 253.

22. The words of a speaker at a public protest meeting held in Beckenham reported in the *Bromley Record*, July 1874

23. 1854 (17 & 18 Vict., cap. ccx)

24. The full text of the MKR-SER agreement is set out in the Mid Kent Railway Act (18 & 19 Vict., cap. clxix)

25. *English Hearts and English Hands*, p.347, gives a good example of the philanthropy of Mr Knight, Jnr who provided free meals for his employees "who have walked many a mile from their last place of work without a penny in their pockets".

26. The Beckenham Agreement is to be found at PRO RAIL 729/8

27. It was continued between the LCDR and SER, successors to the WELCPR and MKR, as a result of s.55 of the LCDR (Works) Act 1861.

28. Walter Mathew in *Beckenham Journal Jubilee Supplement*, 26 September 1936 and quoted in slightly different terms in Copeland, Village. Mathew (1850 – 1941) was the son of the farmer at Copers Cope Farm and was a friend of Frank Moore, the son of Beckenham's first stationmaster. He took a keen interest in local railways and was employed as a telegraph clerk by the LCDR when he personally inspected the wreckage of the 1866 accident. He became a partner with Moore in a coal merchant's business at Beckenham Junction.

29. In the case of Sevenoaks, Sheppard's coach left the

town daily at 7.15 a.m. to connect with the 10.15 a.m. train at Beckenham and provided a return service off the 5.10 p.m arrival at Beckenham.

Chapter 2

1. Report from Directors to shareholders, EKR Half-yearly meeting, August 1853.

2. Mid-Kent Railway (Bromley to St Mary Cray) Act 1856, (19&20 Vict., cap. cxxv)

3. (20 & 21 Vict., cap. cxliii)

4. This well-known partnership between Sir Morton Peto and Thomas Brassey was responsible for the construction of a great deal of railway mileage in Britain and abroad and only came to an end with the eventual bankruptcy of Peto in 1866.

5. *Bromley Record*, June 1858. Walter Mathew, however, states that the first train from Shortlands was greeted by a peal of cannon from Martin's Hill, Bromley – Copeland, the *Village of Old Beckenham*, p.28

6. WEL&CPR Minutes, 14 May 1858

7. Robert Borrowman, (1870 – 1910), a popular local figure who was co-opted onto the Beckenham UDC Railway Accommodation Committee, was a keen local historian and his *Beckenham Past and Present*, (1910), is a seminal and still much sought-after publication.

8. Letter from Walter Mathew to J.A.Bennett cited in Copeland, *Village*, p.28; Bennett was described by Copeland in the introduction to the book as "the leading local historian of 50 years ago."

9. Of the three stations with Penge in their name, only the LCDR station (Penge West) was situated in Penge; the LCDR and WEL&CPR stations were actually in Beckenham.

10. The reference is in s.6 of the LCDR (Metropolitan Extensions) Act passed on 6 August 1860.

11. "So far as it is known, no tickets were issued at the halt" - Norman Harvey, *Railway Magazine*, May 1956.

12. Stanford's 1862 *Atlas of London* is the only non-OS map to show the station buildings and platform.

13. *Beckenham Journal*, 4 November 1911.

14. The original Lower Sydenham station was outside the Beckenham parish boundary but within the Cator estate lands and thus was also subject to the Sunday traffic agreement.

15. Southborough Road was renamed Bickley on 1st October 1860 and Bromley became Bromley South in June 1899.

16. MKR (St Marys Cray) Director's Report to Shareholders, September 1859

17. East Kent Railway (Western Extension) Act 1858 (21&22 Vict.. cap. cvii)

18. The price eventually paid was £120,000 inclusive; previously £105,000 had been offered in November 1858 and £106,200 in February 1859.

19. (23 & 24 Vict., cap. clxxiv)

20. (22 & 23 Vict., cap. xcviii)

21. Lord Harris at the LCDR Half-Yearly meeting, July 1861

22. (23 & 24 Vict., cap. clxxvii)

23. *Railway Times*, 2 June 1860

24. *Railway Times*, 3 November 1860.

25. At this time all LCDR locomotives only had names and not numbers.

26. It is possible, but unlikely, that the Ordnance Survey made an error but no alternative suggestion as to what the "S.B." might have been has been put forward; it seems to have been a much smaller structure than the Saxby type 1a box which in any event was situated on the up side but its position suggests that it was more than a refuge for the signalmen; the two boxes may have co-existed for a time but O.S. maps of that era sometimes still showed features which by the time that the particular edition was published may have been disused or even removed.

27. In a communication to the present author, Peter Kay commented that, strictly, the original location of the box is unknown and, although unlikely, it may have been moved from the up to the down side of the line in or after 1863.

28. Discussion on the Railway Telegraphs and the Application of Electricity to the Signalling and Working of Trains, *Minutes of Proceedings of Institute of Civil Engineers*, Vol.22, p.206

29. Again the source is Walter Mathew – see *Beckenham Journal, Jubilee Supplement*, 26 September 1936; it may be that he was, in fact, referring to a slightly later date as the box was certainly not built with a 36 lever frame but may have had the frame extended when the 1863-4 alterations were carried out at the station; when inspected by Col. Yolland in 1878, in connection with the opening of a new siding, the box had 37 levers.

30. *Railway Times*, 26 January 1861

31. (24 & 25 Vict., cap. ccxl.) but see the minor variations authorised by ss.13 to 16 of the LCDR (Kent Lines) Act 1865 (28 & 29 Vict.,cap. cccxlvii)

32. The name chosen was somewhat curious, given that no part of the tunnel actually lay within the administrative boundaries of Penge itself.

33. E.W.Veale, *Gateway to the Continent*, (London 1955)

34. This money, along with other sums recovered from the LCDR, LBSCR and Crystal Palace Company, funded the new college buildings which, in turn, was to contrib-

ute valuable passenger revenues at West Dulwich even though the governors of the school had negotiated half-fare concessions for college pupils travelling to LCDR stations including Penge, Beckenham Junction and Shortlands.

35.   House of Commons Select Committee on Railway Bills, Vols. 27 and 28 evidence of George Parker Bidder, WEL&CPR Engineer, 17 May 1860 and James Brunlees, C.E. 2 May 1860.

36.   The Beckenham vestry later gave Forbes Road the new name of Mosslea Road after it had unexpectedly acquired notoriety as a result of the Penge Murder of 1877 – see also note 7 to chapter 11.

37.   Details of the tunnels construction were given by the Chief Civil Engineer associated with the project, W.H.Thomas, in his evidence to the Commons Select Committee on the Shortlands & Nunhead Railway Bill, 15 May 1889

38.   The section from Canterbury to Dover Town was opened to traffic on 22 July 1861.

39.   (25 & 26 Vict., cap. ccxxiv)

40.   *Herapath's Railway Journal*, 4 July 1863.

41.   LBSCR (New Lines) Act 1862, (25 & 26 Vict., cap. lxxviii) s.23; regular LCDR trains never ran again between Victoria and Crystal Palace over the former WEL&CPR route. The LCDR had to pay dues to the LBSCR in respect of trains using the section of line between Bromley Jct and Crystal Palace but the Beckenham to Crystal Palace services were not "joint" in any sense of the word.

Chapter 3

1.   LBSCR Act 1859, (22&23 Vict., cap. lxix)

2.   1862 Act, s.26. Although (to use the contemporary expression) a "joint purse" service, the Norwood to Beckenham trains were always operated solely by the LCDR, despite comments in Bradley and others to the contrary; whether the service ever made any money for either the LCDR or LBSCR is a moot point.

3.   (25&26 Vict., cap. cliii)

4.   Section 13 of the 1862 Act specifically provides that the road ascent to bridges was to be on a gradient no greater than 1 in 30 unless the threat of flooding on the line dictated otherwise and "the Company shall not alter the present gradient of the road leading from Beckenham to Penge beyond the east Side of the Road leading to Thayer's Farm on the Western side of the Clock House.

5.   The station was subsequently renamed Croydon (Addiscombe) in April 1925 and became plain Addiscombe in March 1926; it is referred to throughout this work as Addiscombe.

6.   For his local background see J. L. Filmer, *Bromley Palace and Coles Child*, in *Bromley Local History* 5 (1980).

7.   (27&28 Vict., cap. cccxi) and SER (Mid Kent Amal-gamation Completion) Act 1866 (29&30 Vict., cap. ccxxxv)

8.   SE&LCDR (London, Lewes & Brighton) Railways Act 1866, (29&30 Vict., cap. cccxviii)

9.   LL&BR Abandonment Act 1868 (31&32 Vict., cap. cxxiii)

10.   By June 1898 this figure had improved to a mere 3¾ minutes; a century later 90% of all SER/LCDR area trains were noted to be running on time or within five minutes of scheduled arrival.

11.   Letter from A. Gurley Smith (a persistent letter writer) in the *Bromley Record* of October 1873

12.   Comment from William Starling, who was a metal broker in the City and a later director of the Bromley Direct Railway. He was apparently an unpopular figure and was described as being "an arrogant and pompous man."

13.   Bromley SER until 1899.

14.   Captain Tyler's accident report to the Board of Trade on the derailment in Penge Tunnel on 6th January 1868.

15.   The new road names are taken from the *Penge Hamlet Directory* of 1871-2 and 1876; by November 1879 it was said (in the Beckenham council minutes), that "St Johns Road was now principally used as an approach to the station" while in June 1880 the LCDR agreed to put the connecting road between Penge station and Parish Lane into a proper state of repair so that it could then be adopted as a public road.

16.   *Beckenham Journal Jubilee Supplement*, 26 September 1936.

17.   LCDR Act 1874,(37 & 38 Vict., cap. cxiv)

18.   For morc information on thc Pcngc Loop scc Kay, *Penge Forgotten*, part 2

19.   Introduction to the first edition of *The Beckenham Directory*, 1885, p.28-9

20.   The two quotes are from Thorne, *Guide to the Environs of London*, (London 1876) and Pevsner and Cherry, *The Buildings of England: London 2 (South)*, (London 1984)

21.   From a deed relating to a house in Albemarle Road, cited in Inman & Tonkin, *Beckenham*.

22.   T.Unwin, *Guide to Bromley and its Neighbourhood*, 1875,

23.   See *Beckenham Journal*, September 1878 and 27 February 1959. The Society, named after the Yorkshire born philanthropist Dr George Birkbeck, was founded in 1851; it subsequently became the Birkbeck Bank and was absorbed by the London, County and Westminster Bank in 1909

Chapter 4

1.   House of Lords Evidence in Opposed Railway Bills, 1880, Vol W-Y.

2.   The opposition of the SER to the unsuccessful LCDR Bill cost them an estimated £2,000.

3.   Born in 1816, Lennard, a member of both the Farnaby and Cator families, was created a baronet in 1880 "as a reward for his devotion to the Conservative cause" and later became as the first Chairman of the new Kent County Council. He died in 1899 and is still locally regarded as a somewhat controversial figure.

4.   Emily Hall, quoted in Sherrard, *Two Victorian Girls*, (London.1966).

5.   The name "Eden" comes from the family of that name (of whom Sir Anthony was a later member); fortuitously it also describes its formerly Arcadian landscape.

6.   This imposing Victorian building still survives as a licensed premises although the "Hotel" suffix was dropped many years ago.

7.   The pub and cottages have now been demolished and their site is now occupied by that last flourish of pride of Beckenham Council, the West Wickham Swimming Baths.

8.   (43&44 Vict., cap. l)

9. William Bennett, the West Wickham postman, quoted in *Beckenham Journal Jubilee Supplement*, 26 September 1936.

10. E. Garrett, *Our Navvies a dozen years ago and now*, (London, 1885), p.16-17.

11.   Frost, *Croydon to the North Downs - A Handy Guide to Rambles in the District*, (1881).

12.   John Favell, *The Railway Journeys of My Childhood*, London 1982.

13.   LCDR Act 1879, (42 & 43 Vict., cap. xiv).

14.   LCDR Act 1884 (47 & 48 Vict., cap. cxlvii) s.14 extended again by LCDR Act 1886 (49 & 50 Vict.,cap. xl), s. 54.

15.   Cited in Kidner, *London Chatham & Dover Railway*.

16.   Shortlands and Nunhead Railway Act 1889, (52&53 Vict., cap. cxxvi)

17.   LCDR (Further Powers) Act 1896, (59&60 Vict.,cap. cc)

18.   The full text of the Memorial and Report are printed in the *Beckenham Journal* for March 1879.

19.   The never completed tower in Wembley Park may have been of dubious benefit, the Snowdon Mountain Railway less so but the Channel Tunnel does not seem to be such an eccentric idea in the 21st century!

20.   The SER Minutes record the opening date as May 1 but the timetables and local sources insist upon 1 June. The name of the station has occasionally but erroneously been rendered as "Clockhouse".

Chapter 5

1.   SER (Confirmation of Cator Agreement) Act 1897, (60&61 Vict., cap.ccxxxiii)

2.   *Bromley Record*, July 1874.

3.   Quoted in Nock, p. 192

4.   Adrian Gray in his *South Eastern & Chatham Railway*, p. 122, states that the Beckenham Appeal "was the start   of a considerable campaign to force that traffic away from suburban stations."

5.   From March 1956 the ground frame was controlled from the box at Elmers End following the closure of the Clock House box.

5a.   By 1925 4,140 tons of coal were being delivered to the UDC siding and this, along with a good proportion of Beckenhams refuse was being used to generate 4,650 kw of electricity for use throughout the council area and beyond, in addition, to supplying power to the Penge section of the South Met Tramways. Source: Garke's *Manual of Electricity Undertakings*, Vol. XXIX.

6.   Beckenham Urban District Council Act 1903, 3 Edw. 7, cap. Ccxvii

7.   In November 1911 an SECR internal notice "to come into force on a date to be advertised" stated that the Beckenham Jct to New Beckenham, Norwood Jct and Crystal Palace services would be entirely withdrawn but, somewhat confusingly. that "local branch trips" would be worked between Beckenham Jct and Norwood Jct. This was not put into effect immediately but the Crystal Palace service succumbed within four years of the publication of the notice and the Norwood service within five while the New Beckenham spur services lasted until 1939 – it is interesting to note, however, that all of these closures were instigated as a result of war-time conditions.

8.   Originally operated under contract by the General Motor Cab Co Ltd, H & S Taylor took over the direct operation of the route in May 1912 and on 2 July 1914 it became LGOC route 113.

9.   See also D. Gould, *The SE&CR in the 1914-18 War*, Oakwood Press, 1981.

10.   The 109 was renumbered as 227 in 1934 and became in 1952 a Crystal Palace to Chislehurst via Penge, Beckenham and Bromley route famed for the late retention of its RF single-decker buses with conductors; for further details see George West, *The Scooter Run; the Story of a Bus Route in Beckenham* in Wagstaff and Pullen, *Beckenham, an anthology of local history*.

Chapter 6

1.   The London Society recommendations as found in

The London of the Future ed. Aston Webb, (London,1920).

2. The contractors responsible for equipping the substations were the British Thomson-Houston Co in respect of Upper Sydenham and Elmers End and English Electric in the case of Shortlands.

3. Over the next twenty years or so electric train failures in Penge Tunnel, due to blown fuses and short circuits, were not uncommon and on several occasions trains had to be propelled out of the tunnel by following steam trains; much alarm seems to have been caused to passengers by these incidents.

4. *Bromley Mercury*, 17 January 1930; the present author remembers that the Crystal Palace line trains of the 1960s were still being referred to by staff as passengers alike as "the ghost train" because of a general absence of any passengers.

5. Klapper, *Sir Herbert Walker's Southern Railway*.

6. The locomotives were "Fulwood", an inside cylinder model built by the Hunslet Engine Co of Leeds (No. 529 of 1891) and an un-named product of Black, Hawthorn & Co of Gateshead (No. 889 of 1890). On completion of the Bethlem Royal project "Fulwood" was sold by Arnolds to another contractor, Shanks & McEwan Ltd, and put to work on the Farnsfield to Broughton railway construction contract in Nottinghamshire while the Black, Hawthorn locomotive went to Caffin & Co for use on the reconstruction of Leigh-on-sea station.

7, Revd. O'Donoghue quoted in Muir and Manning, *Monks Orchard and Eden Park*.

8. In the case of the Fairley Estate (Merlin, Stanhope and Ernest Groves) the "Tudor" features cost an additional £10 per house.

9. Gordon Maxwell, *The Fringe of London*,(London, 1925) in a chapter entitled "The Passing of Langley Park".

10. p.137; the book, sub-titled "Suburban Development, Life and Transport, 1900-1939, does not deal at any length with Beckenham but gives a vivid picture of work, leisure and the realities of living in the inter-war suburbs.

11. See also "Social and Economic Effects of Suburban Electrification" in Brown, *Southern Electric*, Vol.1 p.80

12. Most, but not all, of the houses were well built; the Coney Hall estate became famous for a mortgage repayment strike in the late 1930s allegedly arising out of accusations of jerry-building and the subsequent litigation instigated by Mrs Elsie Borders.

13. Letter from SR to F. Harmer in Beckenham Library local archives.

14. The Borough was well-prepared and by the start of 1941 some 200 children from the area mentioned were evacuated principally to Wales and the north of England while in other areas many children were removed from Beckenham by their schools or by private arrangements;

many had returned by 1943 just in time to meet the regenerated Blitz and the advent of the VI and V2s.

15. Accounts of the latter appear in Darwin, *War on the Line*, (Southern Railway, 1946) while Brooksbank, *London Main-Line War Damage*, (Harrow, 2007) details the effects of bombing on the system as a whole while Watkins and Manning, *Beckenham, The Home Front*, gives a full account of the war in Beckenham and West Wickham; the latter is also covered by Walker, *West Wickham in the Second World War*.

16. The footage referred to is available on a Ian Allan DVD "*Vintage Southern*".

17. *The Becchamian*, Autumn 1940. The same issue suggests that the contemporary paper shortage meant that there was less writing to be done in examinations and that by filling in all the blank spaces in exercise books homework was more exciting by setting for the masters "a sort of jig-saw puzzle."

18. Lt. Col. Mount's report to Ministry of War Transport, cited in Brooksbank.

19. The unit involved was 1799; one coach was completely destroyed while the other two were subsequently repaired.

20. More properly the Southern Region of the Railway Executive of the British Transport Commission; the Executive was abolished in 1953 and the BTC ten years later when the British Railways Board was set up.

Chapter 7

1. All local stations received SR targets and later, with the exception of Beckenham Junction, Penge East and Birkbeck, totems; some stations like Clock House displayed both simultaneously after platforms were lengthened in the 1950s. The highest price achieved at auction to date for a local totem was the £900 achieved for an Elmers End example.

2. Beckenham Council Minutes, Vol. XXII, General Purposes Committee, 11 March 1957

3. The rebuilding work on the Birkbeck bridge was not completed until 1966, much to the chagrin of the Council and local motorists.

4. Rather whimsically one of the developments on the site of the trackbed is named Bradshaw's Close.

5. The box here survives to the present day as an engineers' store and is thus the last signalbox building to be extant in Beckenham.

Chapter 8

1. Much useful information can be found both on the "unofficial" website www.croydon-tramlink. co.uk and on the official Transport for London website.

2. There had been a previous limited service for lorry drivers. For the full history see Comfort, *The Channel Tun-*

nel Rail Link, (Oakwood Press, 2007).

3. The Railtrack (Shortlands Junction) Order 2001 (2001 S.I. No. 2870)

4. For more details see the BML2.co.uk website.

Chapter 9

1. For a graphic description of such stock see Ahrons, *Locomotive & Train Working of the Nineteenth Century*, Vol. 5 (Cambridge, 1953), pp.4.

2. *op cit.*, p.5

3. Nock, *South Eastern & Chatham Railway,* p. 134

4. Norman Harvey in a letter published in the *Railway Magazine* of May 1956. However in 1913 the stock of the 8.11 am Kent House to Holborn Viaduct service arrived as empty coaching stock from Bickley at 7.43 and as the working timetable shows no overnight stabling of stock here it is possible that he was mistaken about this point even if the siding was otherwise used to stable stock in that period, perhaps the 7.43 may have been backed in to the siding to let other trains pass.

5. *Railway News,* 31st January 1914, states that they were being used on the Norwood service at the time, and Jackson in *London Local Railways* suggests that the service was being worked by railcars "from 1915" but no details are given in either source and there remains some doubt as to the accuracy of both statements.

6. Nock, *South Eastern & Chatham Railway*, p. 141.

7. But perhaps not as surprising as the fact that slip coaches survived until 1960, the last working being at Bicester on the Western Region.

8. Lewis Blake, *Before the War, A portrait of Bromley & District, 1929-1939,* (1985), p.78-9.

9. Brown, *Southern Electric,* Vol.1 p.160

10. Unfortunately the "Night Ferry" was rarely photographed in Beckenham, given the rather anti-social hours at which it passed through the Borough!

Chapter 10

1. Other local private owner wagons included those of H & W Carr, Tyne Main, R.E. and Mary Ann Ray.

Chapter 11

1. The quotations are from Captain Tyler's accident report to the Board of Trade dated 10 October 1864; the second-class carriage involved was No.102 built in March 1862.

2. The driver later received compensation of £20 for his injuries and the widow of the fireman was paid a weekly pension of £1 until such time as she remarried or her eldest son commenced work.

3. Captain Tyler, ibid 1.

4. For details see Ministry of Transport accident report

by Lt. Col. E P Anderson (9 July 1930) and International Railway Congress Association Bulletin Reports, 931, page 732

5. See Tatlow, *St John's, Lewisham, 50 Years On*, (Oakwood Press, 2007)

6. Jackson, *London's Local Railways*.

7. Evidence of the railway staff at Bromley and Penge is found in *The Trial of the Stauntons* (Notable British Trials series, William Hodge,1911). Harriet Staunton is buried at St Georges, Beckenham.

8. The damaged carriage was driving trailer 76893 of 4 VEP unit 3170; it was subsequently repaired and returned to service. The only casualty of the day (apart from the train) seems to have been a local schoolgirl who was knocked down and badly injured by a hit and run driver apparently disorientated by the emergency road diversions in place.

Chapter 12

1. See also letter from Norman Harvey in *Railway Magazine*, May 1956, p. 340.

2. Darwin's correspondence can be found on-line at www.darwinproject.ac.uk and contains much of domestic and railway interest as well as more obvious matters. In September 1856 he tells Lubbock that "I forgot to ask about the [Mid-Kent] Railway, my invariable question" and elsewhere he denounces the "horrid omnibus journey" from Beckenham to Downe.

3. She resided at several Beckenham addresses and her residence adjoining the goods yard at Clock House is commemorated by Malory Close, a road in the redeveloped yard.

4. Some of this footage is available on an ITN/ Timereel DVD *"London's Railways, 1920s – 1970s"*.

5. In 1914 there were four houses in Beckenham called "The Myrtles" namely 35 Barnmead Road, 67 Mackenzie Road, 32 Westmoreland Road and, possibly the most suitable contender, 47 Coper's Cope Road – the latter has, unfortunately, been replaced with a block of flats. In any event "The Myrtles" of the story probably existed only in Conan Doyle's imagination.

Sources and Acknowledgements

"The Railways of Beckenham" was originally inspired by the work of Robert Borrowman and the local historians who followed in his wake. Whenever possible, the author has consulted primary and contemporary sources of information in local, national and private collections and these sources included newspapers such as the *Bromley Record*, the *Bromley Mercury*, the *Beckenham & Penge Advertiser*, the *Beckenham Journal*, the *Beckenham Times* and the *Penge & Anerley Free Press*; the *Sydenham & Penge Gazette*, the *Times* and the *Daily Telegraph*, the Minute Books and other records of the Beckenham Local Board, the Beckenham Urban District Council, the Borough of Beckenham and the London Borough of Bromley Council; the local history archives of the Beckenham, Bromley and West Wickham libraries; local and other parliamentary papers pertaining thereto; the Minute Books and other papers (including timetables (public and working), sectional appendices, special traffic notices and instructions, advertisements and handbills and other publicity relating to British Railways Southern Region, and the Mid Kent, the London, Brighton and South Coast Railway, the London, Brighton & South Coast Railway, the London, Chatham and Dover Railway, the South Eastern Railway, the South Eastern & Chatham Railway, the Southern Railway, the West End of London & Crystal Palace Railway, the West Wickham and Hayes Railway companies; Bradshaw's Guide and Shareholder's Manuals; publications of the Railway Clearing House and Office of the Rail Regulator; Ordnance Survey large scale maps; various local directories including Thornton's *Beckenham Directory*, the *Penge Hamlet Directory*, Kelly's *Beckenham & West Wickham Directory* and their *Bromley & District Directory*; inspection and accident reports of the Board of Trade and Ministry of Transport, and reports in *Herepath's Railway Journal, Modern Railways, Rail, the Railway Magazine, Railway News, Railway Times* and *Trains Illustrated.* Particular thanks are due to the librarians and staff of the Advocates' Library in Edinburgh, Beckenham Library, The Bethlem Hospital Archives, the Bromley Borough local history library and archives, The National Archives at Kew, the National Library of Scotland and its map room and West Wickham library, and also to members of the Signalling Record Society, The Industrial Railway Society and the South Eastern & Chatham Railway Society as well as to many of the individuals listed below who supplied information from their own collections and archives. Mistakes, however, remain the responsibility of the author and he would welcome via his publishers any comments, corrections, observations or additional information.

In writing a book of this character the author has been fortunate to have had the assistance of many individuals who have an interest in and knowledge of Beckenham and its railways including David Banks, the late H. Rob Copeland, Derek Coe, John Denning, Martin Elms, Simon Finch, Colin Gale, Brian Humm, the late Eric Inman, the late Alan A. Jackson, Peter Kay, Laurie Mack, Terry McCarthy, Pat Manning, the late Richard C. Riley, Alan Simpson, Geoff Smith, John Wagstaff and, especially, Cliff Watkins for his willingness to investigate, photograph and report back on even the most obscure aspects of Beckenham history – an invaluable help when the book was being written from a distance of over four hundred miles from its subject. For photographs and the for the permission to reproduce them I am indebted to the above and also to Richard Casserley, Jim Connor, Tony Harden, John Minnis, Tony Riley, the late Richard C Riley, John Scrace, the late J.L.Smith, David E. Wallis and Bill Tonkin for the amazing collection of local postcards of his late wife Nancy and also to the Bethlem Hospital Art and History Collections Trust, the Bluebell Railway Museum Archives, the Lens of Sutton Association, the editor of the *Railway Magazine*, the South Eastern & Chatham Railway Society and Barry Hoper of the Transport Treasury. The author has used his best endeavours to trace the identities of those who originally took the photographs but for wrong or missing attributions he can only apologise. For the front cover illustration "Golden Days at Beckenham Junction" thanks are due to the artist, Eric Bottomley G.R.A. (from whom fine art prints of this picture can be ordered on 01531 660677) and to Terry McCarthy who commissioned it. For the design, production and distribution of the book the author is indebted to Bruce Murray and Kevin Robertson, who were ever patient and calm when faced with a string of alterations to the text and illustrations, often at a late stage.

Finally perhaps the greatest debt of all is owed to John Minnis, the author's oldest friend and fellow traveller for many years on the 3.52 from West Dulwich, whose continuing help, wisdom and encouragement was responsible for this book eventually appearing. It then remains only for the author to sincerely thank his ever patient wife Kate who has had to put up with Beckenham and its railways for all too long but who can now see, with the publication of this book, that there is indeed light at the end of the Penge Tunnel.

Selected Bibliography

Railways

BRADLEY,D.L., *Locomotive History of the LCDR,* (RCTS, 1979)

Locomotive History of the SER,(RCTS, 1982)

Locomotive History of the SE&CR, (RCTS, 1980)

BROWN, D., *Southern Electric, A New History,*Vol.1, (2 Vols, Capital Transport, 2009, 2010)

DENDY MARSHALL, *History of the Southern Railway,* Revised ed. By O.S. Nock (Ian Allan,1983)

GOLDING, Brian, *A Pictorial Record of Southern Electrtic Units: Drawings and Plans.* (Noodle Books, 2009)

GOULD, David, *The SE&CR in the First World War*, (Oakwood Press, 1981)

GRAY, Adrian, *The London, Chatham & Dover Railway,* (Meresborough Press, 1984);

The South Eastern Railway,(Middleton Press,1990)

The South Eastern & Chatham Railways: A Marriage of Convenience, (Middleton Press, 1998)

HAJDUCKI, Andrew, *The Norwood Spur Line,* London Railway Record 5 (1995);

Beckenham Junction: The First 140 years, London Railway Record 10 (1997)

HALL, C.K. (Ed.), *Signal Box Register, Vol.4 Southern Railway*, (Signalling Record Society, 2009)

HART, H.W., *The West Wickham & Hayes Railway*, (Trains Illustrated, December 1955)

HOWARD TURNER, John T, *The London Brighton & South Coast Railway,* 3 vols., Batsford 1977/9

KAY, Peter, *Penge Forgotten*, London Railway Record 20 & 21 (1999)

KIDNER, Roger, *The London, Chatham and Dover Railway,* (Oakwood Press, 1952);

The South Eastern Railway, (Oakwood Press, 1954)

The South Eastern & Chatham Railway, (Oakwood Press, 1956);

The Southern Railway (Oakwood Press, 1958)

Southern Suburban Steam, Oakwood Press, 1984)

KLAPPER, Charles, *Sir Herbert Walker's Southern Railway* (Ian Allan, 1973)

The History of Transport in Bromley and District, (Bromley Local History 1, 1985)

LANE, A.W., *The Development of the Mid Kent Line 1855-1960,* (Proceedings of Croydon Natural History & Scientific Society, Vol. XII)

LEE, Charles E., *The West End of London Railway*, Railway Magazine, Vol. 102, p.634 (1956)

MINNIS, John. *New Century on the SE&CR,*(Didcot, 1985)

MITCHELL, Vic and SMITH, Keith, *Victoria to Bromley South,* (Middleton Press, 1992)

Clapham Junction to Beckenham Junction, (Middleton Press 1994)

London Bridge to Addiscombe including the Hayes Branch, (Middleton Press,1992)

Crystal Palace (High Level) and Catford Loop, (Middleton Press 1992)

MOODY, G.T., *Southern Electric 1900-1979* (5th ed., Ian Allan, 1979)

SKINNER, M.W.G., *Croydon's Railways,*(Southampton 1985)

TATLOW, Peter, *St John's, Lewisham, 50 Years On,* (Oakwood Press, 2007)

WOODMAN, Trevor, *The Railways to Hayes* (Hayes, 1982)

Beckenham and West Wickham local history

BORROWMAN, Robert, *Beckenham Past and Present*, (Beckenham, 1910)

COPELAND, H. Rob, *The Manors and Estates of Old Beckenham* (Beckenham, 1962)

The Village of Old Beckenham (Beckenham,1987)

FINCH, Simon, *Images of London: Beckenham & West Wickham,* (Stroud, 1999)

GRAY, E, *Bromley, Beckenham and Penge :a comparative study of changing geography of three towns on the southern fringe of the metropolis* (Unpublished London University Ph.D thesis)

INMAN, Eric and TONKIN, Nancy, *Beckenham,* (Chichester, 1993)

KNOWLDEN, Patricia and WALKER, Joyce, *West Wickham: Past into Present* (W Wickham, 1986)

MANNING, Pat and WATKINS, Cliff, *The Story of Beckenham Green* (Beckenham, 2008)

MUIR, Ian and MANNING, Pat, *Monks Orchard and Eden Park,* (Tiverton, 2004)

WAGSTAFF, John and PULLEN, Doris (Ed.), *Beckenham, an anthology of local history* (1984)

WALFORD, Edward, *Greater London, A Narrative of its History, its People and its Places,* Vol.2 South (London, 1882)

WALKER, Joyce, *West Wickham and the Great War*, (West Wickham, 1988)

West Wickham and the Second World War, (West Wickham, 1990)

WATKINS, Cliff and MANNING, Pat, *Beckenham, The Home Front 1939-1945*, (Beckenham 2005)

Other published works dealing with particular topics and specialised areas are found in the notes to each chapter.

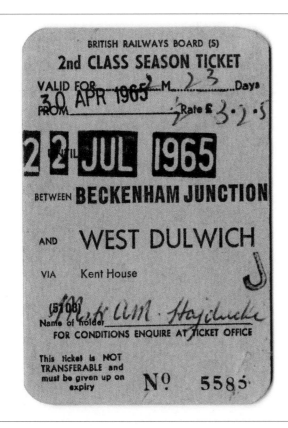

Index

Norwood Spur Junction in 1929 with the singled spur line to Norwood Junction on the left and the re-laid Crystal Palace line to the right. The box, a Saxby type 1b dating from 1862, is on the verge of being demolished and replaced by a ground frame hut. (the late E Wallis)

Bottom Left - A Crystal Palace train fails to stop in the up bay at Beckenham Junction with destructive results, 1st October 1985. (R.C.Riley collection).

Bottom Right - Details of New Beckenham showing the SECR valancing and the wooden lamp room, August 1988. (Andrew Hajducki).

Over Page (Endpiece) - Junction starter signals and locomotive water supply column on the up side of Beckenham Junction Station in 1952 (K R Collection)